The
Antigay
Agenda

The Antigay Agenda

Orthodox Vision and
the Christian Right

Didi Herman

The University of Chicago Press
Chicago and London

The University of Chicago Press, Chicago 60637
The University of Chicago Press, Ltd., London
© 1997 by The University of Chicago
All rights reserved. Published 1997
Paperback edition 1998
Printed in the United States of America

06 05 04 03 02 01 00 99 98   2 3 4 5

ISBN: 0-226-32764-7 (cloth)
ISBN: 0-226-32765-5 (paperback)

Portions of chapter 5 originally appeared as "(Il)legitimate Minorities: The
American Christian Right's Antigay Rights Discourse" in *Journal of Law and
Society* 23, 3 (1996).

Library of Congress Cataloging-in-Publication Data
Herman, Didi.
    The antigay agenda : orthodox vision and the Christian right /
    Didi Herman.
        p.   cm.
    Includes bibliographical references and index.
    ISBN 0-226-32764-7 (alk. paper)
    1. Homosexuality—Religious aspects—Christianity.
    2. Fundamentalism—history—20th century.   3. Conservatism—
    Religious aspects—Christianity.   I. Title.
    BR115.H6H47   1997   96-30354
    261.8'35766'0973—dc20   CIP

⊗ The paper used in this publication meets the minimum requirements of the
American National Standard for Information Sciences—Permanence of Paper
for Printed Library Materials, ANSI Z39.48-1992.

In memory of my father,

George Herman,

who believed this could be a better world,

and for

Kathy Michael,

who deserves to see it.

Contents

Acknowledgments

I was able to undertake the field research for this project because of grants provided by the Centre for Research in Women and Gender Relations, University of British Columbia; Keele University; and the Nuffield Foundation. Thanks also to the Faculty of Law and the Centre for Research in Women and Gender Relations, University of British Columbia, for their hospitality while I was a visiting scholar there in 1994. I am also grateful to my own Department of Law at Keele University for their support, and to the Keele library for a fabulous interlibrary-loan service.

I would also like to thank the following people who gave their time for interviews and, in many cases, provided me with useful resources: Robert Knight, Lon Mabon, Tony Marco, Tom Minnery, Loretta Neet, Will Perkins, Kevin Tebedo, and Jim Woodall. They may not be pleased with this book, but I hope they feel I have used their words fairly.

Several individuals and organizations made my life easier by providing a variety of resources. Thanks to Kitty Cooper, Charles Cooper, Martin Durham, Emma Henderson, Lisa Herman, Nina Klowden Herman, Marlee Kline, Bill Lunch, Julie Nice, and Angie Wilson. And to Lesbian/Gay Law Notes, People for the American Way, Political Research Associates, the Institute for First Amendment Studies, and cc.watch (Internet). Special thanks to Amy Devine and the Citizen's Project in Colorado Springs for all their help, and to Kathryn Stinson for research assistance.

Friends and colleagues have read bits and pieces of this book while it was an ongoing project. Thanks for criticisms and encouragements to Jim Beckford, Larry Cata Backer, Joel Bakan, Paisley Currah, Ruthann Robson, and Kenneth Wald. Special appreciation to Carl Stychin, who resolutely read far more of this than was his duty, and helped, more than a little, to keep me sane while I was writing it.

Many thanks are also due to Doug Mitchell and Matt Howard at the University of Chicago Press, for their encouragement and attention, and to Joann Hoy for copyediting, and also to Anita Samen at the Press.

Finally, thanks, as always, to Davina Cooper, for everything.

Introduction

Context, Approach, Definitions

The extension of political and social rights to lesbians and gay men has been one of the most volatile political issues the United States has seen in recent years. As a consequence of struggles for gay rights, families have been divided, local communities conflicted, and governmental institutions contested and reviled. For some, gay rights represent the just culmination of campaigns for full citizenship. For others, gay rights symbolize the unacceptable but inevitable excesses of a culture out of control. For all those who care, the legal rights of lesbians and gay men is an issue not just close to hearts, but reflective of the individual and collective soul.

Initially, gay rights struggles largely took the form of demands to remove criminal sanctions from same-sex sexual behavior. Throughout the West, and somewhat reluctantly in the United States, the repeal or modification of sodomy, buggery, and other homosexually identified criminal laws was partially successful; one could point to a general public consensus agreeing that what individuals did in the privacy of their homes was either their own business or, at the very least, not the appropriate subject of criminal sanction (see, e.g., Mayer 1992). Campaigns for decriminalization resonated with an antistatist ethos growing in strength during the latter half of this century.

Gradually, what we now call the "lesbian and gay rights movement" emerged: emboldened political subjects seeking the extension of legal equality in a range of social spheres. New gay demands necessitated state activism, not withdrawal, encompassing inclusion in antidiscrimination legislation, as well as spousal/family rights to marriage, pensions, and other forms of social entitlement based on heterosexual partnership. The history of the gay rights movement in the United States, as well as other forms of lesbian and gay activism, have been well documented and analyzed by, among others, Adam (1987), Altman (1982), Cruikshank (1992), D'Emilio (1983), and Vaid (1995).

By the 1990s, then, the lesbian and gay rights movement, despite a setback in *Bowers* v *Hardwick*,[1] had realized a range of objectives. In terms of legal equality, these achievements included the addition of "sexual orientation" to dozens of existing antidiscrimination laws. By 1995, for example, nine states had enacted legislation banning some form of sexual-orientation discrimination (California, Connecticut, Hawaii, Massachusetts, Minnesota, New Jersey, Rhode Island, Vermont, and Wisconsin). Other gay rights successes included the official modification of the military exclusion policy (from an outright ban to "don't ask don't tell"), and the extension of "family/partner benefits" (e.g., health, pension, and other employment benefits) to same-sex couples in a number of local jurisdictions. It now is estimated that approximately one-fifth of the American population live in an area guaranteeing some form of local gay rights protection (Wald, Button, and Rienzo 1996). Some areas of law, however, particularly those to do with children (custody, adoption, fostering), remained more impervious to change (see Herman and Stychin 1995).

Aside from law-reform initiatives, the lesbian and gay movement perhaps had its greatest impact at the level of everyday life and culture. Television, film, media, education, and religious institutions all became terrains of struggle and, in many cases, slowly (but surely) began to act as agents of normalization.

But from the first stirrings of gay rights activism, the move to provide lesbian and gay legal equality was resisted. The opposition to gay rights came from several different quarters. For some, particularly in the early days of gay rights campaigning, homosexuality was a disease in need of cure, not official condonation. Others contested gay rights on economic grounds—the cost of concession would be paid in the unacceptable growth of state bureaucracy, and the diminution of private-sector freedoms. Still others were concerned with the individual rights of those who did not approve of homosexuality; prohibitions on sexual-orientation discrimination, it was argued, would curtail individual liberties unjustifiably.

But for most, opposition to gay rights demands was on religious grounds: homosexuality was a sin condemned, in no uncertain terms, in holy Scriptures. Lesbian and gay rights were akin to "adulterer's rights" or "murderer's rights." Many people experienced the cultural normalization of homosexuality, of which the acquisition of formal equality was only a symptom, as an attack on everything

3

they believed in. The close correlation between religious orthodoxy and opposition to gay rights has been confirmed in a multitude of statistical studies and experiential research.[2] A religious, antigay perspective is shared by many conservative believers of the major American faiths—Christianity, Judaism, and Islam.[3] As I will explain more fully in subsequent chapters, the mainstreaming of gay and lesbian sexuality shook the foundations of orthodox religious belief. For strict observers there could be no tolerance of what was scripturally condemned. The increasing acceptance of homosexuality, particularly within religious institutions themselves, became a sign of godlessness and impending calamity. The opposition of the orthodox, then, became the primary obstacle to the progress of gay rights. The more the lesbian and gay rights movement gathered momentum and achieved successes, the more the disquiet of the orthodox increased.[4]

At the same time as the lesbian and gay rights movement was gaining strength and a groundswell of religious opposition was fermenting, a different political movement was also coming to the fore. From initial public stirrings in the 1970s, the movement that I shall call (and subsequently define as) the Christian Right (CR) was, by the 1990s, one of the most vibrant and effective social forces in the United States.[5] The history, politics, and significance of the CR's activism has been chronicled ably by many scholars.[6] While commentators are divided as to the potential power of the CR,[7] all are agreed that this is a movement worth watching.

For those interested in the progress and politics of lesbian and gay rights, the CR is not only deserving of notice; its activities are of the utmost importance. By the

1980s, as I will argue, the CR had made antigay activity central to its political practice and social vision. From the 1970s onward (there were six antigay referenda in 1977/78 alone),[8] the CR mobilized grassroots opposition to homosexuality, and gay rights were dealt setbacks locally and nationally. Local gay rights ordinances were repealed, and in some cases banned permanently;[9] statewide initiatives prohibiting future similar legislation were launched;[10] state gay rights legislation, and proposed legislation, was challenged or killed.[11] In some cases specific antigay statutes were proposed and/or enacted. For example, laws denying legal recognition to same-sex marriages were passed in South Dakota and Utah, and by 1996 had been proposed in over twenty other states. Practically every state in the nation has been the focus of some form of antigay activity.[12] And, in the summer of 1996, an anti–gay marriage bill had been approved by the U.S. Congress. Behind almost all of these antigay campaigns were activists and organizations of the CR social movement. While orthodox believers of other faiths may oppose gay rights with a similar fervor, it is the CR that has instigated and led the public antigay agenda in the United States. In this area there is little evidence of the "religious right" realignment suggested by Hunter (1991, 47–48).

Academic discussions of social movements have tended to focus on two questions: How does a movement (such as the CR) become an effective catalyst for change (e.g., Zald and McCarthy 1987)? And in what ways do "new" social forces represent a break with the past, and symbolize distinct, postmodern forms of social struggle (e.g., Melucci 1989; Offe 1985; Tucker 1991)? A further question that has concerned sociologists of religion is whether, and to what extent, religious orthodoxy is a product of moder-

5

nity (e.g., Hunter 1987; Lawrence 1989).[13] While I am interested peripherally in all these questions, my analysis takes a different form to these approaches. In this book I am concerned with the underlying antigay politics of the CR, and not the details or success of specific struggles, the nature of the CR's relationship to the Republican Party, or the unpacking of what is "new" or "modern" about the CR. I do not intend to duplicate the excellent efforts of others who have taken these analytic routes.[14]

The purpose of my endeavor is to explore beneath the superficial rhetoric of political campaigning in order to understand what makes CR antigay politics tick. Perhaps most importantly, I am interested in analyzing the diverse discourses relied on by the CR: theology, science, demonology, rights, and governance, among others. The sorts of questions I pose and to which I attempt to respond include: What are the motivations underlying CR antigay politics? How does the CR construct its lesbian and gay subjects? Do these representations draw on the imagery and traditions of conservative Christianity? How, and why, have CR antigay discourses and strategies shifted over time? What does the CR really want?

On a personal level my initial interest in writing this book was to move beyond stereotypical depictions of "religious bigotry" motivated by "homophobia." Such approaches seemed too partial in attempting to come to terms with the clash between lesbians and gay men and religious orthodoxy. As Wilcox, Jelen, and Linzey (1995) have suggested, many conservative Christian responses are reasonable, not loony or psychopathic (see also Harding 1991), nor even necessarily the product of alienation or displacement (e.g., Lipset and Raab 1971). Religious believers are legitimate social-movement actors; faith, as

Stephen Carter has argued (1993), must be taken seriously. This is so particularly in the United States, where
individuals express among the highest levels of religious
commitment in the world—over 90% of the population
believe in God and pray regularly.[15]

Finally, having spent several years of my academic career writing about the politics of lesbian and gay rights
movements, I wanted to take time to consider the opposition forces that consistently turned up in these struggles.
As I argue throughout the book, lesbian and gay activists
must understand, and in some sense come to terms with,
the conservative Christian vision animating so many of
their opponents.

This book, then, attempts to do at least five things:
(1) examine the theological roots of CR antigay activism;
(2) explore the historical emergence of lesbian and gay
subjects in conservative Christian discourse; (3) analyze
the representations of lesbian and gay sexuality by the
CR; (4) consider the secularization of CR politics, particularly within its emergent rights discourse; and (5) analyze
how the CR's antigay politics are shaped by the way in
which the CR understands, and attempts to reorder, the
state. My hope is that, by the end, my analysis will have
helped to illuminate the dynamics of this important social
struggle. Theoretically and methodologically, my analysis
is grounded in the insights provided by several disciplinary approaches, including sociology, legal studies, political science, and history.[16] I hope that this theoretical and
disciplinary eclecticism (and nonorthodoxy) takes a wide
angle to the topic at hand. However, I am also conscious
of not sacrificing attention to detail in order to paint with
a broad brush.

The book proceeds as follows. In this first chapter I

7

begin by defining the terms and parameters of my study. I then introduce some of the main players in the story, and continue by outlining the key themes and arguments of the book. In the final part I spend some time examining what I view as an essential foundation to understanding the CR's antigay politics: conservative Christianity's end-times scenario (eschatology). In chapter 2 I use the journal *Christianity Today* to explore how conservative Protestants engaged with homosexuality over a fifty-year period. I hope to lay the foundation for the rest of the book by introducing and developing several key themes and arguments, for example, the (dis)continuities between antigay and other Christian discourses such as that of anticommunism and anti-Semitism. This chapter is also intended to set the historical context to the CR's subsequent antigay activism.

Chapter 3 considers the CR's representation of gay sexuality and the lesbian and gay movement itself. Using various materials, including books, organizational documents, and videos, I analyze the ways in which the CR has conceptualized both the content and the threat of homosexuality. I pay particular attention to themes of anarchy, paganism, and anti-Christian conspiracy. Chapter 4 is devoted to exploring how the CR understands lesbianism, as distinct from male homosexuality. All too often, the CR's construction of lesbian sexuality is ignored; I hope to remedy this situation by providing a close analysis not only of the representation of lesbianism, but also of the ways in which the CR links lesbianism to their antifeminist agenda.

Chapter 5 is concerned with the CR's rights discourse: How has it changed? What are its implications? I consider how the CR constructs lesbians and gay men as an illegiti-

8

mate minority, undeserving of rights. I then explore the implications of this construction in light of those whom the CR champions as rights-deserving. For, as I argue, the CR's antigay rights discourse poses problems for its "rights" politics generally. Chapter 6 focuses on how these politics played out in one particular instance—the struggle for Amendment 2 in Colorado in 1992. In this chapter I am also interested in exploring the role of law, and the courts, and in considering the nature of citizen democracy in a pluralist society. Finally, chapter 7 shifts the focus away from the CR's antigay politics and onto the question of "the state": How does the CR envision the state? What does the CR really want? In a short afterword I pose some final thoughts and questions to do with the notion of "backlash," and the task of coming to terms with religious vision.

9

Terms and Limitations

To begin with, this book is about the United States. While lesbian and gay rights issues are relevant throughout the world today, no one book can do justice to all of these dynamics. My focus is exclusively on the United States, where, arguably, the movements both for and against are the most active.[17] Throughout the world, particularly in the "postcommunist" era, the American CR is extending its reach and influence. Second, as I have already indicated, I am concerned with the CR. What do I mean by this term? I use the phrase for convenience, and not as a term of art, to refer to a broad coalition of profamily organizations and individuals who have come together to struggle for a conservative Christian vision in the political realm.

I thus make an important distinction between the rela-

CHAPTER ONE

tively secular economic right (see Crawford 1980; Green 1987; Frum 1994) and the CR; antigay activity involves those Rebecca Klatch (1987) has described as *social,* rather than solely *economic,* conservatives.[18] There is much overlap between the two in terms of political agendas, and their antecedents are similar (see Bell 1964; Forster and Epstein 1964; Jorstad 1970; Lipset and Raab 1971). However, the CR speaks on behalf of a different, religious constituency, and I argue that, in the long term, the future visions of the two are significantly different. Furthermore, the economic right is not a major player in antigay activism; indeed, in some cases the opposite has been the case.[19] I should also note that I do not include the CR's potential constituency as itself constituting the CR. Rather, this constituency is composed of a diverse collection of conservative Christian believers who may or may not support particular items on the CR's political agenda.

What, then, do I mean by "conservative Christian"? I use this phrase to refer primarily to conservative evangelical Protestantism (I discuss the essential components of this faith below). In many ways I ought to be using the term "Protestant Right," for, with certain notable exceptions (e.g., Phyllis Schlafly, Paul Weyrich), the key antigay activists and organizations are Protestant. However, I have opted against this term for one reason: it is Christian faith and history as a whole that animates the antigay activity analyzed in this book, and not Protestantism per se. So when I use "Christian Right," I include Catholicism. This is problematic, as I will also show the ways in which the CR is deeply Protestant and anti-Catholic (see Wilcox and Gomez 1989–90). For the most part the CR that I am interested in, and that I will show is the catalyst behind antigay politics, is largely a Protestant movement, and thus my discussion of Catholic individuals and organizations is minimal.[20]

The CR that I discuss is also a *white* movement.[21] Again, while there are nonwhite conservative Christian organizations, activists, and constituencies, I would include none of these in my definition of CR.[22] Few persons of color, and no nonwhite organizations, are to be found at the forefront of national antigay activism. To reiterate, I use the phrase to refer to the leading Christian, profamily organizations only—those that set the agenda and the tone (see below).

I have also opted out of using the phrase "religious right," for similar reasons. While conservative Moslems and Jews have joined with the CR in specific struggles (see, e.g., Redman 1993), and a few prominent allies of the CR are Jewish (e.g., Don Feder, Daniel Lapin, Michael Medved),[23] I would argue that, *in relation to antigay politics*, there is no general "religious right," per se. In the United States the opposition to gay rights is led, invigorated, and inspired by Christians, and the Christian faith. All of this should become clearer as the book progresses.

It is also important for me to state that I am *not* including extremist Christian movements in my analysis. While the Christian Identity and militia movements (see Aho 1990; Barkun 1994; Coates 1987; Diamond 1995), for example, express deep Christian commitments and virulent antigay hostilities, they are not the key players in mainstream, antigay activism.[24] I also, perhaps more controversially, include the self-styled "paleoconservatives," such as Patrick Buchanan, in this group that I exclude from analysis. While Buchanan attracts support from some CR figures and several CR constituencies, his ethnocentric nationalism puts him at odds, in my view, with the public stance of the mainstream CR (see chapter 5). These tensions were apparent, for example, in Pat Robertson's repudiation of the Buchanan presidential bid in 1996.

While these extremist movements and the CR share certain core beliefs, it is far too simplistic to suggest the mainstream CR is nothing more nor less than the racist right (see chapters 5 and 7). Extremist movements, unlike the CR, often exist on the margins of both legality and popularity; perhaps more important, the mainstream CR seeks actively to distance itself (both strategically and normatively) from this extreme and, in my view, with some justification. For example, organizations on the extreme have called for the death penalty for homosexuality.[25] The movement that I discuss here is not of this ilk. For these reasons I also exclude from my analysis the violent wing of antiabortion activism (see Blanchard and Prewitt 1993).

Thus far, I have noted that my use of the phrase "Christian Right" refers, predominantly, to a coalition of organizations one can broadly speak of as a mainstream movement, based, for the most part, on a conservative, evangelical Protestantism. It is now necessary for me to explain what I mean by these words. I use the phrase, as do many others (e.g., Bruce 1984), to describe a specific set of religious beliefs that can largely be reduced to two key tenets: biblical inerrancy and premillennial dispensationalism. Research suggests that approximately one-fifth of the population would subscribe to these views.[26] Very simply (I expand on this in chapter 2), biblical inerrancy is the belief that the Christian Gospels, and to some extent the Hebrew Bible, are to be taken authoritatively as the word of God. The idea that one read these writings in their social context, or interpret them in light of changing values, is an abomination.

Premillennial dispensationalism is the eschatological position held by the majority of American conservative Protestants who believe in a specific end-times scenario: the world will descend into chaos and war, the true believers will be raptured to heaven, the Antichrist will rise and seek to take over the world (the Tribulation), Christ will return to defeat him and usher in the millennium—the thousand-year reign of Christians on earth. At the end of the millennium, Satan will rise again, be defeated, and earth will be no more—only heaven, populated by Christ and the saints. In the final part to this chapter, I explore premillennial dispensationalism in greater detail.

One final point in this discussion. While the CR is often seen to be composed of "fundamentalists," sometimes analyzed as a subset of "evangelicals" (see Wilcox 1992), I have chosen to leave the nuances of these distinctions to others (e.g., Ammerman 1991). I do not use the term "fundamentalist" in this book for two primary reasons. First, it has acquired a pejorative meaning that I do not wish to convey.[27] Those whom I interviewed for this book, for example, would not wish to be described as fundamentalist, and many view it as a term of insult. Second, "fundamentalist" is in many ways a confusing term of art in scholarly literature, and while the debate is interesting, the merits of my project do not hinge on its resolution.[28] The words "conservative" and "orthodox" are sufficient, and accurate, for my purposes. I occasionally use "evangelical" when I refer to a broader movement than the CR.

Thus far, I have tended to focus on the "Christian" part of the term "Christian Right." However, the CR is conservative politically, as well as theologically. Aside from its antigay stance, the CR could be said to espouse a procapitalist, promilitary, antifeminist, and broadly anti-

13

welfarist politics. With the exception of chapter 7, where I move away from an exclusive focus on antigay politics, these issues or positions are not the concern of this book. Excellent analyses of these aspects of the CR agenda have been performed by, among others, Himmelstein (1986), Ingersoll (1995), Klatch (1987), and Lienesch (1993), as well as many sources noted earlier in this chapter. I should reiterate that the antigay activity I focus on is only one part of the CR's agenda. Having said this, however, I do attempt throughout the book to link the CR's antigay politics to the movement's wider social agenda.

Finally, I should note that this project is not a survey of the entire CR. I have endeavored to focus my attention on a selection of texts from organizations and individuals that, in my view, are the key players in articulating a CR, antigay politics. This selection is representative of the CR movement, although not necessarily of conservative Christianity as a whole. My focus is predominantly, although by no means exclusively, upon *national* organizations and personalities, and upon books and videos produced for a Christian readership and easily available in most Christian bookshops.[29] It should at all times be remembered that the CR has a huge potential constituency of Christian orthodox believers; while my focus is on large organizations and key individuals, the opposition to gay rights comes from much wider quarters than these.

Leading Players

There are several organizations and individuals that, I would argue, stand at the forefront of antigay activity in the United States. I do not in any sense wish to suggest that CR antigay politics is reducible to those whom I identify below; I merely introduce several characters who will appear consistently in the book.

One of the most important organizational players is Focus on the Family, a multimedia conglomerate headed by James Dobson, a psychologist by profession, who has written several books and hosts a national program on Christian radio.[30] The "mission statement" of the organization commits it to upholding several principles, including biblical infallibility, the Second Coming, and the resurrection of the "saved" to life, and the "lost" to "damnation."[31] Focus is headquartered in Colorado Springs, Colorado, a center of conservative Protestant organizing (see chapter 6), and provides both pastoral services and political leadership to conservative Christian communities. The organization publishes a range of material, including its pastoral magazine *Focus on the Family*, its political organ *Citizen*, and numerous other books, magazines, and videos directed at either advice giving or political mobilization. Focus has made antigay campaigning one of its most significant activities, and its publications provide important source material for this book.

Another main contender in the antigay arena is the Family Research Council (FRC), a Washington, DC–based organization headed by Gary Bauer, a former adviser to the Reagan administration.[32] The FRC began its life as a subsidiary of Focus on the Family; it is now nominally independent. The chief concerns of the FRC have to do with a broad range of profamily issues: abortion, feminism, education, and, importantly, gay rights. By the mid-1990s Gary Bauer and the FRC were one of the most significant national CR players. Much of their activity centered on fighting the extension of lesbian and gay rights.

Formerly known as the Institute for the Scientific Investigation of Sexuality, the Family Research Institute (FRI) is an important generator of CR "facts and figures"

15

on homosexuality. Paul Cameron, director of the FRI, is a controversial figure whose activities I explore more fully in chapter 3. The FRI relocated to Colorado Springs from Washington, DC, in 1995. Other national organizations I discuss include the American Family Association, Concerned Women for America, the Report, the Rutherford Institute,[33] and the Traditional Values Coalition.

I should say a word here about the Christian Coalition, perhaps the best-known CR organization. The coalition has a history of antigay politics and activity, and its local activists are among the most vociferous antigay campaigners. By the mid-1990s, however, the organization's leaders had clearly asserted a form of pragmatic politics aimed at achieving the widest possible consensus (see Diamond 1995; Levitas 1995; Penning 1994; Wilcox 1994). Part of this move appeared to involve a decentering of antigay politics from the coalition's *national* agenda. For example, there was little hint of antigay material for sale at its 1995 conference in Washington, DC—in stark contrast to previous Christian Coalition "Road to Victory" conferences.[34] Interestingly, the coalition's *Contract with the American Family* (1995) contains few words on the topic of homosexuality.[35]

Also illuminating are the periodic battles that erupt between the coalition and other CR players like Focus on the Family or the FRC.[36] For many on the CR, the Christian Coalition is too compromising and pragmatic; its apparent downplaying of the antigay agenda is symbolic of this. For these reasons the coalition does not appear as a major player in my text, although its role in conservative Christian politics generally (and antigay activity locally) is prominent indeed. Finally, it is worth reiterating that antigay politics is only *one* (but a very significant) aspect of the work of most of those organizations. As I note further in chapter 7, the CR has a comprehensive sociopolitical agenda of which antigay activity is only one part.

Themes and Arguments

One of my objectives in this book is to highlight the ways in which the CR's antigay discourse draws from and plays to preexisting demonologies—particularly anticommunist and anti-Semitic discourses (chapters 2 and 3). I argue that, while there are continuities between these Christian representations, there are also disjunctions and inconsistencies. For example, while "the Jew," "the communist," and "the homosexual" all share certain attributes (e.g., subversive, apostate, infectious, and so on), these discursive subjects are also distinctively dangerous and imbued with particular and sometimes contradictory properties. I am thus interested in considering the resonances of "homosexual" with other "devils," but also the manner in which the lesbian and gay subject is differentiated and (re)produced.

17

Throughout the book I also explore the relationship between the CR's sexuality politics and its construction of gender and race. In other words, an important theme involves analyzing how the homosexual is "raced," how the feminist is "lesbianized," how the African American is "heterosexualized," and so on (chapters 3 and 4). I argue that the CR, in its attempt to reach nonwhite conservative Christian constituencies, constructs a homosexual intended to disidentify these communities from gay rights. Doing so, however, creates paradoxical effects causing complications for both the CR's antigay and race politics (chapter 5).

Another theme I explore has to do with the role of

legal discourse: more specifically, the shifting and contradictory dimensions to the CR's antigay rights discourse (chapters 5 and 6). I argue that a tension has arisen between "old moralists" and "new pragmatists"; the former insist on maintaining an antigay politics of disease and seduction, while the latter wish to bury this discourse under a veneer of liberalistic rights rhetoric. One consequence of these permutations is to place in jeopardy a past key tenet of CR antigay politics—anti-immutability (that homosexuality is made, not born). In chapter 5 I explore these developments generally, and in chapter 6 I examine how CR rights discourse played out in a specific example—the struggle for Amendment 2 in Colorado in 1992. In the latter chapter I also spend some time considering the role of the courts in policing the exercise of citizen democracy.

Ultimately, for religious conservatives, gay rights come from the state, and not from God. How the CR envisions the state, and its own role vis-à-vis the state, is something I probe throughout the book, most directly in chapter 7. The CR is often described in conflicting terms, as either antistatist or theocratic—aspiring to create a religious state. I argue that both these analyses have merit, and they are not as contradictory as they might appear.

The CR's relationship to the state is intimately bound up with conservative Protestant end-times theology, and that is another prominent theme in the book. In my view, the influence of this eschatology on antigay politics in the United States is momentous, and its significance has been underplayed. While I could be accused of exaggerating its effects, I have chosen to correct the balance by risking overemphasis. Paul Boyer (1992, xii) has written, and I agree, that "one cannot fully understand the American public's response to a wide range of international and domestic issues without bearing in mind that millions of men and women view world events and trends, at least in part, through the refracting lens of prophetic belief." The final section of this chapter outlines this theology and serves as a necessary foundation upon which the remainder of the book rests.

Premillennial Dispensationalism: Conservative Protestant Eschatology

Over 60% of Americans have no doubt that Christ will return (Gallup and Castelli 1989, 66). Of these, many millions are premillennialists—they believe that the Bible prophesies the end of the world, followed by the Second Coming of Christ and the arrival of the "millennium." A smaller number are postmillennialists: Christ will not return until God's kingdom rules on earth for one thousand years. I discuss postmillennial theology more fully in chapter 7; it is not an eschatological perspective espoused by many Christians in the United States today. Premillennial understandings largely (although not entirely) animate the CR and its potential constituents.[37]

Premillennialists find the predominant authority for their eschatology in the final book of the New Testament—the Revelation to John.[38] Most historians view the Revelation as an inspiration to believers during intense persecution by Roman tyrants at the time of writing, 81–96 C.E. (see, e.g., Gager 1983). However, orthodox Christians have for centuries considered it a prophetic blueprint for the earth's end, Christ's return, and the ultimate rule of the saints over the world as heaven (Boyer 1992). That these things will happen is beyond question; literally millions of Americans believe it deeply; the disputed matter is *when*, not *if*.

As Paul Boyer (1992) has shown in his study of the apocalyptic genre (see also Bull 1995),[39] versions of the end-times scenario have flourished throughout the history of Christianity (see Dobson and Hindson 1986).[40] Apocalyptic eschatology has been both populist and radical; early white settlers in the "new world" brought a mix of pre- and postmillennialist perspectives of many centuries' duration (see Lippy 1982). By the early 1900s, "new world" optimism (see, e.g., Glanz 1982) had given way to doomsday forecasting, and premillennialism had become the dominant theology—that continues to be the case today.

Historically, there have been various versions of the end-times scenario, more popularly known as Armageddon (the final battle). Broadly, in order for Christ to reappear, most premillennialists believe that Jews must return to Palestine, whereupon the Beast and the Antichrist will engage in battle (the "great tribulation"). Just before the final struggles begin, the saved Christians ("saints") will be "raptured" up from earth to meet Christ. Some of those left on earth will turn to Christ during the final hours—importantly, this will include several thousand Jews. Most of these people will die painful deaths—they are martyrs who will return with Christ and the saints at the end. Everyone else will simply die and go to hell—if not in the Tribulation, then killed by Christ on his return.

Following the defeat of the Antichrist, Jesus and the saints will rule over all the earth for one thousand years. According to Billy Graham (1983, 227), "Jesus Christ will be the King over all the earth in His theocratic world government." At the end of this millennium, Satan and his cohorts will rise again, only to be defeated, forever,

20

at which point earth will be no more, and everyone (left) will live in a perfect heaven. In addition to Boyer's exhaustive study, the details of this scenario have been analyzed, critically and otherwise, by a range of theologians, historians, sociologists, journalists, and others, including Chandler (1984), Dobson and Hindson (1986), Henry (1971), Pieterse (1992), and Wilson (1977).

Popularly, the eschatology has generated a wealth of best-selling literature aimed at predicting and representing the end of earth. Historically, the Antichrist was argued to be embodied in the Ottoman Empire ("the Turk"), and in the pope himself (Boyer 1992, 61–62, 153). In the first half of this century, signs were seen in the ascendancy of fascist dictators, the expansion of Soviet communism (e.g., Lindsell 1984), the creation of the Israeli state, and the nuclear arms race. In a popular 1970s and 1980s scenario the USSR, with its allies Iran, Libya, and others, Revelation's "Kings of the North," would invade Israel. There they would do battle with the "Kings of the East" (China, Japan, and so on) in the final Tribulation (see, e.g., Robertson and Slosser 1982, 213–22).

21

Writers also pointed to the rise of the European Union, sometimes called the New Roman Empire (Robertson and Slosser 1982, 214), the increasing purview of the United Nations, and the role of international financial institutions (Robertson and Slosser 1982; Robertson 1990). In the 1990s many premillennialists believed the Gulf War signaled the coming end (see Jones 1992). As I explore fully in subsequent chapters, in the latter part of this century in the United States, the imminent apocalypse has also been associated intimately with cultural degeneration: secularization, sexual immorality, worship of the state, crime, drugs, and so on (see chapters 2 and 3).

One of the most popular authors is Hal Lindsey, whose

book (cowritten with C. C. Carlson) *The Late, Great Planet Earth* (1970), sketching a scenario similar to the one above, has sold millions of copies around the world. In 1994 Lindsey updated his reading of Revelation in *Planet Earth: 2000 A.D.* Despite the failure of past predictions, "No matter how you cut it," Lindsey argues (1994, 3), "there's not much time left." Lindsey's update downplays nuclear holocaust and highlights the "abortion holocaust" (and other profamily issues; 17), socialistic environmentalism, New Ageism, and multiculturalism. These are all linked to "the globalists at the U.N." (44). Somewhat more fantastically, Lindsey also claims that demons in UFOs are planning to promote one world religion (69).

Despite new developments in global political alignments, Lindsey continues to assert that Russia will meet China in an Israeli Armageddon. He completes *Planet Earth* by explaining how to be raptured and avoid all the catastrophe. Other popular writers of the genre include Billy Graham (e.g., 1992) and Pat Robertson (e.g., Robertson and Slosser 1982; Robertson 1990, 1991, 1993). Interestingly, Robertson's thinking has shifted toward postmillennialism; I consider his views more closely in chapter 7 (see also O'Leary and McFarland 1989; Toulouse 1989). A slightly different scenario was sketched for me by Kevin Tebedo (interview by author, 1994), a cofounder of Colorado for Family Values.

> There will be great Tribulation. See I—I—in my mind, I can see it. Red China, the Soviet Union [*sic*], many of your South American countries, South Africa now, many of those nations that were pure communist, pure Marxist-Leninist, that did not have a capitalist system, that drained their people absolutely dry. But their elites still

drove limousines. They still ate T-bone steaks and had champagne and caviar, and flew around in jets. Well that money was not being provided to them by their people. That wealth was coming to them from a system set up by God called capitalism. Free enterprise . . . Once America, when all the money is gone, and it's liable to be gone, there is no other sugar daddy in the world. There is no one. And it will be over. Economically, there won't be anybody to fly their Lear jets. There won't be anybody to run their cattle so they can eat T-bone steaks. They will have killed the Host, as it were. And when that happens there will be economic upheaval—worldwide—such as the world has never seen before.

Apocalyptic visions also form part of the fiction oeuvre of conservative Christianity (as they do for other belief systems as well). One example is Paul Meier's *Third Millennium* (1993), which I purchased in Jackson, Mississippi, from a Christian bookstore's "bestsellers" shelf in 1995. The story concerns a Jewish family living in California in 1995. A new president, corrupt, calculating, and intent on world domination and the obliteration of Christianity, is in the White House. As he plunges the United States, and the world at large, into greater and greater chaos, Christian believers suddenly disappear, and the Jewish family slowly begins to realize that salvation for them can only come through accepting Jesus. The novel culminates in a series of catastrophic events centered in Israel—most of the world's population (including all those who have refused to accept Christ) perish in a range of horrific holocausts. At the very end, Christ rides down from heaven, with the saints, to usher in the millennium.

Many readers of my text will find these ideas fanciful

at best. However, it is too easy to dismiss them as silly and unimportant. As I noted above, millions of Americans, including political policymakers (see Barkun 1987, 168; Boyer 1992, 141–44) read the Revelation for signs, buy prophetic literature, and believe fervently in the scenarios. The premillennial worldview embodies both what Hofstadter (1966) has called a political "paranoid style" (meaning very imaginative, rather than mentally unbalanced), and a fear of conspiracy that runs deep in American culture (Davis 1971; Johnson 1983). It also helps to shape, in important ways, the stances and understandings believers take on social and political issues generally.

Conservative Protestant eschatology informs many of the political positions adopted by the CR. For example, the CR's enthusiastic support for Israel (see Mouly 1985), particularly in light of its continued anti-Semitism, makes little sense without an understanding of the role Jewish people must play at the world's end (see Henry 1971; Pieterse 1992).[41] Similarly, the CR's prodefense and patriotic stance is, for many, linked to the preordained role the United States is destined to play in the final days (see Boyer 1992, chap. 7; Cassara 1982; Lienesch 1993, 229–33, 240–41).

Finally, premillennialism is not simply, or solely, an eschatology; it is also visionary. Come the millennium, justice and equality will reign everywhere. Poverty, race hatred, and sinful corruptions will be no more. At its heart, conservative Christianity is utopian, hence its appeal, power, and significance as a social force to be reckoned with. These are considerations I return to in chapter 7 and the afterword.

Devil Discourse and the Shifting
Construction of Homosexuality
in *Christianity Today*

In this chapter I examine the emergence historically of the CR's antigay politics, in order to understand current developments more comprehensively. I conduct this study through a reading of *Christianity Today (CT)*, the leading American conservative Protestant publication, over a forty-year period. *CT* was established in 1956 by several prominent conservative evangelicals, most notably Billy Graham, unhappy with the liberal tenor of the preeminent Protestant journal *Christian Century*. *CT* quickly became, and has remained to this day, the unofficial, mainstream voice of the conservative evangelical movement.[1] I have chosen to center my analysis upon *CT* for three primary reasons.

First, the journal represents the mainstream of conservative Protestantism. From its initial appearance in 1956, *CT* has both catalogued developments within its own movement and played the role of spokesperson for conservative Protestantism in the United States. It is by no

25

means a radical right-wing fringe journal; indeed, *CT* has been the subject of sustained criticism by CR activists who believe it to be too moderate. As I indicated in chapter 1, my concern in this book is with the mainstream CR, rather than the extreme/racist right. *CT* thus seemed an appropriate and at the same time difficult place to begin to look for both the emergence of an antigay politics and, just as important, the wider social critique within which the CR antigay agenda is located.

Second, through studying a journal such as *CT,* given its political/religious orientation and longevity, I hope to uncover an early representation of the homosexual subject in conservative Protestant politics. Somewhat to my surprise, I found that writers in *CT* were discussing homosexuality in some detail as early as the 1950s, and with great vigor in the 1960s. Indeed, I will argue that this unofficial voice of conservative Protestantism formed its basic stance toward lesbian and gay rights during this initial period, albeit with some hesitancy. A study of the journal, then, facilitates a piecing together of conservative Christianity's antigay politics, particularly as a specific CR antigay literature was not generated until the 1980s (the subject of the next chapter).

Third, as my concern in this book is with exploring the themes and constructions within CR antigay politics, I was interested in discovering the extent to which these themes linked to older ones, particularly anticommunist and anti-Semitic discourses. Indeed, I began this project speculating a fairly predictable relationship between Cold War constructions of "the communist" and 1980s representations of "the homosexual." As *CT* was a fervent propagator of anticommunism in the 1950s and 1960s, I presumed such relationships could be illustrated by con-

26

sidering these different discourses within the pages of the journal itself. However, as I will show, things are not quite so stark. Yes, there are continuities, but there are also significant differences that bear closer examination.

I should also make three caveats. First, my discussion of material from *CT* is, by necessity, selective. Although it may seem from my review that the journal concerned itself with nothing but railing against moral degeneration in all its forms, this was not the case. *CT* was, and still is, a forum for sophisticated theological debate and informed commentary on the church and its mission. My focus, however, is elsewhere. Second, a great deal of research on the history of conservative Christian sexual politics remains to be done. This chapter makes only a small contribution to that project. Nevertheless, as Mark Toulouse (1993, 243) has written: "[T]he ideology constructed in religious journalism is not unrelated to the real life activities of those who share it or find themselves persuaded by its logic. It therefore becomes necessary to take such constructions seriously." Third, it may be obvious that I do not discuss lesbian sexuality in this chapter, and that is because *CT* has never done so. While I could comment on this absence, I have chosen to do so in chapter 4, where I analyze how the wider CR represents lesbianism.

27

I have chosen to organize the following discussion chronologically, beginning with the birth of *CT* itself in the mid-1950s. While this to some extent encourages a misleading, linear understanding of my themes, overall I believe that, for the purposes of the rest of the book, the material is best laid out in this fashion as it enables the historical context to emerge as a backdrop to what follows. In exploring the politics of each era, I hope to show at least five things. First, for several decades conservative Protestants have been concerned with many of the issues that concern them now. Second, CR antigay discourse has some antecedents in CR anticommunist and anti-Semitic discourses, but the differences between these understandings are also important. Third, conservative Protestant politics have always been fought over, and are in transition. Fourth, the construction of "the homosexual" in the pages of *CT* has itself undergone significant shifts. And fifth, beliefs in biblical inerrancy and premillennial dispensationalism underpin and permeate conservative Protestantism's overall social critique.

THE FIRST ERA, 1958–1965

Sexuality

There is a commonsense story, expressed by both the CR and its opponents, that a groundswell of conservative Christian protest against sexual immorality began to surface in the 1970s—largely as a reaction to the perceived values of the "permissive sixties." With a new sexual license for women, institutionalized by the *Roe* v *Wade* abortion decision (410 US 113 [1973]), a growing culture of drugs and crime, and the demands of the rising gay rights movement, conservative Christians, the story goes, began to wake up and put sexuality issues on their political agenda. This narrative has become commonsense knowledge, and is repeated by CR activists themselves.[2]

But while the *social power* of conservative Christianity clearly underwent shifts during this period, the issues of concern to them were not new. In other words, sexuality had always been discussed in detail, and Armageddon had for some time been associated with increased sexual depravity. Interestingly, the 1950s, now often glorified as an era of exemplary sexual restraint and the widespread observance of traditional family values, were actually assailed as being a decade of extreme licentiousness and perversion.

"A virulent moral sickness is attacking American society. Its obvious symptoms may be seen at any newsstand in large cities or small. American society is becoming mentally, morally and emotionally ill with an unrestrained sex mania."[3] This remark, the opening to an article published in 1958, signaled the start of *CT*'s concern with changing sexual mores. The authors complained that young people were being taught to glorify all forms of sexual sin and perversion and that women, in this increasingly sick society, "are completely depersonalized and are shown merely as pliant machines which men utilize for brutish pleasure" (5). While "unrestrained sex mania" was related to the breakdown of the idealized, traditional family (God's plan for the family[4]), of equal concern was the relationship between sexual license and anti-Christianity. An overall assault on the church was epitomized by the era generally: "If our churches fail to answer it," the authors of the above piece cried, "they will rue the day that their timidity and inaction gave a victory, by default, to the advocates of paganism" (8).

This anxiety about rampant sexual license was heightened in an article published in 1959. Here the author's concerns were "obscene advertising," "pornographic business," "juvenile delinquency," and the "erratic sexual life" of young people.[5] These developments were condemned, using the language of contagion, as "viruses" that "infest and infect not only the young but the adult

29

generation of our population," "infecting their numerous consumers with bodily, moral, and mental diseases" (3–4). The author proceeded to argue that the spread of these viruses led inevitably to the training of young people "in the difficult art of mass murdering of innocent people" (the connection was not made clear).[6]

The tone of this piece, and others like it, signified the level of crisis as it appeared at that time. The 1950s were seen, by many conservative Christians, as a period in which sexual depravity was not merely excessive; it was, in fact, in danger of causing the imminent downfall of the nation. By 1960 events had escalated to such a point that *CT* published an editorial roundtable discussion on "America's sex crisis."[7] Various members of the *CT* editorial board expressed profound distress at how "sex obsession is destined to destroy our nation" (6). Remarkably, one participant blamed the "new freedom of women"; I say remarkably because this was still the period where women, in that commonsense story, were seen to know, and to be confined to, their place in the home. It is also worth noting that some participants blamed the church for making sexuality a taboo subject and not encouraging frank discussions of sexual issues.[8] The following year the editors reconvened their roundtable to discuss "the press and sex morality."[9] According to the participants, the crisis was deepening, the press was contributing, and "the breakdown in morality threatens the very survival of the nation" (21). Communism was mentioned frequently (I address this further below), as was "the Soviet use of sex for espionage" (21).

Throughout the early 1960s, article after article appeared, railing against "an ever-widening cancer of corruption," the effects on "immature youth," and "the new morality" in general.[10] One writer found that the "morals revolution" had even begun to infect Christian colleges.[11] Once again, the "emancipation" of women was blamed, as was the growing consensus that sex was simply about pleasure, or required only love.

Homosexuality was also discussed explicitly. Writers viewed an increase in reported same-sex sexual practice as evidence of sexual depravity generally. Homosexuality was not singled out for special condemnation; rather, writers portrayed it as one of a list of sexual ills. Pitirim Sorokin, for example, accused the theater of promoting "sensational plays alluringly displaying 'the third sex' and other sex abnormalities."[12] In a slightly later article he noted an "[i]ncrease of the homosexuals and other 'sex-deviants,' attested by decreasing prosecution and increasing legalization of such relationships."[13] Homosexuality was also mentioned, together with "perversion" and incest, by *CT*'s editors during their sexuality roundtable.[14]

During this period, conservative evangelicals attacked popular culture for promoting homosexuality. According to one *CT* contributor, "great stress has been laid upon homosexuality in paperback books," and one writer went so far as to find that there was a "cult of the homosexual in our times [that] is hard to grasp for those who do not meet the force of its drive."[15]

The *New York Times* of December 17, 1963 carried a report covering almost a full page on the alarming spread of "overt homosexuality" in New York. A book written by a homosexual under a pseudonym pleads for acceptance of homosexuality as normal and right in Britain. The writer names many well-known men as homosexuals and claims there are at least two million of them in his country. The British public is more aware of this problem than the American, and in the popular mind the "new morality" group is considered the champion and one of the great hopes of these deviates in their campaign to win popular acceptance.

Despite these references[16] *CT* did not seriously concern itself with the emerging lesbian and gay *movement* until the late 1960s, and I will return to that below. Nevertheless, male homosexual *behavior* was a topic of concern to evangelicals during this earlier period, and they did not hesitate to say so.

Within *CT* texts, discussions about sexuality were never far from presentations of cultural degeneration in general. For example, the "moral downfall of youth" was attributed to a range of factors, including growing secularization, family breakdown, progressive education, pornography, alcohol and switchblades, and stringent labor laws.[17] Emma Fall Schofield, one of the few women to write for *CT* during this period, associated the destruction of youth with "latch-key children," alcoholism, and, in terms reminiscent of conservative discourse today, "fatherless homes."[18]

Yet another writer, in a two-part series, accused the "postmodern mind," typified by an avowal of moral relativism, of wrecking havoc on American culture.[19] And, in an article in 1962, Charles Lowry found communism's bedfellows in the "widening gulf between our intellectuals and the great body of the American people," "an unconscious secularism," and a "spreading moral decline, linked with progressivism in education, the removal of religion from life, and the thrust of materialism and the sensate in American culture generally."[20]

A specific emphasis on youth and education runs throughout this discourse. American young people were portrayed as being in imminent danger from the corruption or disease of moral decay, and the schools were clearly identified as sites of struggle between evangelicals and those doing the devil's work: "We should be roused from slumber by the spectre of a society where every school may become an instrument of state policy, every classroom a center for inculcating a totalitarian creed, every lecture an occasion for delineating truth and goodness as personal prejudices instead of durable distinctions."[21] This author employed the "spectre" of the Soviet school to show that godlessness led to "the worship of antichrist" (13), and that this was the direction in which the United States was headed if Christians "surrender our public schools needlessly to the spirit of the age" (14).[22]

Perhaps one of the key events for evangelicals during this period was the U.S. Supreme Court decision in 1963, placing restrictions on religious exercises in the schools.[23] Despite conservative Protestant support for the separation of church and state during this period, this judgment was roundly condemned as going well beyond the remit of the historical "wall."[24] While I discuss the church/state question in more detail in chapter 7, it is worth noting now that one of the effects of the case was to confirm public education as an important site of struggle for evangelicals.

In addition to the prayer issue, the schools were also seen as a key fighting ground in the battle against Catholicism (see below) and against left-wing ideology generally, as "educational administrators have by and large nurtured socialistic tendencies."[25] The universities too were lamented as almost lost to the degeneration process, and this was still several years before the period of campus radicalism was perceived to have begun. Universities were "vast temples of spiritual ignorance," and intensely liberal.[26] The university student was easily influenced, "pliable and submissive to what is being said, whether fact or fiction," while the "no-gospel of secularism has darkened the minds of many members of academic communities."[27]

In the pages of *CT* the theme of cultural degeneration inevitably was articulated with that of the end-times scenario.

> The long night of human barbarism seems to have begun. To many observers, the horizon of this third night exhibits little, if any, prospect of a sunrise. . . . Descending from its pinnacle of lofty achievement, the Christian West in becoming pagan is headed for inevitable doom. The light men shun today is blinding, for the post-Christian era revolts against the most sacred inheritance of the race. To assume that an anti-Christ culture will escape perdition is sheer madness.[28]

This prediction, penned by *CT*'s editor during the journal's first year of operation (1956), was repeated at regular intervals by various writers. America of the 1950s and early 1960s, far from being viewed as a place where religion and family values were respected, was instead represented as spiraling out of control in its descent to the very depths of preapocalyptic degeneration.

CT's writers differed in their assessments of how close to the end America was. And levels of apocalyptic rhetoric also varied considerably. However, several themes remained constant. First, there was a general view that American society was in a period of deep crisis. Politically,

34

evangelicals perceived several phenomena that were both serious threats to and yet fulfillments of their belief system: communism and, in particular, its attendant atheism; a growing Catholic population; the black civil rights movement (discussed further in chapter 7); expanding secularization; and a crisis in sexual morality. The increasing prevalence and acceptance of homosexuality was simply further evidence of this degeneration. Themes of contagion, corruption, and indoctrination, while quite prevalent in discussions of sexuality, were most clearly evident in other discourses, and I turn now to examine several of these.

Homosexuals and Other Devils

ANTICOMMUNISM. In the 1950s conservative Protestants, like the rest of America, were caught up in the fervor of anticommunism. Indeed, as several writers have documented, right-wing Christians were behind many of the leading anticommunist organizations.[29] That is not to say that the CR spoke as one voice during this period; on the contrary, for many on the right, the mainstream conservatism epitomized in journals like *CT* did not go nearly far enough (see Bell 1964; Forster and Epstein 1964). Indeed, in examining *CT*'s anticommunism it is important to keep in mind that its editors and journalists were writing in a climate where the anticommunist credentials of professed conservatives had to be constantly renewed and proven. In fact, the Protestant churches were themselves the focus of significant anticommunist witch-hunting and even a direct investigation by the House Committee on Un-American Activities (Roy 1960). In addition, then, to enunciating a sincerely held political position, *CT* was also clearly operating in this climate of fear and suspicion, and

35

to some extent, its anticommunist politics must have been a pragmatic response to the times. Yet, as Kenneth Wald (1994) has argued, anticommunism was not simply a knee-jerk, opportunistic reaction; it was a reasoned, principled position for Christian orthodoxy to take.

For, while *CT* was clearly concerned with communism's anticapitalism, of even greater concern was its professed atheism. Indeed, it is difficult to separate *CT*'s economic conservatism from its critique of communism as a totalizing belief system, one without God at its center. In article after article, communism was criticized as "intrinsically atheistic"; indeed, the words "communism" and "atheistic" were more often than not used in conjunction, as qualifiers of each other.[30] J. Edgar Hoover, in a series of contributions to the journal, described communism as "a bitter enemy of religion" and consistently emphasized its anti-Christian essence.[31] Fred Schwarz, founder of the Christian Anti-Communism Crusade and a frequent critic of less fervent conservatives, wrote in *CT* that communism had the "germ of godlessness" and was a "spiritual pathology."[32]

Communism was accused of having a "hideous, inner ugliness"; "evil," "brutal," and "bloodthirsty," its propagandists "cruel and cunning men" with a "nefarious program."[33] Blood imagery was frequently deployed: Communists engaged in "blood purges" and, with "sadistic cruelty," created "rivers of young blood."[34] Communism, thus articulated with atheism, equaled barbarism and inevitable carnage.

At the same time as Communists were constructed as blatant, bloodthirsty barbarians, aggressive spillers of "young blood," they were also represented as accomplishing their work through "brainwashing," and "clever pro-

36

paganda," and through stealth, smuggling, and covert action.[35] But these constructions were not paradoxical, for the devil can take many forms. The theme of conspiracy, often implied but occasionally explicit, is something I take up more fully in later chapters. At root there is little question that many conservative Protestants believed that communist power exemplified "the power of the demonic and the satanic in history,"[36] and that communism's victories signaled the coming end.

The link between communism and conservative Protestant eschatology (see chapter 1) was made directly by several writers. According to Fred Schwarz: "The hour is late. The enemy is gaining on all fronts. Christian civilization appears in its death throes."[37] The ultimate success of communism, its achievement of world domination, followed by the final battles of Armageddon, was imminent. For William Harrison it seemed "that now is the time for every believer in Christ to be looking expectantly for that blessed hope, the glorious coming of the Lord and in that expectancy to hold forth unceasingly to the world the Word of Life."[38]

Charles Lowry in a 1957 article brought together many of the themes I have traced above.

Communism is as far as ancient Gnosticism from being in the normal sense of the phrase a Christian heresy. It is rather an opposed and a competing system, controlled by diametrically antagonistic premises; and it is in a very nearly exact sense the expression in twentieth-century terms of the spirit of the Antichrist. It seeks deliberately, strategically, uncompromisingly and with fierce, inhuman hostility to extirpate the influence, teaching and name of Jesus Christ.[39]

In 1962 Billy Graham wrote an anticommunist piece advising readers to make their preparations for the Second Coming.[40]

Ultimately, these Christians were concerned that communism presented a total belief alternative to the Christian faith.[41] Much like conservative Christianity, orthodox communism explains the past, predicts the future, and offers a stinging critique of contemporary society and a strategy for change. At the same time it expressly denies the authenticity of conservative religious belief; indeed, as is well known, Karl Marx likened organized religion to a drug, stupefying the masses into obedience. In fact, Marx's characterization of religion resembles conservative Christianity's characterization of communism. It was no wonder that those who believed in the literal truth of the Bible, the rapture of the saved to heaven, Armageddon, and the inevitable return of Jesus found communism's entirely different (but similarly prescriptive) orthodoxy so threatening (see Wald 1994).

ANTI-SEMITISM. In contrast, the image of "the Jew" in the pages of *CT* during this period was somewhat different. While the Christian construction of Jews as bloodthirsty child stealers was common in earlier centuries, in the 1950s, in the immediate aftermath of the Holocaust on the one hand and in a climate of unquestioned citizenship rights for American Jews on the other, mainstream conservative Christian anti-Semitism was bound to take a different form. Although it is tempting to argue that right-wing anticommunism went hand in hand with anti-Semitism during the 1950s, with a few notable exceptions,[42] I did not find this to be the case in the pages of *CT*. Rather, "the Jew" tended to make its appearance in discussions about Israel and evangelism.

In one early exchange, for example, two writers debated how Christians ought to respond to the new Israeli state. Oswald T. Allis argued that "Zionist agitation" had resulted in a spurious claim to "repossess a land that has not been theirs for nearly two thousand years. What other people in the world would venture to demand that the clock of history be put back two millennia for their benefit?"[43] According to Allis the Jewish people were condemned long ago: "The destruction of Jerusalem by Titus and the resultant dispersion of the Jews was the punishment for their sin of rejecting and slaying their long-promised Messiah" (8). For Allis this fundamental truth, that the Jews killed Jesus, left only one response to the question of whether Christians should support Israel: "Should Christians be willing to plunge the nations into a third world conflict just to restore unbelieving Jews to, and to maintain them in, a land from which they were driven nearly two thousand years ago? We believe the verdict of history will be, No! May God grant that this verdict not be written in rivers of blood!" (9). Interestingly, it was not long before this sort of overt language disappeared from the pages of *CT*. During this period, however, anti-Semitism of this sort, couched in the rhetoric of anti-Zionism, was seen as acceptable by the journal's editors.[44]

In this same issue a response to Allis was offered by Wilbur M. Smith. For Smith the return of the Jewish people to Israel signaled a fulfillment of divine ordinance (see chapter 1). Indeed, for the millennium to arrive, there *must* be Jews in Palestine. Smith asked, "If we take the unauthorized liberty of cancelling these prophecies, why may we not with equal liberty cancel any other prophecy with which a particular theory would lead us to disagree?"[45]

The names of Palestine, the prophecies regarding Palestine, the disappointing history of the Jews in Palestine in
ancient times and events in the newly created state of
Israel bear a united, indisputable testimony to the fact
that the greatest glory this land has ever seen will yet be
unfolded. Jerusalem shall truly become a city of peace,
and the people of God will dwell in unwalled villages,
each man sitting in quietness and confidence under his
own tree. This will be God's victory for that portion of
the earth which He has called His own land. No anti-
Semitism, no wars, no unbelief, no pogroms, not Antichrist himself will be able to prevent the fulfilment of
these divinely given promises. (11)

It was Smith's position that quickly became the line *CT*
took on Israel, and in many ways this was the honest position for premillennialists to take. If one believes in biblical
inerrancy, the scenario Smith sketched must surely come
to pass. Nevertheless, even in his construction, Israel was
not to be supported for its own sake, but only as a necessary precondition for the return of Christ—and this fact
remains as true for conservative Protestants today (see
chapter 1).

The second predominant manner in which "the Jew"
appeared in *CT* was in discussions about conversion. In
early contributions one can find echoes of Allis's portrayal
of the arrogant and stubborn Jew. According to one
writer, evangelizing the Jews was very difficult because
"he [the Jew] has never considered himself inferior to any
other people; he has never thought he had anything to
learn from them. On the contrary, he has always been
conscious of his own superiority."[46] At the same time,
however, the author, a converted Jew, argued that Chris-

tians had not been as welcoming as they ought to have been, and that the contributions of Jewish converts to the movement were often overlooked.

Arguably, *CT*'s anti-Semitic discourse was more patronizing than it was demonizing. In several respects it differed from anticommunist rhetoric. For conservative Christians of this period, Judaism, unlike communism, was not a serious threat to the Christian mission. While the creation of the Israeli state *could* have been seen as the first step in a plan for Jewish world domination, for these premillennialists it was not. On the contrary, they believed, and still do believe, that there must be religious Jews in Palestine in order for Jesus to return. At the same time, prophecies insist that many Jews be converted—hence the obsession with Jewish "obstinacy and stubbornness." Furthermore, Jews were, after all, both God's chosen people[47] and a God-fearing people—even if they did continue to reject the Truth of Jesus.

41

Communists, on the other hand, were simply to be opposed; there was no salvation for atheists of any political persuasion; atheism, unlike Judaism, was clearly in the service of Satan. For premillennialists in this era, then, Jews were not really devils; rather, they were arrogant, pathetic, and necessary, all at the same time—but they were not, as in Christian imagery from previous centuries, evil. Communists, however, were the devil incarnate, sweeping Christianity away in their deadly advance. Homosexuals during this period thus had the "benefit" of both these constructions: on the one hand, they were both obstinate and pathetic, willfully rejecting the Bible's prescriptions; on the other, the apparently growing prevalence of homosexual behavior signaled the ascendancy of satanic cultural forces.

I should also note that one of the reasons conservative Protestants did not perceive a huge threat from Jewish quarters was that Judaism is not an evangelical religion— Jews are not interested in competing with the Christian mission. Communists, on the other hand, sought both to debunk and to surpass this mission through promoting their own form of evangelism. Although in this early period homosexuality was identified with the evils of secularism, lesbians and gay men themselves were not perceived to have an "agenda"—in other words, they were not viewed as counterevangelists.

It is also worth pointing out something I will pursue in more detail at a later stage. Within conservative Protestant discourse, there is a very important role played by the "ex" or "former" subject. The former Communist, the former Jew, and the former homosexual provide hope for change, on the one hand, but even more importantly their contributions tend to temper more virulent ones. These authors nearly always plead for understanding, often accuse the church of discrimination, and give an "insider" view of the target community. With respect to this last point, it is often the "former," or "ex," who will paint a picture of Jews, or lesbians and gays (less so Communists), as tragic, rather than dangerous; to be pitied, rather than vilified. But this is certainly a generalization; the "formers" can often be among the most virulent—McCarthyite America witnessed many such examples. I will return to the ex-gay (to use their term) genre later in the chapter.

ANTI-CATHOLICISM. During these decades, there were several other concerns of *CT* that bear some scrutiny. One of these is the perceived increasing political power of Catholics.[48] For obvious reasons, notably the failure of Protestant fears to be realized, this theme died out by the late 1960s. For many years, however, the need to combat perceived Catholic encroachment was an important part of the conservative Protestant agenda.

According to one former Catholic, for example, the Catholic faith in France was responsible for that country's rising rates of prostitution and child delinquency.[49] Like their construction of communism, writers in *CT* characterized the Catholic church as having "vast power" and as using "the cleverest of propaganda."[50] In language reminiscent of later discussions of gay activists, Catholics in the United States were accused of moving from being an "ineffectual minority" to being a "high-powered lobby" (11–12).

In their drive to dominate America, "Catholics have simply taken over the public schools. . . . Roman Catholic hierarchy is now within sight of its goal. Success has come even faster than its leaders dreamed. . . . Now, as a powerful minority . . . [i]t intimidates Congress, censors and silences opposition, collects vast sums from the public treasury and drives towards official recognition and establishment" (13). According to one writer, identified only as a "former Jesuit trainee":

> One thing is clear to me. Protestants are sooner or later either going to have to stand up for their religious beliefs, or see themselves go down to defeat before the machinations and power of Rome. They are losing the fight for the minds and souls of America's future generations today. . . . It is massive indoctrination, a process of education designed to make America in the future a Catholic country, utterly submissive and obedient to Rome.[51]

One of the chief Catholic "crimes" during this period was to imply an end to church-state separation by calling for state funding of Catholic schools. In light of current conservative Christian attempts (though not necessarily *CT*) to reinterpret American constitutional history as never intending such a wall to be built (see chapter 7), the motivation for this anti-Catholic rhetoric seems ironic indeed. This discourse petered out, no doubt as it became increasingly clear that the Catholic lobby was not the threat initially envisaged.[52] In drawing historical parallels with gay rights, it may be worth keeping this example in mind.

THE SECOND ERA, 1965–1980

44   During the journal's next fifteen years, concern with all the issues discussed above, with the exception of anti-Catholicism, remained consistent refrains for *CT*. New moves to incorporate sex education classes in the schools were vigorously debated (and not per se condemned);[53] themes of cultural degeneration and satanic force, partly evidenced by sexual license, were again emphasized by some writers;[54] and anticommunist and anti-Semitic themes played out, with some exceptions, much the same. In the remainder of this chapter, I narrow my analysis to focus exclusively on the question of gay rights, which began in this period to occupy an increasing number of pages in the journal. *CT* responded to the challenge of the emerging lesbian and gay movement in three primary ways: through biblical commentaries, by analyzing the role of the church, and through reporting on the campaigns of gay activists.

By the mid-1960s *CT* began to take note of a sea

change in social attitudes to homosexuality. *CT* news analysis reported criminal-law reforms in Britain implementing aspects of the Wolfenden Report,[55] and growing discussions among American Protestants about the status of gay members and clergy.[56] During this period much of the language used was fairly neutral. In other words, the writers employed, with some exceptions, standards of "objective" journalism and were not themselves partisan speakers in the debate.

One report, for example, in 1970 detailed the founding of the gay Metropolitan Community Church in Los Angeles.[57] The story noted that the church's establishment "reflects both the growing willingness of homosexuals to assert themselves as a movement and a more relaxed attitude toward homosexuals by religious groups" (48). The report went on to discuss several personal stories of members, and concluded: "Although the congregation includes a sprinkling of limp-wrist stereotypes, leather-clad boys, colorfully frilled men, and Mack-trucklike women, the great majority are indistinguishable in appearance from a typical WASP congregation. Like those in straight churches, most who attend Metropolitan come with problems of all kinds in the hope that God, with a little help from his friends, will make his love known to them" (50). Other stories during this period reported on rising gay militancy, and growing divisions within the church, but still in relatively neutral terms.[58]

One exception to the general tenor of *CT* journalism at this time was a piece written by a self-proclaimed "non-practicing homosexual" (18, 15 [1974]: 13–14). Identified only by the initials I. M., the author, in a piece provocatively titled "Metropolitan Community Church: Deception Discovered," argued that the MCC "encourages non-practicing homosexuals to express themselves by relating to one other member of their own sex," and fails to tell its members that homosexuality stands condemned by God (14). The inflammatory tone of this piece stood in some contrast to the ex-gay genre generally, which tended to approach the topic more sympathetically (see below).

While *CT* journalists were taking note of the rising lesbian and gay movement, the journal also took pains to explain thoroughly the correct biblical position on homosexuality. During these years *CT* published several writers who, through biblical exegesis, presented what they perceived to be the inevitable, negative opinion on homosexuality found in the Scriptures.[59] Some engaged directly with liberal evangelical interpretations, and all concluded that the Scriptures were clear—homosexual behavior was sinful.[60] At the same time almost all emphasized the "love the sinner, hate the sin" principle, and some chastised the church for its failure to show compassion.

Despite this understanding, the construction of homosexuality and homosexuals in these texts was unequivocal. One early editorial argued that prohibitions against homosexuality were "divinely inspired"; often, as here, gays themselves were represented as sad and pathetic, their own bodies evidence of the Scripture's Truth: "[h]omosexual relations are almost never lasting, and the dominant mood in 'gay' bars or in the 'cruising' areas of our cities is one of loneliness and compulsive searching. . . . Seldom do relationships last beyond the moment. Former partners frequently engage in blackmail schemes, thus further debasing the relationships."[61]

But while these pictures were clearly unflattering, it is worth vigorously making the point that condemnations

46

of homosexuality did not necessarily result in support for criminalization, or any other repressive measures. On the contrary, one writer indicated his support for the Wolfenden recommendation to decriminalize same-sex activity in private, believing the individual homosexual to be "more sinned against than sinning."[62] One commentator went even further, arguing that "the time is surely gone when, in the name of Christ, anyone may justly persecute a homosexual or mount a political effort that deliberately seeks a public policy of discrimination."[63]

During this period *CT* also published a series of articles concerned with how the church should respond to gay rights. The first editorial on the subject was unequivocal, clearly indicating that any debate within the church had only one correct resolution.

47

> Scripture pronounces its own judgment on homosexuality and states clearly that those who practice it shall not inherit the kingdom of God. . . . Romans 1:18–32 shows that homosexuality is contrary to nature, and that it is part of the degeneration of man that guarantees ultimate disaster in the life and the life to come. . . . We are quick to point out that grace is for the homosexual too. But grace does not legitimize what is sinful. The Church had better make it plain that Christianity and homosexuality are incompatible even as it proclaims deliverance for the homosexual from his sinful habit through faith in Jesus Christ.[64]

By 1969, in terms reminiscent of anticommunist and anti-Catholic rhetoric, the journal also began to associate the gay movement with having a wider agenda, particularly one centered on promoting homosexuality in the schools. One article, questioning a federal sex education curriculum, directly noted the perceived advantages to "perverts" of all kinds: "Homosexuals, voyeurs, exhibitionists, and other deviates will be tempted to join the teaching ranks in an attempt to gain either an outlet for their sexual drives or a platform from which to propagandize for public acceptance of their irregularities."[65] A follow-up editorial in 1970 expressed dismay that "homosexuals have become more and more demanding of late," and a third, in 1972, noted that the "Gay Liberation Front is gaining ground"; this contribution also made several explicit links between homosexuality and child molestation.[66]

Harold Lindsell, one of *CT*'s chief editors during this period, found an occasion to write a feature article upon receiving a Presbyterian magazine portraying homosexuals as "whole, healthy, appealing persons."[67] Lindsell, appalled by the magazine's naïveté and disregard for Christian tenets, wielded strong language to condemn his wayward brethren. In referring to a "homosexual murder case" (although he noted that this was an "extreme"), and accusing the Presbyterian magazine of making "effective use of the technique of brainwashing," Lindsell also states that the "lack of compassion many Christians show for homosexuals is inexcusable." Nevertheless, he clearly has no misgivings about how the church ought to respond.

> A church that decides to show compassion toward the homosexual by admitting him to full rights and privileges shows a false compassion that confirms the sinner in his wicked ways. . . . It is discrimination on the part of the church to exclude homosexuals, but it is not oppression. Discrimination lies at the heart of Christianity. The ax of God's holiness and righteousness divides the saved

48

from the lost. The church does not admit atheists and agnostics to its fellowship, and this is discrimination; it does not admit unitarians either. Nor should it admit fornicators, adulterers, and drunkards, whom the Scriptures say are not eligible for admission to the fellowship of saints. . . . The final and conclusive argument against homosexuality does not come from the psychologists, the sociologists, the secularists, or the humanists. It comes from God, who has spoken his word against it and has never stuttered in his speech. (12)

It must also be pointed out that, while the editors' opinions were absolute, other articles, published in *CT* at the same time as these others, took a more lenient approach. One of the leading evangelical feminists, for example, wrote a feature extolling the biblical virtues of same-sex friendship, noting that "it seems especially regrettable that so much homophobia exists among evangelicals."[68]

CT's hard line on homosexuality was also challenged in the mid-1970s from a different quarter, as a new genre of literature gained some currency. Although it is difficult to establish just when the ministries to homosexuals took off, it seems clear that by this period there were several large organizations working with individuals who wished desperately to be straight. Perhaps because the leaders of these organizations were often ex-gays themselves, their writings in *CT* were often (but not always) more sympathetic to the "plight of the homosexual." In 1975, for example, a founder of one such ministry expressly argued in favor of antidiscriminatory legislation for lesbians and gay men: "The churches can and should support legislation that would give the homosexual equal rights in employment, housing, and public accommodation."[69] The

49

author's argument was that, once legal discrimination ended, "Gay Lib" would have little left to fight for, and the church could "then pursue in ministry the problem of the homosexual's relation to God." The role played by these ex-gay ministries increased in the 1980s, and I continue on that theme below.

So for *CT* the late 1960s and 1970s were characterized by the journal's growing awareness of homosexuality as a sin with a movement behind it. While the journal reported on the movement's activities with a fairly objective eye, *CT*'s editors chose to publish biblical condemnations together with their own clear statements on the appropriate response of the church. It is also possible to discern a growing concern with "gay militancy," and an increase in the linking of homosexuality to sexual crime.

50　　Arguably, as the gay rights movement grew in force, lesbians and gays began to be seen less as Jews, and more as Communists. By this I mean that by the late 1970s the dominant representation of the homosexual in *CT* was no longer the pathetic, wayward individual. Rather, the gay movement was increasingly being portrayed as "counter-evangelistic"—as an anti-Christian force, promoting a heresy increasingly sanctioned by the state in the form of decriminalization and the extension of civil rights.

Yet at the same time no direct position on legal rights for lesbians and gay men appears to have been taken. It was a silence (in *CT*) reminiscent of an earlier period— that of calls for a civil rights act for African Americans in the late 1950s and early 1960s (see chapter 7). One of the first direct references to civil rights for lesbians and gay men came in 1980, during the height of the Reagan/Carter election campaign: "From the governing principles contained in the Bible many inferences can be drawn.

Legislation should benefit family structures, not penalize them. It should preserve the civil rights of all, including homosexuals, but not approve and advance immoral lifestyles."[70] No guidance was given as to how these two seemingly incompatible objectives ought to be achieved.

The Third Era, 1980–1989

In the 1980s, as in the previous period, homosexuality was again much discussed by the journal. However, biblical expositions receded,[71] perhaps because no more needed to be said, and a new species of article gained ascendancy—that of the ex-gay genre. As I noted above, writing of this type tended to adopt a largely sympathetic tone, while at the same time clearly asserting that homosexuality was wrong and, ultimately, unsatisfying on a personal level.

A feature piece, published in 1981, epitomized this approach, and it is worth considering it in some detail.[72] The article was written by Tom Minnery, who later became an important antigay campaigner as an official with Focus on the Family. The front page of the feature presented a photograph showing, presumably, two gay men, with their backs to the viewer, walking with their arms around each other in an intimate embrace. In the text the author was intent to convey, in strong terms, that many conservative Christians themselves had been going about opposing homosexuality in the wrong way. Minnery included interviews with lesbians and gay men who recounted how they were helped to change through "love," rather than "condemnation, hatred and fear" (37), while he commented that "[t]he important fact emerging from the CHRISTIAN-ITY TODAY investigation is that Christians won't get

51

through to homosexuals until they overcome their understandable fears and learn to accept them as people and take the time to develop their trust" (40).

Minnery also took great pains to refute the accusation that gays pose a threat to children: "The trouble with such sweeping accusations is that there's not much solid evidence that homosexuals are any more likely to commit sex crimes than are heterosexuals" (16). He quotes, with apparent approval, a psychiatrist who argues that "there is no persuasive evidence that homosexuals are more likely to be child molesters"; indeed the psychiatrist suggests that they may be less so (41). Minnery even goes so far as to accuse Anita Bryant, at that time leading a Florida antigay campaign, of "unwittingly provid[ing] ammunition for homosexuals wanting an excuse to fight rather than change."

As we shall see, this was a rather different tone to one being adopted by other conservative Christians during this period, and later by *CT* (and Tom Minnery himself). In the ex-gay genre the lesbian or gay man was represented as being deeply unhappy in the homosexual lifestyle, but in need of love and compassion to come out of it. Vitriolic attacks, or "antihomosexual hysteria" as Tom Minnery put it (16), were viewed as obstacles to this process. Throughout the 1980s *CT* published several other articles in this same vein.[73]

As before, *CT* continued to print news reports on gay activism. Whereas previously these items had centered upon developments within the church, by the 1980s the journal covered gay rights struggles generally, as well as the response to these demands made by local conservative Christians. It is worth noting, however, that these reports continued to be written in relatively neutral language—

the activities of both gay activists and their opponents are conveyed in a journalistic fashion, with only a slight bias evident in favor of antigay campaigners.[74]

At the same time the editorial stance of *CT* remained far more assertive in its position. In one editorial, written in 1983, the journal noted that heterosexuals "need to repent—of our un-Christianlike attitude to homosexuals."[75] However, in the same piece the editors clearly differentiated homosexuality from race and sex, arguing that "homosexualism" cannot "slide in under the same rubric of basic human freedoms" (8). This would appear to be one of the first instances in which *CT* confronted the argument that sexual orientation *is* analogous to race or sex; it is a claim that the conservative Christian movement continued to dispute with increasing vigor (see chapters 3 and 5).

Aside from the significant increase in the ex-gay genre, there were few other differences between *CT*'s response to gay issues in the 1980s, as compared to the 1970s. In contrast to what I expected to find, the journal's tone did not escalate, few references were made to the phrase now uttered routinely by the CR—"the homosexual agenda"—and fears about children were not only largely absent, but often expressly discounted. While *CT* certainly maintained its theological opposition to homosexuality, only by implication can one infer a similar resistance to gay rights legislation. Once again, no direct stand was taken. Perhaps even more remarkably, *CT* showed little concern with the AIDS epidemic, and rarely articulated AIDS and homosexuality together (but see Toulouse 1993, 256–57). Arguably, *CT* was in danger of losing touch with its constituency and its fears. Interesting as well is that rhetoric about general "cultural degeneration"

53

also decreased during this period, as did articles dealing with prophecy and satanism. However, these themes, as well as a new perspective on homosexuality, picked up considerably in the 1990s.

THE CURRENT ERA, 1990s

"[E]vangelicals need to reappropriate the Bible's gritty recognition that the presence and reality of the demonic affects how we do ministry and carry on our witness. In a time like ours, when people dabble in counterfeit spiritualities and have hair-raising brushes with evil, and when evil clearly assumes institutional and social proportions, we need to know how to recognize and resist the work of the Adversary."[76] The editorial from which this quotation is taken appeared in a 1990 issue that contained a lengthy feature piece on the devil. Perhaps a response to the impending millennium, it signaled a renewed passion on the part of *CT*. Perhaps because the editors realized the journal was in danger of becoming stodgy and out of touch or, even worse, not conservative enough, *CT* seemed to wake up to how far forces of evil had come. In quite a significant shift from the previous decade's approach, the world of the early 1990s was once again represented as preapocalyptic—in language reminiscent of *CT*'s discourse during the 1950s and 1960s.

54

In one of the features accompanying the above editorial, Clinton E. Arnold detailed Satan's powers, advising readers how to recognize those under his sway.[77] He contended that "Satan and his forces can exert their influence on the social, economic, political, and even religious order within a culture," and observed that prominent murderers had confessed to being under Satan's influence (17–

18). Arnold argued, in advising on how to "detect the direct influence of Satan," and in terms clearly relevant to any discussion of homosexuality, "that those who persistently and wilfully continue in certain patterns of sinfulness may experience increasing amounts of direct demonic influence" (19).[78]

By implication "the demonic" was a chief concern in the issues *CT* now emphasized—particularly education. Certainly, a concern with children and education was evident in the pages of *CT* from its earliest issues. However, the 1980s had been a period in which the journal seemed to evince a rather lackluster response to contemporary developments—their rhetoric in the 1950s and 1960s was far more extreme. As the 1990s began, however, a renewed concern with these sites of struggle was evident. By 1992, for example, the journal began to publish articles condemning notions of political correctness and the resulting "new orthodoxy" of social control.[79] The catchphrase "culture wars" appeared more often—referring to "struggles over ideas and values, rights and responsibilities"—struggles which *CT*'s news reporters claimed were "reaching new levels of violence and intensity."[80]

One of the most significant forces in these battles, *CT* increasingly began to argue, was the gay rights movement. The journal rather abruptly, given its focus in the 1980s, moved away from its concern with ministry to homosexuals toward a far more aggressive response to what its editors now perceived as a highly dangerous political movement. The ex-gay genre faded to the background[81] and was supplanted by a discourse of "gay power," and for the first time news reporting on gay issues began to take on a clearly antigay hue.

One of the first incidences of this was an editorial, pub-

55

lished in March 1992.[82] The editors, writing ostensibly about the ex-gay ministries, carefully chose language signifying gay power—clearly drawing upon the literature of the wider world of conservative Christianity, to which I turn my attention in the next chapter. The editorial referred to "the gay PR machine and its media missionaries" while condemning "gaybashing" and "antigay rhetoric" (16).

Less than a year later, *CT* finally took a clearer stand on rights questions—choosing the "gays in the military" issue, then a controversial policy question for the Clinton administration.

> There may still be time to deter the President from a tragic decision that would adversely affect the moral and spiritual health of both the armed forces and the American commonwealth. . . . Homosexual practice is wrong, and it is not homophobic to say so. No faithful Christian, or any advocate of virtue, should acquiesce on this issue just because discussion of it is couched in the twisted terminology of "gay rights". . . . Nor is the issue one of equal rights or unfairness or discrimination or bigotry. Advocates of "tolerance" for practicing homosexuals in the military and society at large are generally disingenuous in this appeal: It really cloaks what amounts to a political *validation* of an unnatural, unhealthy, and ungodly lifestyle. . . . Sodomy, no matter how it is legitimized, is still a filthy practice at odds with human anatomy.[83]

But, on closer examination, this editorial was actually "guest" written, the author described as an "orthodox priest" and army chaplain (16). How much it reflected the stance of *CT*'s editors was left to the reader's imagination.

CT's news coverage also underwent a sea change in

the early 1990s. For nearly the first time since the 1960s, the journal critically examined gay activists' attempts "to encourage acceptance of homosexuality among public-school students."[84] This piece, an item in the news section, continued to report on particular examples using highly charged rhetoric previously avoided by *CT*'s journalists.

> The National Education Association is training teachers how to offer "equal opportunities" to gay and lesbian students. Lesbian couples are reading politically charged children's books to San Francisco Kindergartners during story time. In fact, around the United States, homosexual activists—seasoned by their political successes over AIDS, abetted by the educational and social-work establishments, and strengthened by the support of the Clinton administration—are pushing harder than ever for schools to promote their sexual orientation as being on the same moral plane with heterosexuality. (70)

57

The journalist, Dale Buss, went on to accuse gays and lesbians of "wrapping themselves in popular ideas about mutual tolerance"; indeed the words "tolerance" and "understanding" were several times written with quotation marks, perhaps indicating the author's derision (72). An insert in this piece listed the various "tactics" used by "homosexual activists" in their "bid to occupy the high ground in the battle over schools."

But it was several months later, in July 1993, that the Christianity Today Institute (the journal's think tank) finally took on the gay rights movement directly. In a two-page editorial and eight-page feature report, *CT*'s editors resolved to "speak the truth." The editorial, written by David Neff, set the tone and to do so relied on comments by conservative blacks and gays disputing the notion that homosexuals were an oppressed minority.[85] He then proceeded to stake out *CT*'s position on gay rights: "At base, we must reject the civil-rights approach to gaining gay acceptance, not just because it locks homosexuals into a victim identity, but, more fundamentally, because it locks them into a homosexual identity. . . . Enshrining gay identity in civil-rights legislation does not bring freedom, but bondage. True freedom is found in growing toward what God, not biology, calls us to be" (15).[86] With this statement, then, *CT* both put an end to any doubt about its position and made a different choice than it had twenty-five years earlier when confronted with imminent civil rights legislation for African Americans (see chapter 7).

The main article in this institute feature resuscitated the theological grounding for opposing homosexuality, urged Christians to be compassionate, and advocated increased support for the ex-gay ministries.[87] This author's tone was quite different from, for example, Dale Buss's earlier piece on the gay agenda in the schools. While the author urged Christians to "speak the truth" about "God's view of homosexual behavior," at the same time he noted that

58

> we can fail by saying the right things but in the wrong way. Too many Christians have let hate slip into their rhetoric on this issue. The challenge here is to be the loving opposition, to imitate our Lord, who chases down his sinful creatures with aggressively open arms while all the while saying no to our sins. We all need to repent of our arrogant and intolerant attitudes toward those whose struggles are different from ours. Our goal must be to become a community that embodies the welcoming grace and love of our Lord Jesus Christ. (25)

Arguably, this article existed in some tension with others from the early 1990s. Indeed, these themes of tolerance and understanding stood in contrast to Dale Buss's use of these words in quotation marks, and to other conservative Christian texts of this period (see chapter 3). It thus seems fair to say that *CT*, while clearly taking a stand against gay rights legislation, also displayed a certain amount of ambivalence as to where, on the antigay spectrum, it wished to place itself.

By the middle of the decade, this tension was revealed as more general, with *CT* attempting to position itself in the center of contemporary conservative Christian politics. Indeed, in the mid-1990s the journal's concern with gay rights became, once again, more muted, perhaps in reaction to the ascendancy of populist, conservative rhetoric following the 1994 election of a Republican Congress.[88] Nevertheless, the journal's construction of the homosexual, once largely a benign portrait of unhappiness, had clearly shifted over the decades. The lesbian and gay movement had become a power to be reckoned with. In contrast to the main photograph accompanying the 1982 feature on homosexuality, of two embracing men walking away from the viewer, the 1993 feature opened with a picture of a young man, facing the camera, fist in the air, yelling. In the next chapter I explore the ways in which this image more accurately reflects how the CR represents the lesbian and gay movement.

Representing Homosexuality
and Its Agenda

This chapter analyzes, in some detail, the extent and manner in which the CR has identified the lesbian and gay movement as a serious threat. First, I am interested in establishing that the CR has indeed come to list the fight against gay rights among its foremost political priorities. The homosexual agenda is not a peripheral issue requiring a modicum of energy; rather, the struggle against the social and political demands of lesbians and gay men now ranks among the CR's most important objectives. Second, I hope to illustrate and explore the forms within which the CR's homosexual movement takes shape. What is it about this movement that is so threatening? Is it the demands themselves or the actual bodies (and souls) of the claimants that the CR opposes? In short, how are lesbians and gay men, their social movement and perceived agenda, represented in CR discourse?

The CR, like any social movement, does not espouse one view on this—there are many representations. Some are more vitriolic, others more tempered in their assessment. I consider a range of discourses, pointing out connections as well as contradictions between them. I begin the chapter by illustrating the manner in which the CR has prioritized the antigay agenda. The rest of the chapter is concerned with analyzing the discourses within which the homosexual enemy is constructed.

PRIORITIZING THE ANTIGAY AGENDA

As I suggested in chapter 2, conservative Protestant perspectives on gay issues underwent shifts in tone and substance over several decades. By the early 1980s the CR increasingly began to occupy itself with the lesbian and gay movement, no doubt in response to the growing visibility of gay rights demands and the grassroots antigay activities of local organizers (see chapter 1).[1] By the late 1980s and into the 1990s, these developments precipitated the emergence of a new CR cultural genre, consisting of books, videos, and special reports, specifically dedicated to identifying the gay threat, and calling Christian believers to arms.

At the same time, leading CR organizations began to reorient their agendas to include, and in many cases to prioritize, the struggle against the lesbian and gay movement. Their newsletters, magazines, workshops, and other resources soon featured this new urgency. Conservative Christian antigay activities, previously ad hoc and largely the product of localized conflict, began to assume more of a national, coordinated, organized character.

One of the first books to emerge devoted entirely to gay issues was Tim LaHaye's *Unhappy Gays* (later reprinted as *What Everyone Should Know about Homosexuality*), published

61

in 1978. Aside from being married to Beverly LaHaye, president of Concerned Women for America, Tim La-Haye's CR connections are deep and long-standing. He has been a leading figure in a number of organizations, including the Moral Majority, the Council on National Policy, the Traditional Values Coalition, National Empowerment Television, and the Coalition on Revival.[2]

At the start of *Unhappy Gays* (1978, 10), LaHaye explains the decision to turn his attention to homosexuality in the mid-1970s: "Everywhere I turned, newspapers, television, and many individuals bombarded me with the realization that America is experiencing a homosexual epidemic." According to LaHaye, "straights" had better wake up fast to the fact that "[t]he homosexual community, by militance and secret political maneuvering, is designing a program to increase the tidal wave of homosexuality that will drown our children in a polluted sea of sexual perversion—and will eventually destroy America as it did Rome, Greece, Pompeii, and Sodom" (179).

Another early work was Enrique Rueda's *The Homosexual Network* (1982). Rueda, a Catholic priest active in CR organizations, wrote the book at the behest of Paul Weyrich, a leading CR activist and president of the Free Congress Research and Education Foundation.[3] *The Homosexual Network* went out of print but was incorporated into a subsequent publication by Rueda—*Gays, AIDS, and You* (1987). Both books were published by Devin-Adair, a company that allegedly produces Holocaust denial material (Anti-Defamation League 1994). In these texts Rueda undertakes a study of homosexual "subculture," concluding that homosexuals are wealthy political players who have successfully advanced the forces of liberalism (see below). However prescient in flagging the issue, the early

62

warnings provided by LaHaye and Rueda languished in relative obscurity until rejuvenated in the early 1990s by subsequent developments.

By this time the antigay genre had been supplemented by several more texts, one of the most notable being William Dannemeyer's *Shadow in the Land: Homosexuality in America* (1989). Dannemeyer, a U.S. congressman at the time with a long history of antigay activism, writes in tones reminiscent of rhetoric that might have fueled medieval crusades. Even the cover highlights the forbidding, threatening character of the problem. It features a drawing of two identical-looking men (white, dark hair, bushy eyebrows and moustache) with arms raised and fists clenched (fists possibly interlocked in the air). Their mouths are open (one appears to have his tongue extended), and they are shouting. They march behind a banner that reads, in huge red letters, "Gay Power." The U.S. Capitol looms in the background. The tone of the book is signified by the shadow metaphor—an evil presence is stalking America.

63

Shadow in the Land canvasses several topics, including the causes of homosexuality, the role of the church, the power of the gay movement, and AIDS and public policy. William Dannemeyer, then a Republican member of Congress and sponsor of a California ballot initiative to eliminate anonymous HIV testing, begins his book by detailing the successes of the gay movement and then asks: "How are we, as supporters of the Judeo-Christian ethic, supposed to respond to this well-planned and well-financed attack on our civilization? The question faces us wherever we turn, demanding an answer—not in ten years, not in two years, but this year, now! . . . We must either defeat militant homosexuality or it will defeat us"

(17–18). Elsewhere, Dannemeyer's rhetoric becomes even more urgent, reminiscent of earlier anticommunist discourse (see chapter 2): "the United States . . . is surrendering to this growing army of revolutionaries without firing a single shot, indeed, without more than a word of protest. The homosexual blitzkrieg has been better planned and better executed than Hitler's. . . . we don't even know we've been conquered" (121).

As the book reaches its climax, Dannemeyer describes lesbians and gays as "the ultimate enemy" (134), a horde likened to "Genghis Khan's army" (139), and their reorientation of language (e.g., "homophobia") as a "putsch" (141). He tolls the bell on the final page: "we have the capacity to make the wrong choice and plunge our people, and indeed the entire West, into a dark night of the soul that could last hundreds of years before the flame is again lit. It has happened before. It can happen again. It is in full knowledge of such a grim possibility that I have written this book" (228).[4]

Shadow in the Land, given the legitimacy of its source (a U.S. congressman) and its arrival at an opportune moment in CR resurgence, has become a foundational CR antigay text; it is cited authoritatively in subsequent genre publications, of which there have been many. In one of these, entitled *When the Wicked Seize a City: A Grim Look at the Future and a Warning to the Church*, the authors reiterate Dannemeyer's theme of the need for urgent response. "Either the Church becomes militant in its opposition to sin, and aggressive for righteousness and healing, or we will see the collapse of our entire culture into a hedonistic nightmare—with deadly consequences for millions" (McIlhenny, McIlhenny, and York 1993, 27).

The authors of this text, Chuck and Donna McIlhenny, have become folk heroes of the antigay genre.

Their attempts to "clean up" San Francisco and the violent backlash their activities provoked, chronicled in *When the Wicked*, have been lauded as inspirational by subsequent writers. Two of these, dedicated to explaining the true nature of the homosexual movement, are George Grant and Mark Horne. They deploy a similar apocalyptic rhetoric in declaring that the writing of *Legislating Immorality: The Homosexual Movement Comes out of the Closet* "involved the fiercest spiritual warfare that either of us has ever experienced" (1993, xii).

In other books with a wider focus, the lesbian and gay movement is also represented as one of the most portentous current threats. Dobson and Bauer, in *Children at Risk* (1990, 107), write that "today there are few political and social movements as aggressive, powerful, or successful as 'gay rights' advocates"; in *Winning the New Civil War* (1991, 177), Robert Dugan suggests that "homosexual rights may provoke the bitterest and most prolonged battle of all"; Steve Farrar's call (1994, 114, 118) to Christian men describes the gay issue as "high noon for America"; "the destroyers," he writes, are "in the streets"; and Roger Magnuson (1994, 13), a lawyer and prominent public speaker on family issues, states that "militant homosexuals are on the march . . . to drastically alter the fabric of American culture."

All of these books are targeted primarily at Christian believers and are intended as a wake-up call. They tend to be available solely at Christian bookstores or by mail order, and are published by small and large Christian presses. In the antigay genre, publishers that figure most prominently include Huntington House (Louisiana), Moody (Illinois), Multnomah (Oregon), and Word (Dallas).

The sometimes fevered rhetorical pitch of this literature is to be expected of what are essentially inspirational and action-oriented texts aimed at a preexisting but lethargic constituency. In attempting to set gay rights as a national Christian priority, the genre tends to share several key themes. The most prominent of these is that "ordinary Americans" are in a state of war (see Linder 1982). The enemy is profoundly powerful; it is an enemy that invisibly stalks its prey (the shadow) and, at the same time, is out in the streets, aggressively and visibly battling for supremacy (the militant). In this scenario it is now or never to take up arms for Jesus.

The emergence of a specific antigay genre reflected new developments within CR politics. It is not simply that some books were published exhorting believers to make antigay struggle a priority; at the organizational level, this had already begun to occur. As I noted in chapter 1, CR antigay activity was apparent from the 1970s. In the early 1980s Jerry Falwell's Moral Majority was also engaged in vociferous antigay campaigning (see Jorstad 1987).

More recently, the mantle has been taken up by other organizations, such as Focus on the Family.[5] They have produced volumes of antigay material, including several front-page stories in the organization's political magazine, *Citizen*. One of the first of these, appearing in June 1991, was entitled "How Homosexuals Push Their Agenda." It accused "homosexual activists" of making backroom deals with legislators in a bid to achieve gains secretly that they could not win democratically. For the most part the piece detailed the brave efforts of "pro-family activists" who refused "to give up despite long odds" (2). Another front-page gay feature was published in 1992, and in 1993 an entire issue of *Citizen* was devoted to the media bias against conservative evangelicals, as exemplified by the backlash against the passage of an antigay rights amendment in Colorado.[6] Yet another front-page feature appeared in 1996, this time to oppose same-sex marriage rights.[7]

Throughout these years, antigay news stories were published regularly in *Citizen*. Focus's Canadian office in Vancouver has been even more preoccupied with the perceived successes of the gay movement in that country. In 1994–1995 alone, at least five front-page stories appeared in the Canadian version of *Citizen*.[8] In one, entitled "Why You Should Get Involved," Focus on the Family Canada lists "Gay Rights" at the very top of its political agenda.[9]

Focus on the Family's close affiliate, the Family Research Council (FRC), has also made homosexuality one of its key advocacy issues.[10] The FRC publishes a special collection of materials on homosexual issues covering a range of topics, including sex education in the schools and the "hidden gay agenda."[11] The packet also provides information on ordering the controversial video series *The Gay Agenda* (discussed below) and contains several "parental advisories" to keep "shocking" material away from young children.

Many other national conservative Christian organizations have also targeted the lesbian and gay rights movement, for example, the American Family Association, Concerned Women for America, and the Free Congress Research and Education Foundation.[12] All of these organizations have put the fight against gay rights at the heart of their political campaigning, and workshops on "the gay agenda" have become more frequent and sophisticated at annual conferences of these and other profamily organizations.

The immediacy and significance of the antigay agenda

67

is particularly highlighted by the emergence of dozens of conservative Christian organizations devoted solely to antigay activities. These include Paul Cameron's Family Research Institute, Ty and Jeanette Beeson's The Report (producers of *The Gay Agenda* videos and former publishers of Peter LaBarbera's *Lambda Report*) and state/municipal organizations such as Family First (Massachusetts), Yes! Repeal Homosexual Ordinance (Tampa), Idaho Citizen's Alliance, and Equal Rights—Not Special Rights (Cincinnati), to name just a few (see also chapter 1). Interestingly, some organizations with gay rights as an initial raison d'être, for example Oregon Citizen's Alliance and Colorado for Family Values, have since branched out into other right-wing activities as well (see chapter 7).

Finally, some measure of the prominence gay issues found on the conservative Christian agenda by the mid-1990s was evidenced by the nature of the attendance at a national antigay strategizing conference, held in 1994. Several dozen representatives from over thirty national and local organizations met in Colorado Springs, to hear speeches by campaigners and theorists and set future strategy.[13] Clearly, antigay activism had achieved a profile and coherence not seen before.

Mirroring these organizational developments, the prominence of gay issues for the CR was most publicly visible in its waging of antigay law-reform initiatives (see chapters 1 and 6). The CR's antigay agenda was not simply rhetorical; grassroots campaigning had frequent success in rolling back the gains achieved by the lesbian and gay rights movement. Indeed, it is not an exaggeration to say, and no doubt many conservative Christians themselves would agree, that by the mid-1990s the battle between the CR and the lesbian and gay movement was one of the most significant arenas of social struggle in the

United States. This view was echoed by all of the CR activists I interviewed for this book, many of whom were active on other fronts as well. Nevertheless, they ranked gay rights among their "top five" priorities; for several, it headed the list.

Constructing the Enemy

My concern is with the underlying sexual politics of the CR, rather than the details of its success and failures on the gay rights front. I therefore now wish to explore the diverse knowledges informing CR representations of homosexuality. In order to do this, I have divided my discussion into three parts: homosexuality itself, in other words, how the "condition" of homosexuality is represented; homosexual practice, how the "condition" manifests itself in particular behaviors; and the gay movement and its agenda. In these sections I focus on how the dominant representation of the homosexual is the gay man. In chapter 4 I examine the CR's presentation of lesbianism.

69

The Homosexual Condition

There are two key themes in CR characterizations of homosexuality. First, homosexual practice is an incontrovertible sin. Biblical inerrancy demands this conclusion; any other is not truly Christian. Second, homosexuality is a chosen behavior, and not an immutable genetic or psychological trait. In keeping with this notion, many conservative Christians operate homosexual therapy clinics intended to help and keep individuals out of the "lifestyle."[14] In the previous chapters I spent some time tracing biblical injunctions against homosexuality. Here I focus instead on the second, but not unrelated, theme.

The vast majority of CR literature reiterates, again and

again, that homosexuality is a behavioral choice, not an innate affliction. Every book on the topic spends at least several pages on this question,[15] and organizational publications similarly rehearse anti-immutability arguments.[16] Their public case is made largely on scientific grounds, although, as I discuss below, theological beliefs continue to loom large here as elsewhere. As is usual in these sorts of debates, the CR seeks both to demolish the arguments of their opponents, particularly the "gay gene" and brain-differentiation scientists,[17] and to construct their own, secularized explanation for homosexual behavior.

The scientific data upon which the CR literature relies is drawn from a range of sources; most can be traced back to a small number of primary texts that tend to be recycled throughout the movement's literature. These in turn can be subdivided into those that focus on either biological or psychological causation. In terms of biology, two particular studies are consistently cited to refute gay gene/brain theories (Byne and Parsons 1993; King and McDonald 1992). These data dispute the conclusions of the biological determinists by questioning their methodology. The critics do not attempt to prove the opposite case—that there is *no* biological cause of homosexuality—but that is the general presumption in the antigay genre.

On the psychological front the response of the CR is somewhat more ambivalent. Here the work of two authors figures prominently—Elizabeth Moberly (1983) and Joseph Nicolosi (1991, 1993). Moberly's thesis is that, in early childhood, homosexuals suffer a developmental deficit. In her view, homosexuality is caused largely by a dysfunction in the parent-child relationship. Nicolosi has extended these ideas in his influential work *Reparative Ther-*

apy of Male Homosexuality (1991).[18] Perhaps unsurprisingly, these authors suggest that gay men overidentify with their mother (due to an absent or dysfunctional father), while lesbianism may result from sexual abuse or weak mother-modeling. Importantly, CR "psy" theories insist that, with proper counseling, gays can (and should) be made straight.[19]

In contrast to the biological literature, CR activists are more responsive to these psychological theories as they both pathologize homosexuality and provide further ammunition in the fight against single parenthood and inappropriate gender modeling. This "psy" genre also presents homosexuals as pathetic and unfulfilled; gay men and lesbians constantly seek parental substitutes as love objects—a doomed and tragic quest. Homosexuality is, in these terms, the "sexualization of an emotional pathology" (Kevin Tebedo, interview by author, 1994). Importantly, "psy" theories implicitly refute biological ones; however, by focusing on deep-seated childhood trauma they also undermine the preferred CR reading that homosexuality is nothing more than a sinful, behavioral choice.

In the realm of sexuality, there are two key reasons for the CR's opposition to immutability theory, one theological, one practical. On religious grounds it cannot be possible, within the conservative Christian worldview, for God to have "made" homosexuals. Clearly, God made Eve for Adam (not Madam, as one campaigner reportedly put it[20]), and subsequent Scripture expressly condemns same-sex sexuality. Homosexual conduct is, therefore, a sin akin to adultery—individuals are no more "born gay" than they are born adulterers.

For most conservative Protestants, human agency is a

71

key determinant of social life. While God has an overall plan that will eventually come to pass, he does not (usually) intervene to manipulate individual behavior on a day-to-day basis. Furthermore, Satan constantly attempts to thwart this plan, and Jesus' armies are in continuous battle with satanic forces. Homosexuality, then, is a sinful choice, the practice of which, like all sinful behaviors, furthers Satan's agenda.[21]

On a practical level the CR came to perceive the immutability question as a crucial political issue, largely because the mainstream lesbian and gay rights movement had made it so. In many countries, but particularly in the United States, where constitutional equality law has been seen to demand it as a criterion for inclusion, gay activists have often made the immutability argument an important plank of rights campaigns. While this has proved controversial within lesbian and gay communities, the public face of the rights movement has, for the most part, continued to point to scientific evidence suggesting that sexual orientation is innate.[22]

The argument is an important one on both legal and moral grounds. Constitutionally, the more sexual orientation could be held to "be like" race, or even sex, the more likely lesbians and gay men would be found to deserve constitutional rights.[23] Because immutability was seen to be a significant characteristic of these other categories, establishing it became central to the pursuit of lesbian and gay legal equality.[24] In addition, many gay rights activists have proceeded on the belief that the heterosexual public is likely to be more sympathetic if they believe that homosexuals are unable to change their sexual orientation.[25] A failure to provide legal protection can then look mean and intolerant. For these reasons the CR identified immutability early on as a significant battleground of debate on gay issues.

For conservative Christians anti-immutability is perfectly consistent with their theological knowledge. A "gay identity" did not exist in the Bible; the sins of Sodom were behavioral, not ontological. Homosexual identity is thus a modern and, in their view, a human invention.[26] Interestingly, this understanding of sexuality resembles that of radical feminist and gay theory, rather than the mainstream gay rights movement.[27] In contrast, however, the CR is quick to dismiss with derision any suggestion that *gender* is socially constructed. Masculinity and femininity are neither behaviors nor identities; rather, they are God-given, biological essences (see Herman 1994, chap. 5). This perspective is confused and hazy in several respects, particularly when it comes to discussing the need for appropriate gender role modeling. In chapter 4 I examine more closely the CR's understanding of the relationship between gender and sexuality.

73

It may also be worth noting three further points to do with conservative Christianity and immutability doctrine. First, this is one area where the CR has been able to enter the gay rights debate on secular ground. Indeed, the ground is that of science—often referred to as a false god in conservative Christian discourse. But the immutability debate has allowed the CR to pose as objective researchers and to publish documents ostensibly containing no religious content whatsoever (e.g., Burtoft 1994).[28]

Second, the extent to which the CR has viewed the immutability debate as crucial is evidence of the seriousness with which they have taken both mainstream America's commitment to liberal equality and the cultural power of constitutional inclusion (see chapter 6 on the latter). In other words, the CR has proceeded against gay rights, rightly or wrongly, on the understanding that if people think homosexuality has a biological foundation then the CR will be less likely, and less able, to stand in the way of protective law reform. Sexuality, like race and sex, will be seen to be beyond an individual's control, and therefore not the appropriate subject of discrimination.

The CR's focus on demolishing immutability theory thus may have reflected its perception that in the United States a general climate of liberal tolerance and antidiscrimination existed during the period in which these arguments were most emphatically voiced. As I explore further in chapter 5, this climate began to chill in the early 1990s and the CR's preoccupation with immutability diminished similarly. Arguably, by the mid-1990s the CR was speaking less about causation and more about power and greed (and this too provides a secularized entrée into the debate). But that is not to say that these latter themes were not present in earlier discourse (as I go on to consider in the final section of this chapter).

Finally, and this is paradoxical given the emphasis on anti-immutability, the CR is keen to establish that the condition of homosexuality occurs in no more than 1–2% of the population. The reason for this position is twofold. First, if lesbians and gays form an insignificant percentage of the population, then the case for civil rights protection may be less compelling than it might be if the 10% figure usually cited by gay activists were accepted.[29] Second, in demonstrating the fallacy of the 10% figure, the duplicity of the gay movement is revealed and its credibility seriously undermined. An entire trajectory of the CR antigay genre has developed to support this claim.[30] Most of this can be traced back to the work of Judith

Reisman, whose coauthored book, *Kinsey, Sex, and Fraud: The Indoctrination of a People* (1990), is held by the CR to have thoroughly succeeded in discrediting the sex research of Alfred Kinsey, upon whose data the 10% figure usually rests.

Reisman's main argument is that Kinsey's research methodology was fatally flawed; hence his conclusions, particularly those to do with the prevalence of same-sex sexual activity and the so-called Kinsey rating, are completely unsubstantiated.[31] Kinsey's data are the usual reference point to support the "10% of the population is gay" statement. Reisman argues that this is a fallacy and that the actual incidence of homosexuality is much lower. These conclusions, in turn, are deployed by the CR, together with survey data from the 1990s, as evidence that the gay population is so small as to be negligible, and that gay activists are deliberately misleading the public.[32]

Perhaps obviously, the "10% fallacy" argument is highly contradictory for the CR; it may be a case of wishing to have their cake and eat it, too. In other words, one cannot logically argue that sexuality is mutable and chosen, while insisting that lesbians and gays form an unchanging and minuscule percentage of the population. The perceived gay agenda for children, discussed below, can hardly be so dangerous unless greater and greater numbers of youth are capable of being indoctrinated. Arguably, these two propositions are irreconcilable.

One final paradox is worth noting here. Religious affiliation is clearly a "chosen" identity. For evangelical Protestants this is nowhere more evident than in the need to be "born again"—a freely chosen, adult (re)commitment to Jesus (see Lienesch 1993, chap. 1). If the religious are rightly afforded constitutional protection, why must lesbians and gay men prove genetic causation to gain the same? CR activists tend to have one primary response to this point: religious freedom is singled out in the Constitution and is thus a "special case." This response is far from satisfactory, not least because it means the CR is claiming for itself the very sort of "special rights" it denies to gays and lesbians. I take up this point further in chapters 5 and 6.

Homosexual Behavior

For the most part the CR is concerned with the manifestations of homosexuality in men. In chapter 4 I discuss the CR's response to lesbianism, such as it is. Here, however, I will focus on how gay male sexuality is represented. But I will do no more than mention several themes, that, with one exception, I will leave relatively undeveloped. Of any aspect to do with the CR and gay rights, the representation of gay male sexuality has been the most analyzed.[33] Critical scholarship in this area has tended to focus on two themes in particular: disease and seduction. These, then, I will do little more than mention in passing. A third dimension, that of anarchic hypermasculinity, has been less explored, and thus the bulk of this section will attempt to outline the contours of this theme.

DISEASE AND SEDUCTION. CR discussions of homosexual behavior are replete with images of disease-ridden gay men. Gay sexual practices, according to the CR, not only lead to the acquisition of devastating illness—AIDS being only one of these instances of "divine judgment" (Chilton 1987, 91)—but are filthy, disgusting, and unnatural at their core.[34] Gay men are accused of playing with urine and excrement, of having a hugely disproportionate incidence of sexually transmitted diseases, and of being generally ravaged, physically and spiritually. Indeed, Concerned Women for America finds gay sexual behavior so horrifying they assign a male vice president to the issue so as not to offend "the ladies" (Jim Woodall, interview by author, 1995).

For many years the primary knowledge producer for the CR in this area has been Paul Cameron, a psychologist who heads his own antigay organization, the Family Research Institute.[35] Cameron is a controversial character, both within and outside the CR. Thrown out of the American Psychological Association for violating ethical principles, and repudiated by the American Sociological Association for posing as a sociologist, Cameron and his research have been widely discredited by mainstream science.[36] His claims, and the rhetoric within which his claims are advanced, are extremist in tenor, and the mainstream CR often prefers to keep Cameron himself in the background while continuing to rely on his research in their own publications. For example, Cameron's appearance as an expert witness in the Colorado Amendment 2 litigation (see chapter 6) was widely seen by the Colorado CR to have backfired, as the press latched onto his checkered past, rather than the content of his testimony. "Actually, every time he appears anywhere, they brought him in here at the urging of the fighting fundies, I told them, I said the minute he comes on the scene he will become the issue. . . . And that's exactly what happened when over my strenuous objections he was brought in. Immediately he dominated the headlines and the whole amendment got a tremendous amount of negative press" (Tony Marco, interview by author, 1994). Despite these misgivings, Cameron was a featured speaker at the national antigay strategizing conference held in Colorado Springs.

With some exceptions CR antigay disease assertions

find their empirical origins in publications of Cameron's Family Research Institute. His data is cited by, among others, the American Family Association, the FRC, Colorado for Family Values, and Stanley Monteith, a physician appearing as an expert in *The Gay Agenda* videos (see below). Cameron's claims include that 75% of gay men regularly ingest fecal material, that 70–78% have had a sexually transmitted disease, and that all are wildly promiscuous.[37] Cameron's disease model does not stop there; he also claims that homosexuality is so perverse as to cause its practitioners to kill, and be killed, disproportionately.[38]

It is important to note, however, that Cameron's largely discredited research is not the sole source of CR antigay disease rhetoric. CR material makes frequent reference to two other sources: mainstream HIV epidemiology studies[39] and the texts of gay writers themselves. With respect to the latter, gay oral histories, gay sex manuals, advertisements in gay magazines, and lesbian and gay theorizing, all provide a significant source of information on sexual practices from which conclusions about disease are drawn. This material is also used to support the second CR behavioral theme, that of "seduction."

Gays, CR literature asserts, target children, hoping to seduce them into a life of depravity and disease (e.g., La-Haye 1991). The newsletter *Lambda Report* is perhaps the best example of how the gay press is used to make this case. *Lambda Report* began as a publication of The Report, Ty and Jeanette Beeson's antigay organization, producer of *The Gay Agenda* video series. The newsletter is now published independently by Peter LaBarbera, its editor, a journalist with past ties to several leading CR organizations who spends some of his time poring over participation lists from lesbian and gay conferences in order to harass attendees.[40] *Lambda Report*'s subtitle is "Monitoring the Homosexual Agenda in American Politics and Culture," and that is just what LaBarbera does.

The newsletters contain stories about gay-related events and activities, interviews with antigay activists, and vitriolic attacks on "pro-gay" government appointees. Perhaps even more important, *Lambda Report* reproduces extracts and advertisements from gay publications. These tend to consist of photographs of half-naked men and women, often in bondage regalia, and quotations advocating pedophilia and other practices gays supposedly aim at children. The activities of NAMBLA, the controversial gay intergenerational sex organization, are featured regularly.

Children, in this discourse of seduction, are seen to possess a malleable sexuality, vulnerable to persuasion. Homosexuals are represented as predators, subverting God's plan for youth. Debates within lesbian and gay communities, particularly those centered on the status of NAMBLA, provide significant fodder for this attack, as do the assertions of populist critics such as Camille Paglia.[41] Judith Reisman, author of *Kinsey, Sex, and Fraud,* is also an important contributor to developing the link between homosexuality and child seduction, as is Paul Cameron.[42]

These themes of disease and seduction are strongly reminiscent of older, anti-Semitic discourses. Jews historically were associated with disease, filth, urban degeneration, and child stealing (see, e.g., Gilman 1991; Mosse 1985). Some of these antigay themes also draw upon anticommunist discourse, discussed in chapter 2. Although Communists were not represented as carrying physical disease, their ideology was likened to a germ, in-

79

festing and desensitizing the innocent. Jim Woodall of Concerned Women for America (interview by author, 1995) similarly used the word "desensitization" in relation to the "gay agenda" and youth. The fate of children is paramount within both genres. In another respect, however, the construction of homosexual behavior is very different. While Communists were accused of being totalitarian dictators intent on producing a docile, compliant, and regimented public, gay sexuality, in contrast, is imbued with an inherent anarchic paganism that threatens to spiral out of control.

ANARCHIC, HYPERMASCULINE, PAGANISTIC. While it might be supposed that the CR antigay genre would draw at least in part upon the traditional stereotype of the effeminate, limp-wristed, ineffectual homosexual, this is rarely the case. Indeed, with the exception of somewhat marginal psychological causation studies, this caricature is almost absent from the literature. Instead, gay sexuality is represented as masculinity out of control, as aggressive, powerful, and unrestrained. It is an inherently "anarchic impulse" (Dannemeyer 1989, 25) and essentially an acting out of unbounded masculinity.

This theme is most visible in *The Gay Agenda* video series. Springs of Life Ministries, Ty and Jeanette Beeson's charismatic church located in Lancaster, California, has produced several antigay videos under a ministry offshoot known as The Report.[43] The most well-known of these is the first, *The Gay Agenda*, released in 1992. *The Gay Agenda* has sold many thousands of copies, has been distributed to hundreds of CR organizations, and even had a screening by the Joint Chiefs of Staff.[44] This video was followed by three others, *The Gay Agenda in Public Education* (1993),

80

The Gay Agenda: March on Washington (1993), and a feature follow-up to the original, *Stonewall: 25 Years of Deception* (1994). All of these videos contain interviews with antigay experts, and they are largely intended to be an exposé of the lesbian and gay movement's secret plans for America. The series is widely available through CR organizations (such as the 700 Club and Focus on the Family) by mail order, and comes with parental warnings. Each film opens with sensationalist commentary informing the viewer they are likely to be stunned and shocked by what they are about to see.

Visually, each film draws from similar stock footage, allegedly compiled by The Report at gay pride marches. The viewer sees shot after shot of half or wholly naked men (occasionally women; see chapter 4), usually sporting some form of sadomasochistic paraphernalia. The men scream, stick their tongues out, push their naked bums in the camera lens, and engage in sexual activity with each other in the streets. Many of the figures are covered in body paint, and there are almost always hundreds, congregated together, in any one shot. Penises, erect and otherwise, are depicted graphically, as is any sexual act the camera can get close enough to film. Images such as these also find expression elsewhere as well. Grant and Horne (1993, 2), for example, describe gay sexuality as "raucous revelry, perverse promiscuity, orgiastic opulence, and apollyonic abandon." Robert Knight of the FRC (interview by author, 1995) speaks of the "fundamental narcissism of the gay movement."

These images of gay sexual behavior contain an extraordinary combination of power, degradation, excitement, pleasure, savagery, and bacchanalian hedonism. The gay man embodies a hypermasculinity, a maleness

81

so extreme it literally ex(im)plodes. Combined with this hypermasculinity, and essential to it, is a paganistic savagery—most clearly symbolized by the shots of men in body (war) paint. Here, the videos suggest, are men "gone Native"—the half-naked, painted man signifying "brutal Indian" in racist iconography—potentially inspiring viewers to constitute themselves as late-twentieth-century pioneers, girding their own loins to take the Nation back to God. Steve Farrar (1994, 115, 131–35), in his call to Christian men, underscores this theme, drawing parallels between homosexual behavior and ancient Baal worship; Christian believers correspond to the Hebrews who drove Baal from Palestine.

Gay sexual behavior, thus, is not simply anarchic; it is fundamentally pagan—it lacks spiritual, as well as physical, discipline. Ultimately, gay sexuality is satanic in origin—and this is most clearly expressed when the CR discusses the lesbian and gay movement as a whole.

82

The Homosexual Movement and Its Agenda

These images of savagery sit uncomfortably with how the CR represents lesbians and gays as a social movement. From the first CR treatises on gay issues (e.g., Rueda 1982), writers sought to portray the lesbian and gay movement as an elite cadre of well-to-do professionals insinuating themselves into the fabric of American institutional life. The movement is portrayed as organized and powerful, its agenda as dangerous in the extreme.

According to James Dobson and Gary Bauer, authors of the influential text *Children at Risk* (1990, 107), "today there are few political and social movements as aggressive, powerful, or successful as 'gay rights' advocates." Others echo these sentiments: "the homosexual movement in America is perhaps the most well organized and most disciplined pressure group in the country today" (Dannemeyer 1989, 22); "they're talented and ruthlessly aggressive in the pursuit of their goals" (McIlhenny, McIlhenny, and York 1993, 17); "we are talking about a very powerful and wealthy group of individuals who have a clear strategy and agenda" (Farrar 1994, 117). Material published by a range of CR organizations also characterizes the movement as a whole in this way.[45]

The media particularly are represented as being in the pocket of the lesbian and gay rights movement.[46] According to Focus on the Family, for example, gay activists during the Colorado campaign for an antigay amendment managed to manipulate the media into printing a series of inaccuracies and misleading distortions all leading to a negative characterization of the individuals and organizations supporting the amendment.[47] At the same time the mainstream media, *Citizen* reporters argued, showed only positive images of the gay movement.

But it is not just the media that CR activists argue have become "gay." Other key institutions of American life have been seized (it is not clear from whom, other than an amorphous "us"), including the arts and education establishments,[48] the military, and the government itself.[49] CR literature very clearly argues that this takeover has been secretive, and that it is a fait accompli: "we don't even know we've been conquered" (Dannemeyer 1989, 121).[50] For many, HIV/AIDS education in particular was used by the gay movement as a cover for homosexual designs on youth (Robert Knight and Jim Woodall, interviews by author, 1995).

The investing of the gay movement with such potency serves to highlight imminent danger, increase fear, galva-

83

nize reaction, and construct the counteridentity of the conservative Christian activist.[51] It also helps to erect an important division for the CR: "gay militants" versus "gay others." Others may include duped troops, conservative gays, and quiet, closeted lesbians and gay men who disapprove of the movement's agenda. Importantly, "others" also includes those struggling to overcome their gay identity, as played out in the ex-gay genre. The militants who have seized power can then be distinguished from the others; the former can be demonized, while the latter are pitied: "Some of you reading this have struggled firsthand with homosexuality because of a missing emotional piece in your relationship with your father. The only response to a man who is working through this issue is biblical love and compassion. But there is another group who demands their actions be accepted and approved. Any hesitancy to do either prompts them to cry 'bigot' or 'homophobe.' These are the *militant* gays" (Farrar 1994, 117). Jim Woodall (interview by author, 1995) makes a similar distinction between "militant homosexuals" with an "in-your-face attitude," and others who simply live their lives quietly. Farrar's and Woodall's device is not an unusual one; those opposed to the CR similarly draw distinctions between the "religious fanatics" and the less blameworthy "faithful."[52]

The theme of gay power runs throughout the antigay genre. Coupled with this is the assertion that gays are inordinately wealthy in comparison to the "normal" population. I take up both these themes in detail in chapter 5, where I discuss the manner in which the CR constructs lesbians and gay men as an undeserving minority. For now, I move on to examining the representation of the gay "agenda." This agenda, according to the CR, is simple and secretive. It is, first and foremost, to "steal our children": "Children are the prize to the winners of the second great civil war. Those who control what young people are taught and what they experience—what they see, hear, think, and believe—will determine the future course of the nation. Given that influence, the predominant value system of an entire culture can be overhauled in one generation, or certainly in two, by those with unlimited access to children" (Dobson and Bauer 1990, 35).

Several gay texts form significant source material for CR claims here. Heavily cited is an article that appeared in a 1987 issue of *Gay Community News (GCN)*, a Boston newspaper. The same paragraph is quoted in dozens of CR publications.

> We shall sodomize your sons, emblems of your feeble masculinity, of your shallow dreams and vulgar lies. We shall seduce them in your schools, in your dormitories, in your gymnasiums, in your locker rooms, in your sports arenas, in your seminaries, in your youth groups, in your movie theater bathrooms, in your army bunkhouses, in your truck stops, in your all-male clubs, in your house of Congress, wherever men are with men together. Your sons shall become our minions to do our bidding. They will be recast in our image; they will come to crave and adore us.[53]

85

The article in its entirety is an outrageous, perhaps tasteless, satire; however, the CR reproduces this piece as if it constituted the secret truth of a homosexual conspiracy. Indeed, one is struck by the similarity between the deployment of the *GCN* article and past uses of another document of false conspiracy, "The Protocols of the Elders of Zion," a forged pamphlet detailing plans for a Jewish takeover of the world. Extracts from the *GCN* piece circulate and recirculate throughout CR antigay texts; authors refer to each other and rarely to the original article.

In addition to the *GCN* piece, the CR has also taken up another gay text, Marshall Kirk and Hunter Madsen's *After the Ball* (1989), which details the authors' strategy for advancing gay rights. *After the Ball* was widely criticized and uninfluential within lesbian and gay communities, but it was taken up by the CR as representative of the movement as a whole in its advocacy of "stealth techniques."[54] According to Jim Woodall (interview by author, 1995), "most of us would never pick up a book like this, and read it, but if you read it, it tells us what their strategy is." The strategic use of this text by the CR is highly disingenuous for several reasons, not least of which is the CR's own well-established embracement of stealth tactics. The claim that the agenda is secret is also paradoxical considering the CR's concurrent assertion that gay sexuality is so visibly victorious.

In detailing achievements of the gay agenda, CR literature focuses on a range of issues, most particularly those to do with children (principally, sex and HIV education in the schools), the redefinition of "family" (gay spousal and marital rights), and the inclusion of sexual orientation in civil rights laws. But for conservative Protestants, and particularly for those active in the CR, the gay movement, while powerful and dangerous, is not acting alone, and its agenda is not solely to do with gay issues. For the CR the success of lesbians and gay men is intimately linked to that of several other groups, particularly feminists, environmentalists, and New Age spiritualists, all of whom are seen to be linked by an anti-Christian ethos. For some, class politics continues to play an important role as well.

You have the extreme environmentalists, the extreme labor movement. . . . the homosexual debate is the actual frontlines. It's the no man's land, during World War I, between the trenches, it's where the actual hand-to-hand combat is goin' on right now. They're almost the vanguard of the effort on behalf of what we call the "radical left." They also have a religious left too. The abortionists, and the radical feminists, the homosexual activists, the environmentalists, the extreme labor movement, and so forth, and that's the coalition out there that is advancing that agenda. (Lon Mabon, interview by author, 1994)

These links are found everywhere in CR literature, one of the most detailed studies being Texe Marrs's *Big Sister Is Watching You* (1993). Primarily an antifeminist tirade directed at Hillary Clinton and her band of "feminazis," *Big Sister* offers portraits of Clinton women appointees, each of whom is described as a member of a secret cabal. Significantly, however, these women are not simply, or only, "radical feminists." Marrs insists, or insinuates, that most are lesbians (I discuss this further in chapter 4), New Age spiritualists (Marrs has also penned *Dark Secrets of the New Age* [1987]), and economic conspiracists (e.g., members of the Federal Reserve and Trilateral Commission). While *Big Sister*'s tone is excessive, and perhaps intentionally amusing (particularly the photographs), its sentiments are echoed by CR leaders and organizations and by the antigay genre generally.

For example, Kevin Tebedo of Colorado for Family Values (interview by author, 1994), argues that "the politics of homosexuality is Marxism-Leninism." Tebedo's views, that communism is alive and well and the animating force behind several American social movements, be-

87

lies the notion that the CR has moved away from an anticommunist politics in the "post–Cold War" era. Indeed, Tebedo and others have no faith that communism has died; they insist that its values (and cadres) are actively seeking and winning political power (see Kintz 1994).[55]

But it is also important to recognize that even these forces—of liberalism/communism—are not acting alone; on the contrary, they are in the service of Satan, who behind the scenes is orchestrating their performance. As I explained in chapter 1, and developed historically in chapter 2, premillennial conservative evangelicals believe fervently in the apocalyptic scenario. They see all around them signs of impending finality. It is therefore understandable and consistent that they view opposing social movements as a satanic conspiracy.[56] In tract after tract the lesbian and gay movement is described as a "malevolent force" (Dannemeyer 1989, 18), and the gay agenda as "symbolic of the all-encompassing plan of the kingdom of darkness as a whole" (McIlhenny, McIlhenny, and York 1993, 232). Pat Robertson (Robertson and Slosser 1982, 88–89) has explicitly linked homosexuality to the "antichrist."

In *Legislating Immorality* (1993) Grant and Horne liken conservative evangelicals in America to the biblical people of Israel, standing up to the Philistines and other opponents with God on their side (see Meigs 1995). Steve Farrar (1994, 115) also employs biblical analogies, arguing that modern satanic forces bear a striking resemblance to the Old Testament people of Baal.

#1. Baal worshippers were pro-choice after the child was born.

#2. Baal worshippers held the environment in high

88

esteem and considered Baal as the one who determined
and controlled the environment. . . .

#3. Baal worship encouraged and promoted rampant
sexual immorality, particularly homosexuality, as a normal and natural lifestyle.

#4. Baal worship sought to coexist as a legitimate reli-
gious viewpoint alongside Judaism.

Each of my interviewees, when asked if they believed
that the lesbian and gay movement was part of a larger
satanic agenda, agreed that it was: "from a religious perspective, and from what I read of my Bible, I would conclude the same. Yes" (Loretta Neet); "if those behaviors
are contrary to [a] biblical or God's perspective in that
sense, well you'd have to say yes, he is an influence there"
(Will Perkins); "I believe that there is evil. Real honest to
goodness evil. [There] is an opposite side of God" (Kevin
Tebedo); "If you're not working for God, you're working
for Satan" (Jim Woodall).

89

> I believe in the personification of evil. . . . I know the
> ultimate struggle is between good and evil, between God
> and the devil, and I do believe that we do side with one
> or the other in this cosmic, ageless struggle that's been
> going on. . . . you're either advancing the principles of
> either a set of moral absolutes or a divine being, or you're
> advancing the principles of immoral absolutes or immoral
> principles, or an unholy being. (Lon Mabon)

The uniting theme here is godlessness: a failure to comply
with conservative Christian tenets is synonymous with
atheism, and atheism is most definitely a satanic strategy.
The gay agenda is the secular agenda is the liberal agenda
is the devil's agenda. Perhaps, after all, it is the presence

of out lesbians and gay men in the churches that most effectively challenges these articulations.[57]

Many of the themes I have discussed, and their contradictions, can be observed in one important but somewhat marginal trajectory of the antigay genre. In the early 1990s a rash of material from CR sources asserted that most leading Nazis in the Third Reich were gay (e.g., Magnuson 1994, 56–57). The proof offered largely consists of references in histories of the period to same-sex sexual activity between Nazi men. One example is a long feature piece by a self-identified orthodox Jew, Kevin Abrams, appearing in an issue of *Lambda Report* (2, 4 [1994]: 6–11). Using an assortment of unknown and mainstream documentation, Abrams constructs the Nazi movement as inherently homosexual. Peter LaBarbera's introduction to the piece suggests that gays were far more powerful than persecuted during the Nazi era (6).

The association of homosexuality with Nazism has been picked up by CR activists and deployed widely. Lon Mabon, for example, head of Oregon Citizen's Alliance, repeated the allegations to me during an interview (1994): "most of the early Nazis were homosexuals. And in fact Ernst Roehm, who headed up the Nazi Brownshirts, was an open homosexual and most of the Brownshirts were homosexual. In fact, many of the early founders of the National Socialist Party used to meet in a gay bar in Germany."

The articulation of gay sexuality with Nazism is noteworthy in several respects. First, this discourse is highly reminiscent of anticommunist rhetoric (see chapter 2) emphasizing the totalitarian, jackbooted character of the enemy. Interestingly, however, this stands in stark contrast to antigay discourses of anarchic paganism. While the Nazis were perceived as godless, they were constructed more as "control freaks" than out-of-control animists. The articulation of "gay" with "Nazi" invests the latter with signifiers of disease and seduction, and the former with conspiratorial plans for world domination. The "gay Nazi," then, is a figure saturated with historical devil discourses: the anticommunist, anti-Semitic, and antigay genres are fused with potent imagery from the Second World War. The revisionism of this historiography is also reminiscent of the manner in which the anti-Jewishness of Nazism has been rewritten by later anti-Semites: the refusal to recognize the persecution of gays synonymous with the rejection of Nazi responsibility for Jewish deaths, or the denial that genocide occurred at all. More moderate conservative Christians disown this trajectory of the antigay genre; however, for others it is powerfully evocative. On another level the figure of the "gay Nazi" is perplexing; if Nazis were gay and gays are Nazis, what does that make the racist, extreme (and Christian) right who idolize the Third Reich? It is also interesting to note that it is not just the CR that has associated Nazism with homosexuality; as George Mosse (1985, 186) has shown, such allegations were made at the time by Hitler's socialist opponents.

91

No Lesbians, Gay Lesbians,
Feminist Lesbians

If the key figure of antigay discourse is the male homosexual, how easy is it for the CR to fit lesbians into this caricature? Do they try? Do they argue that lesbians also carry terrible diseases and prey on children? Or do they simply add the word "lesbian" to a sentence without giving it any specificity? Alternatively, if lesbians lack prominence in CR antigay discourse, are they more visible in a different genre? It would seem that the CR takes all these routes. More often than not, they simply add the word "lesbian" to a paragraph that clearly has no application to women at all. Yet they also increasingly seek to discuss lesbianism explicitly and, on occasion, to present lesbian-specific evidence to prove their arguments. Finally, lesbianism also rears its head within the CR's antifeminism—a discourse that overlaps, yet unsettles, its antigay counterpart.

In this chapter I examine each of these lesbian incarnations in turn. Given the increasingly prominent role played by lesbians in many gay rights organizations, the CR has been, to some extent, forced to confront its denial of the specificity of lesbian sexuality. Paradoxically, any real engagement with lesbian feminism to some extent destabilizes the gay male devil of CR discourse. But there is also a counter to this possibility, evident in the deployment within CR discourse of lesbian "sex radical" literature. This development has enabled the CR to further entrench the image of anarchic, gay paganism (see chapter 3). In its entirety, however, the CR's construction of lesbianism is irretrievably contradictory, predominantly because lesbian politics itself is so fragmented, disparate, and internally antagonistic. It would be far easier to promote the CR antigay agenda if there were no lesbians. Many, therefore, simply write as if this were the case.

93

Invisibilities and Add-ons

As I indicated in chapter 3, the key character of CR antigay discourse is the gay male. The most prevalent depiction of lesbianism is either as an absence—in other words, simply ignored—or as an add-on, appended to a sentence having little or no application to women. An example of the former approach is Roger Magnuson's *Informed Answers to Gay Rights Questions* (1994), a book explaining how to counter "gay myths." In discussing the "truth" that gays abuse children, Magnuson writes, "Every time a cruising homosexual picks up another boy for exploitation, another victim is created" (139). The gender specificity of the language is simply of no consequence to the author. Tim LaHaye goes even further, using without comment the pronoun "he" throughout *What Everyone Should Know about Homosexuality* (1978).

The second method is illustrated by Steve Farrar (1994). Several chapters of *Standing Tall: How a Man Can Protect His Family* focus on homosexuality, and like many other writings in the genre, much of his discussion involves reciting reams of statistics on perverse practices and disease-laden lifestyles (see chapter 3). Farrar occasionally adds the word "lesbian" to a sentence, but his account of behavior can have little application to women: "[100%] of homosexuals engage in fellatio, [93%] engage in rectal sex, [92%] are active in 'rimming,' [29%] of homosexuals participate in 'golden showers'" (124–25). This latter practice, Farrar notes, "is where one man lies naked on the ground and is urinated upon by others" (125). Chuck and Donna McIlhenny (1993) also take this path, occasionally using the phrase "gay and lesbian," but in practice speaking only of men. Within this approach to lesbian sexuality, the word "lesbian" tends to appear most frequently when gay publications or organizations with "lesbian" in the title are being referred to directly.

The focus for these writers is male sexual practice, the danger to male youth, and the power of the gay movement as a whole. Lesbians are somehow irrelevant to these concerns. Arguably, there are several reasons for the lack of attention paid to women, perhaps the most obvious of which has to do with the erasure of lesbian sexuality in culture generally. For many on the CR, as for people more widely, women are the "gentler" sex, and the less sexual sex. Lesbians are simply uncontemplated or, when observed, thought harmless. For example, all of those whom I interviewed for this book had difficulty responding to a question specifically about the dangers of lesbian sexuality. Indeed, when pressed, several suggested that lesbians posed little threat at all.

A related, but more pragmatic, reason for the absence of lesbianism has to do with the nature of the science upon which the CR relies. As I explained in chapter 3, information about gay sexual practice tends to rest upon three cornerstones: Paul Cameron's studies, mainstream HIV epidemiology research, and survey data published in gay media. All these sources focus on male practice, and therefore the CR simply does not have the resources upon which to base lesbian pronouncements. Or, perhaps more accurately, many CR activists have not turned their attention to the material that does exist. If it is necessary to take account of lesbianism, it is easier to do so by adding the word, unthinkingly, to a sentence or phrase.

There is a different sort of add-on approach, however, one where the specificity of lesbianism does receive some notice. This is seen most clearly in the psychological causation genre (see chapter 3). Larry Burtoft (1994), in reviewing this literature for Focus on the Family, suggests three specific causes of lesbianism.[1] The first, he argues, is rooted "in the incomplete fulfilment of maternal needs; an emotional breach occurs during the early mother-infant bonding period" (42). In support of this statement, he provides a quotation from a psychiatrist, Theo L. Dorpat, who asserts that lesbian children are produced by mothers who seek their own sexual satisfaction through "playing" with their daughter's genitalia (42).[2]

A second reason for female homosexuality, according to Burtoft, occurs "when the girl disidentifies with her mother whom she experiences as weak, pathetic, vulnerable or in some way inadequate" (43). The girl then identifies with the father, as a result experiencing severe gender-identity problems, finding herself incapable of living as an authentic woman. Other than noting a personal conver-

95

sation with Joseph Nicolosi (see chapter 3), Burtoft provides no references at all for this remark, or for his next assertion—that a third type of lesbianism is based on a "psychopathology [of] fear." This, he notes, can result from the experience of male sexual abuse, creating "heterophobia, or more specifically, a fear of male sexuality, a fear which can be alleviated through therapy and experiences with positive, affirming masculinity."

Various versions of these ideas are also found throughout the ex-gay literature, a different genre trajectory where lesbianism is occasionally referred to directly (e.g., Bogle 1990; Davies and Rentzel 1993). Here lesbians confess their sin, usually find its origins in their own or their family's dysfunctionality, and explain how faith in Christ led them to reclaim their femininity and to find happiness as wives and mothers.

> I used to view men as unfeeling, insensitive and preoccupied with sex. I related to them only superficially, keeping them at arm's length. I felt they could never understand me, and I certainly had little desire to understand them. Now I see men as having emotions and sensitivity and do not believe they are obsessed with sex. I also appreciate the way men express their thoughts and feelings. The strongest influence in changing my heart has been to be around godly men. I have good friendships with a few men and am open to marriage, should that be God's will.[3]

The ex-gay genre deserves a study in its own right, and I cannot do it justice here (but see Pennington 1989). It is worth noting, however, the similarities between the CR's depiction of the gay "ex" and the role and status of "exes" in other genres. In chapter 2, for example, I noted the role of the "ex" in anticommunist and anti-Semitic discourses.

Similarly, the "moral career" of the gay or lesbian "ex" resembles that of several ex-cultists (see Beckford 1985; Ebaugh 1988).

These forms of attention to lesbianism, then, invest it with a unique, but equally tragic, pathology. The effects of the invisibility and add-on approaches are twofold. In the first, lesbians simply do not exist, women are not homosexual, and therefore the maleness of homosexuality, particularly its hyper and bacchanalian aspects (see chapter 3), is at the fore. Disease, promiscuity, and seduction characterize homosexuality in its essence—any manner in which the presence of women might trouble this arrangement is simply ignored. The risk of this strategy is that it is too easily characterized as outdated, inaccurate, and dismissable. Perhaps more important, invisibility cannot provide ammunition against a movement that is clearly both gay *and lesbian*.

97

In the second, the occasional add-on approach, lesbians are presented, but in an obscure or pitiful manner. If gay men are sad and tragic, lesbians are even more so. They not only suffer gender-identity problems, but also have probably experienced sexual abuse perpetrated by pathological mothers and familial males. As in the ex-gay male genre, former lesbians learn properly how to practice their gender; through Christ they accept who they really are. Taking some account of lesbianism, however, does provide an acknowledgment that lesbians exist; in the long term this is a more useful development for the CR.

There are few mysteries as to why the invisibility and add-on approaches endure. Historically, in almost every genre lesbianism has often been erased, ignored, or marginalized (see, e.g., Faderman 1980). Given that the self-presentation of the gay community was largely male, it was not surprising that its foes took so little notice of its women members. But this is no longer the case. Given the composition and leadership of modern lesbian and gay movements, the erasure or depreciation of lesbian sexuality by their opponents is not sustainable, and many in the CR have become aware of this. Increasingly, then, the lesbian presence has been attended to, but in very specific ways.

The "Gay" Lesbian

There is a robust strand of CR antigay literature that seeks to establish that there is little to distinguish between the practices, and the dangers, of lesbian and gay sexuality. According to Jim Woodall of Concerned Women for America (interview by author, 1995), "we don't need to differentiate between sex between women and sex between men. It is all, as far we're concerned, homosexual sex." As I discuss below, the lives of both lesbians and gay men are disease-ridden, while lesbians, too, prey on unsuspecting and vulnerable children. Occasionally, the CR will suggest that this behavior by lesbians goes against "women's nature"; however, to explain it, they will argue that either lesbians have been corrupted by gay men and made "like them," or that sexual perversion has progressed to such an apogee that women are simply no longer women.

> [G]enerally speaking, most people would agree that in a natural setting males seem to be more sexually aggressive. . . . Male homosexuals, by and large . . . seem more capable of that . . . somehow unrestrained . . . so it's more

98

easily identifiable—the examples are more pronounced, and more exaggerated. Females . . . are sweeter, nicer. . . . But I think as the attacks on what I would call the normal sexual roles continue, and the presentation of the traditional male and female are portrayed more and more as stereotypes, rather than the norm, you see even within the lesbian side of this thing terms like bull-dyke and so forth that tend to represent a male-oriented, female lesbian. . . . I think it's probably lagging behind the male side of it. But females are the gentler side of the human race—it's going to take longer for total breakdown. (Lon Mabon, interview by author, 1994)

As Mabon suggests, this strand of the antigay genre represents lesbians as becoming more like gay men, more aggressive, hypersexual, and anarchic.

Part of painting this picture also requires that the physical dangers of lesbianism be proven. Once again, the CR substantially relies on the research of Paul Cameron, head of the Family Research Institute (see chapter 3). For example, Brad Hayton (n.d., 16), whose tract *The Homosexual Agenda: Changing Your Community and Nation* is intended as a community action manual for Christian activists, presents the following data published by Cameron's former think tank: "In comparison to heterosexual females, lesbians are 19 times more apt to have had syphilis, 2 times more apt to have had genital warts, 4 times more apt to have had scabies, 7 times more apt to have had an infection from vaginal contact, and 12 times more apt to have ever had an oral infection from penile contact."

Cameron's conclusions, as with those on gay male practices, are drawn from his own professionally discredited research (e.g., Cameron et al. 1985), and from se-

99

lected mainstream studies of people with HIV in prisons. In addition to claiming these disproportionate disease rates, Cameron also asserts a significant relationship between lesbianism, drug abuse, and criminality.[4] He also misrepresents data contained in a book about violence within lesbian relationships to prove that "rape and battering are more frequent among lesbian couples than among married heterosexual couples."[5]

But the CR also makes use of more important material than this in-house research. In establishing continuities and consistencies between gay and lesbian sexuality, CR texts draw upon the writings of lesbians themselves. Particularly adept at this are Grant and Horne, authors of *Legislating Immortality* (1993). They quote, for example, from Pat Califia, whose book *Sapphistry* they describe as "a best selling handbook to lesbian sexuality" (38). In it, according to Grant and Horne, Califia argues that lesbians should have no boundaries when it comes to sexual experimentation (38, 44). Grant and Horne quote from other lesbian writers they characterize as similarly "prominent." One is described as having "confessed to sexual encounters with between twenty and forty cadavers during four months of employment at a suburban California mortuary" (45).

Another important figure who explicitly discusses lesbian sexuality is Peter LaBarbera, editor of *Lambda Report*, the antigay monitor. In addition to priding himself on exposing a leader of the National Gay and Lesbian Task Force as a "sadomasochist,"[6] he regularly reprints extracts from lesbian sex manuals and magazines, particularly those to do with anal sex, dildos, and fetishisms.[7] Thus, in this genre lesbians can be as bad or worse than men—gay or straight.

A parallel with heterosexual masculinity is also found in how lesbians are represented vis-à-vis the "seduction" motif. For example, Concerned Women for America's publication *Family Voice* (16, 5 [1994]: 8) implicates lesbians in an article entitled "Gays Revenge: Recruiting Children." A photograph accompanying the piece shows two largish women, one carrying a small child. The article begins, "Outside our schools, young children are being accosted by gay activists before they can get inside," and goes on to describe how the Lesbian Avengers (a direct-action group) hand out "leaflets and candy stamped with the lesbian symbol in an overt attempt to recruit students." The Lesbian Avengers are mentioned frequently throughout the more recent CR antigay genre; the emergence of this "in-your-face" group has played a key role in sustaining the "gay lesbian" theme.

101

Lambda Report, for example, watches the Avengers closely, reproducing extracts from leaflets (e.g., "girls who love girls and women who love women are OK!!! Happy Valentine's Day"), and publishing photos of leather-clad women accosting buses full of children.[8] LaBarbera also reprints pedophilia from the lesbian pornography genre.[9] Other antigay organizations propagate these resources or produce their own. For example, The Report's *Gay Agenda* videos (see chapter 3) also take the lesbian-as-gay approach; lesbians are pictured rarely, but when they are, it is as part of a seething, riotous mass of half-naked flesh. Individual lesbians are shown topless, their pendulous breasts bound in leather straps or flapping out of control like surrogate penises.

The gay lesbian is also vaguely present in CR discussions about the comparative wealth of the lesbian and gay community. While I explore this topic more fully in chapter 5, it is worth noting here that, at the outset, lesbians were simply invisible in CR presentations of a disproportionately wealthy gay community. By the mid-1990s, however, more attention was being paid to considering lesbian-specific data; when this occurred, lesbian incomes were also presented as disproportionate—although the comparative group was "heterosexual women," and not the population as a whole (see chapter 5).

This, then, is a lesbian-aware discourse in which lesbians are "colored gay." By this I mean that, while lesbians are acknowledged, they are simply seen through the CR gay lens; lesbians are simultaneously aggressive and covert, probably wealthy, and fundamentally dangerous to children. Lesbians within this approach also possess a hypersexuality, but it is a malelike sexuality they display; in other words, lesbians, too, are hypermasculine. While "good" women wait for their children at the school gates to take them home for milk and cookies, lesbians cluster there also, conspiring to steal these children away. While gay men act out their, in some way, primal desires in such an unrestrained manner as to render the behavior unnatural, lesbian sexuality is antiwoman at its core. If gay men are men undisciplined, lesbians are really much the same. Indeed, they may be more dangerous: "Unlike homosexuals, lesbians are not at high risk to contract AIDS. In addition, they are able to bear children and thus 'multiply'" (LaHaye and LaHaye 1994, 114).

It is worth noting that this lesbian portrait is at serious odds with the one painted in the ex-gay genre. There women, often telling their own stories of how they overcame their sin, do not appear as rich, bed-hopping, disease-carrying abusers. Instead, and in some contrast to the ex-gay male stories, lesbians are depicted as sad, weak, and searching for something never found. Occasionally, though, the ex-lesbian does refer to an abusive woman who initially led her astray; so here the lesbian who finds Christ was never "gay," while the lesbians who corrupted her were.

Thus, in constructing the possibility that lesbians are quasi-men, a problem in the antigay genre can be resolved. Without a highly sexualized, predatory heterosexual aggressor, "Christian women" are not obviously at risk. The opportunity to draw upon the many discourses of female vulnerability, deployed so successfully, for example, in the iconography of "raced" sexuality (see, e.g., Davis 1981), remains unexploited. Through representing lesbian sexuality as promiscuous, deadly, and most certainly aimed at "our girls and women," a range of fiercely resonant fears can be exploited.

103

But even this approach is not the primary site of lesbian presence in the CR antigay genre. Interestingly, "our women" are seen to be more at risk from the perils of "radical feminism" than from lesbian abuse. In fact, the two are indistinguishable, and the CR's antifeminist discourse is rooted in exposing feminist leaders and feminist philosophy as "lesbian." Paradoxically, however, the feminist lesbian is not a man; the feminist lesbian stands apart from the gay lesbian, as an *anti*male militant, attempting to construct a world without men.

THE FEMINIST LESBIAN

The antipathy of the CR toward feminism is considerable; in many respects this dimension to CR politics has been subject to several excellent critical analyses.[10] I do not intend to explore the CR's engagement with feminism; this is an important topic in its own right and deserves more than cursory reflection here. What I wish to do, however, is consider the presence of lesbian sexuality within CR antifeminist discourse. Lesbianism is far more visible here than in the antigay genre.

For the CR, "radical feminism" (the expression they use to connote feminism of any non-Christian variety) is lesbian feminism. According to William Gairdner (1992, 300–301): "The male is said to be the prime agent of exploitation, from which all women are urged to free themselves. . . . We shall see that lesbianism is but the logical end-result of feminist autonomism, which, pushed further, leads to the glorification of masturbation as self-assertion and freedom from males, to self-insemination, and to single parenthood as the crowning liberty."

104   Each of the CR activists I interviewed for this book drew similar conclusions, suggesting that the agendas of feminism and lesbianism were one and the same. For example, Robert Knight of the Family Research Council (interview by author, 1995) claimed that "lesbianism is the animating principle of feminism. Because feminism, at its core, is at war with motherhood, femininity, family, and God. And lesbians are at war with all these things."

These connections are made most clearly, not unsurprisingly, by the antifeminist activists of the CR, particularly those involved with Concerned Women for America and Eagle Forum, the two dominant CR antifeminist organizations. Jim Woodall (interview by author, 1995), for example, vice president of Concerned Women for America, describes feminism and lesbianism as "partners." Indeed, he believes that feminism's "embracement" of lesbianism has signaled the death knell for the feminist movement because lesbianism is "so far out of

the mainstream." Phyllis Schlafly, longtime Christian activist and president of Eagle Forum, associated feminism
with lesbianism from early on in her antifeminist career
and successfully linked the two in her campaign to stop
the progress of the Equal Rights Amendment (Felsenthal
1981; Mathews and de Hart 1990). Realwomen, the Canadian equivalent to these organizations, has consistently
highlighted the lesbian phalanx dominating the women's
movement in that country (Ross 1988; Herman 1994,
87, 95).

Lurking behind Texe Marrs's "big sister" in his anti-
Clinton *Big Sister Is Watching You* (1993, 14) are militant
lesbians intent on turning America into a "global, Marxist
paradise." Marrs's approach, that of uncovering leading
feminists as lesbians, is a favorite tactic of the CR. Pat
Robertson, for example, in *The Turning Tide* (1993, 187),   105
intends to discredit the president of the National Organization for Women by calling her a "bisexual." Indeed,
several of those whom I interviewed for this book were
keen to give me this information that had traveled the
Christian circuit via a mainstream news story.

Ironically, the depiction of feminists as hard-core lesbian soldiers sits uneasily with another CR discourse—
that of women in combat. Phyllis Schlafly, for example,
argues vociferously against women's direct involvement
in warfare.[11] To do so, she constructs womanhood as pas-
sive and demure: "Men are attracted to serve in the military because of its intensely masculine character. The
qualities that make them good soldiers—aggressiveness,
risk taking, and enjoyment of body contact competition—
are conspicuously absent in women" ("Women in Combat"). How, in the absence of these characteristics, feminists have managed to cause "our military officers to

cower in fear" is left unexplained. Feminists must possess a strange chameleon power, indeed.

There is therefore an underlying tension or incongruity between antifeminism and antilesbianism. On the one hand, CR antifeminist military discourse relies, to a great extent, on asserting biological sex difference, particularly the primal difference of hunter versus nurturer. But if feminists (read lesbians) are "taking over," and/or lesbians are like gay men, this antifeminist anchor becomes somewhat wobbly. The fact that lesbians can apparently subvert their gender, and that feminists can become masculinized, ironically calls into question the manner in which the CR chooses to see sexuality as "made," and gender as "inborn." As I explained in chapter 3, this distinction is important, both for the CR's antigay and anti-feminist agendas. However, a construction of lesbians and feminists as "anti-" or "un-"woman suggests that gender itself may not be all that secure.

Interestingly, the ex-lesbian genre clearly makes the point that lesbians must relearn how to be women. Former lesbians tell stories of how they learned to value their femininity and appreciate men. Just as important, they learned to detect the lies of feminism, for example, that paid work can be fulfilling in itself, or that bodily autonomy is an absolute good. In this sense lesbians are simply acting out against their nature; with proper assistance, through an ex-gay ministry, they can be brought back to the light.

The feminist "colored lesbian" represents autonomy, independence, and woman-centeredness; "lesbian" functions as a metaphor for a world without men. In many ways this is a construction rather inconsistent with the image of the lesbian "colored gay"—the diseased, preda-

106

tory anarchist (Antichrist). Two quite different images materialize here; on the one hand, "gay lesbians" who associate with men, who do more or less the same things in bed as men, and have an identical agenda. On the other hand, the feminist lesbian (or lesbian feminist) wants nothing to do with men; indeed she rejects men and masculinity and intends to create a world of androgenous sexuality. But to do so, paradoxically, she acts like a man— is aggressive, frightening, and potentially omnipotent. Perhaps, then, this is the ultimate deception; lesbians join in with gay men but intend, at some future stage, to remove all men from the scene entirely. More realistically, perhaps these different CR discourses are simply contradictory and irreconcilable. It is easier for members of the CR to ignore lesbian sexuality, and that is partly why so many of them do.

107

Yet another complication is the image of the "lesbian mother"—a nonsensical impossibility in CR discourse (see Kintz 1994). That lesbians have and want children of their own is a fact the CR acknowledges. Contrary perhaps to expectations and to the practices of the tabloid press, however, they do not make much of it. Issues to do with lesbian parenting (e.g., alternative insemination) are raised, but rarely scrutinized. Arguably, this is partly because lesbian parenting arrangements often take place in the private sphere, and do not necessarily entail demands for state intervention. More significantly, to consider lesbians as mothers is to inject a fundamental incoherence into CR antigay discourse. One cannot be a masculinized, aggressive predator *and* a mother, as conservative Christianity defines "mother." Thus far, the prioritization by the gay movement of civil rights struggles in the public realm, rather than the traditionally women's issues of the private arena, has facilitated the CR's indistinct rendering of lesbian mothering.

There are two points with which I would like to conclude. First, in thinking about the challenge lesbianism may pose to the CR's antigay agenda, it may be that it is lesbian feminism, not lesbian "sex radicalism," that complicates the CR's antigay agenda. Within lesbian politics, one section of the community has claimed that lesbian "sex radicals" are the ones whose practices (e.g., promiscuity, sadomasochism, pornography) are truly subversive of the status quo. The less lesbian sexuality mimics an idealized heterosexual norm, and the more it reveals the truly perverse foundations of heterosexuality, the more likely those norms will be transgressed and transformed.

Sex radicals position themselves in opposition to those they label "vanillas," the latter being, generally speaking, old-style, often feminist lesbians who insist that personal sexual practice be prefigurative of a radically egalitarian society: in other words, that lesbians should not uncritically adopt all forms of sexual practice simply because such forms exist. Rather, personal choices, including sexual ones, must be made on some kind of ethical basis, informed by an understanding of social inequality. Sex radicals, on the other hand, by breaking sexual taboos and refusing "discipline," argue that they are the ones whose actions more truly reflect the pursuit of freedom; as a result they are more radical in outlook and consequence. Indeed, several sex radicals condemn those they view as promoting a "feminist moralism," often accusing this group of "being in bed with the right," particularly, for example, around the pornography issue.[12]

But it may be that those lesbians who assert a proporn

and sadomasochistic politics are easily assimilated into the gay lesbian genre, and pose little challenge to the CR's representations. They are held to display all the qualities traditionally associated with gay sexuality—disease, anarchy, excess, deceit—and simply act as fuel added to fire. Lesbian feminism, on the other hand, may compel the CR to come to terms with the political and moral dimensions of a lesbianism with something other than a "keep the state off our back," libertarian agenda. It is precisely the morally transformative project of lesbian *feminism* that proves most troubling to right-wing forces.

My second and final point has to do with the race dimension of the CR's construction of lesbian sexuality, a subject on which I have thus far been somewhat silent. This is for one reason, that there is little to distinguish between the representation of gay and lesbian sexuality. In other words, homosexuals as a group are, within CR discourse, implicitly white. With the exception of a very few faces shown in *The Gay Agenda* series, gay men and lesbians, when represented in CR photography or artwork, are invariably pictured as white.

This white portrayal, I think, occurs for three main reasons, the most obvious of which parallels the absence of lesbianism. In other words, nonwhite gays and lesbians are simply ignored in their absence, and unrecognized when present. The invisibility of race within the wider culture has been subject to intense critical examination, as has the issue of race politics within lesbian and gay communities.[13] Two other explanations are perhaps less apparent.

While the discourse of gay, anarchic paganism *could* have drawn from a racist literature of primitivism, this possibility was largely closed off due to the CR's reference

109

point for this sort of debauchery—Greco-Roman antiquity. This reference point (they would see it as a white one) stands not so much for the missionary battling the heathen primitive, but for the persecuted Christian believer holding on to faith in the face of extreme wickedness. Thus, while the characterization of the gay movement as a whole may have racist undertones (as an "alien other"), and some gay images clearly conjure up other, raced ones (the gay man in war paint; the lesbian New Age goddess worshipper), the CR for the most part, as I read the antigay genre, does not make much of racist discourses available to it. One exception is the association of homosexuality with the city; the urban is gay, black, and, implicitly, not "home." I have discussed this further elsewhere (1994, 93).[14]

110

Clearly, the CR's reticence here also has an important pragmatic impetus, and this is the third explanation for the whiteness of homosexuality. As I go on to explore in chapter 5, part of the CR's antigay agenda involves a very deliberate attempt to court nonwhite communities and bring them on board antigay campaigns. It is therefore quite convenient for there to be no nonwhite gays and lesbians in CR discourse; their absence then becomes a telling indication both of the intrinsic whiteness of homosexuality and of the threat that gay rights may pose to the rights of other "others." Constructing gay rights as a "white" issue, then, becomes part of building bridges between white and black conservative Protestantism.

5

(Il)legitimate Minorities

The Construction of Rights-(Un)deserving Subjects

Thus far in this book I have considered both the historical emergence of the homosexual subject within conservative Protestant discourse (chapter 2) and the representation of gay and lesbian sexuality by the CR today (chapters 3 and 4). In the last two chapters I focused on three key themes: disease and seduction, anarchic hypersexuality, and feminism. I briefly mentioned another—wealth and power. Here I take up this theme in more detail, by exploring the shifting character of the CR's rights discourse.

One aspect to this issue I do *not* address is the debate around the "politics of rights" generally. The mainstream lesbian and gay movement framed its demands in terms of "rights" from early on. As I explained in chapter 1, the rights movement demanded legal protection, primarily through inclusion within antidiscrimination statutes, and the extension of social benefits to lesbian and gay couples. An extensive literature exists about rights discourse and its efficacy in achieving social change. Most of this work focuses on how and why left-wing/progressive forces deploy rights claims, considering questions such as, Are rights inherently libratory or obfuscatory? Does the deployment of rights discourse propel a social movement forward or set it back? Elsewhere (Herman 1990, 1993, 1994) I have considered these questions and others in the context of movements for lesbian and gay rights, arguing that rights struggles need to be assessed in their specificity, and that their effects are complicated, contingent, and contradictory.

This chapter addresses the other side of the equation—*anti*rights discourse deployed by *conservative* social forces. But I do not consider here to what extent the CR is empowered, or not, by its antigay rights rhetoric. Instead, I focus on analyzing or deconstructing this discourse with the aim of providing a more complicated explanation of CR politics than is often presented. I particularly focus on the contradictory and entangled relationship between religious orthodoxy and political strategy.

I consider how one section of the CR—those I term the "rights pragmatists"—have articulated powerful, secularized arguments to construct lesbians and gay men as a minority undeserving of rights. In exploring this development my argument is twofold. First, this newer discourse, and its accompanying retreat from older rhetorics of disease and seduction, has caused palpable tensions within the CR. Second, in order to represent one group as "counterfeit," others must be constructed as "authentic"; given the CR's antipathy to group rights of all kinds (with the exception of religious rights), this too has proved problematic for CR politics—particularly for its race politics.

RIGHTS REASSESSMENTS

By the early 1990s several activists within the CR began to reassess the discourses upon which CR opposition to homosexuality had been based historically. Traditionally, two key discourses were used: biblical injunction and a rhetoric of disease and seduction. I do not in any way wish to suggest that these discourses have faded from view; for many members of the CR, they are as significant as ever (see chapters 3 and 4). But activists of a different ilk, the rights pragmatists, began to insist that these older discourses give way, on the grounds that they were no longer useful and, indeed, were mobilizing support for, rather than opposition to, gay rights. Instead, the pragmatists advocated secular arguments rooted within the traditions of mainstream rights discourse. This shift was mirrored by similar ones in other spheres of CR activity, for example, prayer in schools (see Hertzke 1988; Moen 1995). If the lesbian and gay rights movement was going to use rights discourse to its advantage, perhaps the CR could meet this challenge on its own terms.

113

One of the most important theorists in the gay rights arena is Tony Marco. Marco, an ex-hippie and left-winger, had a "born again" experience in the early 1970s and has since become one of the leading (and independent) intellectual lights on the CR.[1] Working from his home in Colorado Springs, Marco has produced an impressive array of position papers and documents on gay rights issues.[2] He was instrumental in orchestrating the campaign to pass a statewide, antigay initiative in Colorado in 1992 (see chapter 6) and with his wife operates an ex-gay ministry. Marco's ideas have been deployed widely by other CR actors, and thus my focus in this part of the chapter is on his work.[3]

Marco's initial forays into antigay politics were hardly novel; for the most part he propagated traditional rhetorics of disease and seduction.[4] However, he gradually began to shift his thinking. While conservative Christians may subscribe to the traditional beliefs in private, Marco was adamant that, in the public realm, these old discourses be repudiated.

> What gives gay militants their enormous power are money and the *operative presumption that gays represent some kind of "oppressed minority."* It is the fear that we may be "denying an 'oppressed' group rights" that has induced widespread enough guilt in the American people to allow for the progress of "gay rights" we have seen to date. If this is true, I conclude that (a) forcing gay activists to spend tons of money, and (b) demolishing the presumption that gays are an "oppressed minority" are the *only* means by which gay militants' political power can be destroyed *at its roots*. All other approaches to opposing "gay rights" are doomed to failure. . . . If this is so, as I believe it is, we need to immediately drop the "disgust" and "public health threat" arguments we have been depending on for 25 years. Besides being irrelevant to the issues gay militants are really raising, these arguments are no longer credible, appeal only to the "choir" and actually allow our opponents to once again tar us with the role of aggressors—and clumsy, lying ones at that. (emphasis in original)[5]

With sentiments such as these, the rights pragmatists insist that the CR fundamentally rethink its antigay strategizing. As Marco himself was no stranger to the old rhetoric, his conversion from it signaled important developments in CR politics.

Marco and others recognized that the old-style arguments contained several hazards. First, the traditional views sound extremist and hateful to a less orthodox public. As the new pragmatists acknowledged, lesbians and gay men have been more successful than not at dispelling the stereotype of the diseased pedophile. Second, the rhetoric of sin and seduction is saturated with a moralism that is easily recognizable as *religious*. Although, as I noted in chapter 1, Americans express high levels of religious faith, this does not necessarily correspond to support for religious discourse in the public realm.

Third, the old arguments were legal nonstarters. Astute CR strategists conceded that many key battles would be fought within the formally secular arena of the law. For example, the presentation of disputed data, particularly when collected by discredited professionals (see chapter 3), about how gay men ingest fecal material, or speeches on the fall of Sodom and the Second Coming, would make little headway in combating the extension of civil rights protections to lesbians and gay men. Instead, the rights pragmatists argued that the CR had no choice but to fight the gay movement on liberal democratic turf; this necessitated acquiring an arsenal of secular discursive strategies aimed at undermining the legitimacy of lesbians and gay men as a rights-deserving group. At the same time the pragmatic rights discourse would resonate with, and play to, a "backlash" culture fed up with "special" interests of all varieties (see afterword).

Tony Marco (interview by author, 1994) asserts that gay rights demands represent "the nadir of hypocrisy, fraud, greed, and flat out injustice" and constitute "the greatest political scam ever run in the history of the United States." How does the CR substantiate such a claim?

115

The Undeserving

The primary theme of the CR pragmatists is that, while rights may be due to the "truly disadvantaged," the gay movement does not fit this description. Their argument contains two fused limbs: first, gays are immensely wealthy; second, the gay movement is not only one of the most politically powerful in the country, but lesbians and gay men as individuals actually hold vast amounts of political power and unfairly wield it over others. As a result, the CR contends, civil rights protections will simply extend and entrench the extraordinary privileges of this elite and deceitful (because they portray themselves as "oppressed") group.

To make the economic case, the CR deploys a range of statistics.

> Homosexuals claim they are economically, educationally and culturally disadvantaged. Marketing studies refute those claims. Homosexuals have an average annual household income of $55,430, versus $32,144 for the general population and $12,166 for disadvantaged African-American households. More than three times as many homosexuals as average Americans are college graduates . . . a percentage dwarfing that of truly disadvantaged African-Americans and Hispanics. More than three times as many homosexuals as average Americans hold professional or managerial positions . . . again, making homosexuals embarrassingly more advantaged than true minorities in the job market. 65.8 percent of homosexuals are overseas travellers—more than four times the percentage (14 percent) of average Americans. More than 13 times as many homosexuals as average Americans (26.5 vs. 1.9 percent) are frequent flyers.[6]

It is worth considering this income data in some detail. The key source for CR claims that gay incomes far exceed the national average is an article appearing in a 1991 issue of the *Wall Street Journal* (18 July). The figures in this piece were derived from a marketing study undertaken in 1988, surveying readers of several gay magazines. The result, that gay households earn an average of $55,430 per year, has been reiterated not only by Tony Marco for Focus on the Family as in the quotation above, but also by several other CR actors, including the Family Research Council and the American Family Association.[7] These figures have also found their way into grassroots campaigning literature, for example, that of Take Back Cincinnati!, Colorado for Family Values (CFV), and the Oregon Citizen's Alliance (OCA).[8]

A preliminary comment on this data might be to note the perhaps obvious point that self-selecting readers of glossy gay men's magazines are likely to be among the most affluent members of the lesbian and gay community. Second, lesbian income data has been collected rarely; where it has, research shows lesbian households earning anywhere from far below, to somewhat above, the national average.[9] Third, other market research, for example that cited by Roger Magnuson in his antigay book (1994, 100), suggests the differentials are more complex and less dramatic. Fourth, the comparative statistic on the average income of "disadvantaged African-American households" is misleading to say the least. It creates the impression that like is being compared to like. This is not the case; the gay average is not being contrasted with the African-American average, but with the average of the *poorest* black households. Furthermore, these comparisons, while seemingly powerful and persuasive, fail to acknowl-

edge that some affluent gays are black, and many poor
blacks are gay. Recent U.S. census data, for example, suggest that the earnings of black female same-sex households are equal to the national average household income.[10]

This last statistic underscores the complexity of inter-
preting CR economic data. Differentials in average earnings are due primarily to dynamics of gender and race:
gay and lesbian households are more likely to have two
earners than heterosexual ones are; women earn on average less than men; and black people earn on average less
than white. At the end of this section, I consider the extent
to which the CR is truly concerned with the disadvantage
suffered by those it implies are "legitimate minorities."
For now I continue on this theme of gay prosperity.

118

Intimately tied to the construction of gay individual
and household affluence is the CR's depiction of the
wealth of the gay community as a whole.

Gay militancy is also a motherlode of political action dol-
lars. Counting legal expenses, gay militants trying to defeat and overturn Colorado's Amendment 2 have out-
spent proponents 10 to 1. The Human Rights Campaign
Fund (HRCF), a gay national political action committee,
ranks among the top tenth of one percent of America's
PACs. . . . Gay militants have now established a Washington, DC–based "Victory Fund," with a current budget
closing in on $1 million a year, to war-chest the political
campaigns of municipal candidates willing to claim gay
"orientation." According to Tim McFeeley, current
HRCF Executive Director, gays and lesbians spent "con-
servatively" $100 million during their 1993 "March on
Washington." . . . This kind of money gives gays much

more protection and clout than average people enjoy and exponentially more than true, disadvantaged minorities. That's why opposing "gay rights" can't, as gay militants claim, "make gays second-class citizens"—people with this kind of money and clout are never "second-class citizens." Gays are no "minority"; gay militants constitute a rich, powerful *special interest.* And, to coin a phrase, enough money makes anyone a "majority."[11]

The vast opulence of the gay community was highlighted in the earliest CR antigay treatises (e.g., Rueda 1982). Today, according to the CR, these riches are evidenced by the huge assets of gay rights campaigning organizations; however, the only such organization the CR actually identifies as commanding large sums is the Human Rights Campaign Fund, a gay political action committee. The HRCF is vilified similarly by William Dannemeyer (1989, 148–50) and Roger Magnuson (1994, 104), among others.

119

The theme of gay wealth is intimately bound up with the second limb of the secular rights discourse: gays are hugely powerful political actors. This theme appears over and over again in conservative Christian literature. Evidence of this power is found throughout the cultural and institutional life of the country. According to the CR, gays hold hundreds of top political posts; they are effectively "running the country." The world of the arts—film, television, theater, and so on—is completely under the sway of the gay elite. Other institutions (the schools and the media) have similarly been taken over: the military is under threat (see discussion in chapter 3).

According to Loretta Neet of the OCA (interview by author, 1994):

They're not politically disadvantaged, they're not politically incapable of politically advocating for themselves by any way, shape, or form. They are the most powerful lobby in the United States today. Their situation is nothing like what it was for black people in America. . . . they could not advocate for themselves. Politically, they were segregated from bathrooms, from public fountains, they were not allowed in certain businesses. . . . they had to sit in the back of the bus, all those sorts of things. You don't find that for the homosexual community. People would be scared to death to do that, you know, for retribution, lawsuits, whatever.

The theme of "no special rights" inexorably follows from this logic. Gay rights, according to the CR, single out gay people for special privileges—privileges they already have in abundance. Within this discourse gays are already special: especially wealthy, especially powerful. Lesbians and gays, then, are far from being an "oppressed minority"; their wealth and power vastly exceeds their numbers. Indeed, "normal" people, particularly orthodox, practicing Christians, need protection from them and their "retribution." These sentiments were echoed explicitly by Justice Scalia in the *Evans* v *Romer* dissent (see chapter 6).

In considering these discourses of wealth and power, I take note of two themes in particular (see also Schacter 1994).[12] The first is the desirability of homosexuality, and its impact on the CR's traditional stance of anti-immutability (see chapter 3). Ironically, the pragmatists' rights rhetoric, in a manner reminiscent of older themes of disease and seduction, also represents homosexuality as highly desirable—a sure ticket to economic affluence and unlimited influence in the corridors of power. Gays, according to this literature, will get better jobs, higher wages, and travel extensively. They will also be part of one of the most powerful interest groups in the country and, individually, achieve influential positions throughout the institutions of American life.

This picture of gay life, as represented by the rights pragmatists, poses several dilemmas for traditional CR antigay politics. It may be particularly problematic in light of the CR's commitment to the view that homosexuality is a willful behavioral choice, and not an immutable attribute (see chapter 3). If sexual desire is animated by individual agency, as the mainstream CR believes, then why would any reader of its literature not opt for this gay pathway to prosperity?

Ironically, the pragmatists' success depends on the less orthodox public believing sexuality to be immutable: genetically or psychologically innate and impervious to change. What I mean is that the effective reception of the CR gay economic data should encourage envy, resentment, and ultimately anger. It would not do for "straight America" instead to "choose to be gay," yet the logical consequence of the CR position on immutability might lead to this option for those who do not govern their lives according to biblical definitions of sin. There is therefore a fundamental instability between these two pillars of CR antigay discourse: on the one hand, gay power is immense and rights are not needed; on the other, sexual behavior involves strong elements of personal choice, and is not inborn. For the nonorthodox to believe the first, they must doubt the latter—otherwise, to overstate the case, why not choose "the gay lifestyle" and get rich quick?

Public opinion data tend to show that Americans are divided as to whether they believe sexuality to be predetermined and immutable.[13] For many years the CR fought against immutability, deriding the "gay gene" scientists and presenting their own studies arguing that sexuality had no genetic base whatsoever (see discussion in chapter 3). While many conservative Christians continue to beat this drum, others are recognizing that they may be gaining little through it.

In response to these complications and others, many CR antigay activists are opting out of the immutability debate altogether. Several of those I spoke with, for example, argued that the causes of homosexuality were actually irrelevant; all that mattered was that gays possessed immense power and needed no special rights. This position is far more consistent with the rhetoric of the newer pragmatists; a continued attack on immutability both diverts their energies and explicitly undermines the new pragmatic antigay rights agenda.

Perhaps, then, the "new" CR would have more success if it dropped another element from its "old" discourse—anti-immutability—in addition to those of "disgust" and "public health threat" noted by Tony Marco earlier. The sidelining of anti-immutability arguments brings the CR's position on sexuality more into line with mainstream liberal thinking, which arguably is what they need to do to achieve gains in the short term. In other words, the CR loses little by conceding that homosexuality may have genetic origins; their argument is simply that gays do not need so-called special laws and ordinances, given their disproportionate share of the nation's resources, regardless of whether they were born or made. The rights pragmatists would have to live with the odd effect that, in the process of making their case, they present homosexuality as quite appealing.

But things are not quite that simple; for many in the CR, the view that homosexuality is a willful, disgusting, and dangerous deviance from God's plan is fundamental to their *public,* as well as their private, politics. Indeed, several of the organizations actively promoting the pragmatic rights rhetoric are at the same time continuing to compile their own evidence that sexuality has no biological foundation, and that it is inherently repugnant, disease-ridden, and heretical. Robert Knight, the Family Research Council's director of cultural studies, embraces the newer rights discourse while insisting that homosexuals are disease-ridden and a threat to children.[14] Larry Burtoft (1994), who produced a monograph on gay issues for Focus on the Family, takes a similar approach. Both the OCA and CFV, in their antigay material, attempt to combine rights discourse with religious rhetoric and the language of disease and seduction,[15] as do several other writers on gay issues (e.g., Magnuson 1994; Grant and Horne 1993). The purists among the pragmatists, intent on keeping the old rhetoric at bay, pose several dilemmas for CR antigay politics.

At the same time, however, the pragmatists, despite deriding the old rhetoric, need it to succeed. In other words, in order for the newer rights discourse to be effective, its audience must be able to back up their resentment with traditional beliefs about the filth and sinfulness of homosexual behavior. Otherwise, as I have suggested, they might find this picture of gay life too appealing. The interdependency of these "old" and "new" discourses is well illustrated in the campaign for Colorado's Amendment 2 in 1992.

Despite CFV's professed embracement of the rights-oriented strategy, the organization nevertheless fell back on provoking outrage over the homosexual "threat" to children and public health. A CFV broadsheet (CFV 1992), distributed midway through the campaign, contained lurid pieces titled "Target: Children," "Homosexual Indoctrination in the Schools," "Objective: Destroy the Family," and "Homosexual Behavior: Should Government Protect *This*?" The tabloid even reprinted an extract from the absurd *Gay Community News* article I discussed in chapter 3. One CFV activist has described this newspaper (of which 750,000 copies were distributed statewide) as "the single greatest contribution to the '92 campaign" (Bransford 1994, 145). In addition, CFV in the final week of the struggle ran television ads featuring excerpts from *The Gay Agenda* video (see chapter 3). In contrast to Justice Scalia's protestations in the *Evans* v *Romer* dissent, as I discuss in chapter 6, it is not so difficult to see the "animus" behind the initiative.

It is, then, rather difficult to isolate and assess the pragmatists' success.[16] What one can say is that it is clearly important to the CR's antigay agenda that it not throw out the baby with the bathwater; both discourses, old and new, need each other. However, so long as anti-immutability continues to be central to the "old," the "new's" presentation of gay prosperity and power continues to beg the question, Why not me? The pragmatic discourse, then, far from being neutral on immutability, in order to be more effective ought to embrace *im*mutability: "it cannot be you because you were not born this way." But, for two primary reasons, this is unlikely to occur. First, the old traditionalists are still very dominant (the CFV tabloid also contained an anti-immutability piece). A second, and more complex, reason is that some of the rights pragmatists themselves rely on one further argument that directly challenges an immutability stance: the fluidity of gay identity.[17]

Often using lesbian and gay theorizing and "queer" politics, several CR pragmatists argue that the notion of "gay" is meaningless, that lesbians and gays themselves are discarding these labels, and that civil rights protections based on gay sexuality will actually be open to anyone claiming any sort of sexual identity at all (e.g., pedophiles, necrophiliacs, and so on). Furthermore, this fluidity, the CR suggests, is additional evidence of the deceit of the gay community; on the one hand, lesbians and gay men persist in advocating immutability, and on the other, they insist on the shifting terrain of sexuality signified by the word "queer." Tony Marco (interview by author, 1994) argues that "gay militants say sexual orientation is immutable, and it's innate, and yet among queer theorists—the intelligentsia—you hear a completely different tune which is that sexual orientation should be fluid and changeable, depending on one's current status and desires. . . . I think it's fraud."

Arguably, the new pragmatists also wish to have it both ways: they explicitly rely on mutability but implicitly depend on a popular belief in immutability. As I have argued, gay sexuality represented as privileged, in order to be effective, must be perceived as inaccessible, a state to which the average American cannot gain entry. This in turn feeds the second discursive theme I wish to discuss: the ways in which the CR's construction of the gay community draws from and plays to preexisting anti-Semitic ideologies.

This process of racialization, or the ways in which gays are "Jewed," involves gays being constructed, like Jews historically, as a symbolic "fat cat," getting rich off the

125

backs of the average American. I am not suggesting that gays have replaced Jews in this role or that anti-Semitic ideologies are no longer operating. I am also not suggesting that the representation of gays is as monolithic as the myth of the "Jewish conspiracy"; it is certainly not as deep-seated in the popular imagination. Nevertheless, I would argue that there are historical parallels here that are more than coincidental (see also chapter 2).

The notion of greed provides one example. When interviewing Tony Marco (1994), I asked him why, if gays were so rich and powerful, they were asking for human rights protections—for what possible reason would such people put so much energy into demanding laws for which they clearly had no need? According to Marco, "sheer greed and lust for power" lay at the root. Subsequent to this interview (4 November 1994), Marco sent me a follow-up memo with further explanation.

> In every era of history there always seem to be an elite few people compelled to seek extraordinary wealth. And once they achieve wealth, their hunger for affluence is usually supplanted by a hunger for power and influence. . . . No manifestation of the will to power has its origins in any one ethnic, cultural, religious, political or economic class. . . . Greed manifests itself in both the poorest of the poor and the richest of the rich.

In linking Marco's views here to the racialization theme, my intention is not to portray Marco as anti-Semitic; I have no evidence that he is. Rather, I wish to suggest how this construction of gay avarice draws from and plays to a preexisting mind-set sympathetic to the view that America is controlled by a wealthy elite furthering its own agenda.

126

The conspiracy theme (see Davis 1971; Johnson 1983), prevalent in anti-Semitic discourse, is also evident in the CR antigay genre. As I discussed in chapter 3, the CR constructs the gay movement as engaged in a sinister alliance with "liberal forces." These forces are opposed to "ordinary people," who have lost all control over their families and sociopolitical environment. This, too, is a kind of "Jew imaging," which draws upon historical discourses of conspiracy and world domination. I also noted how particular texts are circulated, much like "The Protocols of the Elders of Zion," to prove the existence of the gay demon.

Several CR activists indulge in yet another anti-Semitic strategy—"outing." Uncovering the "secret" Jewishness of prominent individuals has always been an important part of the politics of anti-Semitism (and anticommunism). Similarly, the CR is keen to identify gays and lesbians in "high places." Peter LaBarbera, editor of *Lambda Report,* regularly engages in this strategy, as do many others (e.g., Marrs 1993). I would also suggest that the *effects* of "Jewing" representations are very similar: they engender a populistic envy, resentment, anger, and rebellion. The "gay community" thus becomes synonymous with the world of elite, overly privileged people who take more and more for themselves and have no comprehension of the problems of ordinary folk. "Gay," then, signifies both "Nazi" (see chapter 3) and "Jew"; fascistic, sexually depraved, superrich, and intent on domination. As part of these effects, CR writers clearly hope their readers will identify a huge gap between their own class position and that of lesbians and gay men. This effect in turn ties neatly into a more general resentment against elite liberal values building for some time (see Crawford

127

1980; Edsall and Edsall 1992) and reflected in the 1994 midterm elections. (For further discussion see afterword.) The literature also seeks to feed the resentment of African Americans particularly, and it is to the CR's deployment of race discourse that I now turn.

THE DESERVING?

An integral part of the CR's antigay rights discourse involves making direct comparisons between the status of "homosexuals" and that of "truly disadvantaged minorities" (see Schacter 1994). Their argument is that a few very powerful people are passing themselves off as deserving of a status justly accorded only to those who have proved their need for it. Quite explicitly, then, the CR antigay genre represents "true minorities" as discriminated against, and deserving of the rights they have won. But how easily does this reasoning sit with the CR's race politics generally?[18]

This is not an easy question to answer—partly because activists are very careful about what they say, and partly because there are indeed divisions within the CR on this question.[19] While the antirights position of many white CR members is rooted in long-held racist understandings, others, in my view, sincerely advocate antiracist ideologies (though they may be critical of rights-related strategies). For this reason, as well as because the CR has several nonwhite constituencies,[20] it would be trite to argue simply that the entire movement is racist.

But there is clearly a tension between the CR's courting of nonwhite constituencies and the historic racism and antiwelfarism of many white supporters. On the one hand, the CR is actively seeking to broaden its base and

128

win support among black, Asian, and Hispanic Christians.[21] On the other, this needs to be done without alienating the traditional backbone of the CR—white conservative evangelicals especially, although by no means exclusively, in the South. Several organizations, such as Focus on the Family, tread a careful line between acknowledging some of the social difficulties facing nonwhite families and stressing personal responsibility, the transformative potential of religious faith, and the destructive effects of "welfare dependency."[22] Promise Keepers, the conservative Christian men's movement organization, walks a similar tightrope.[23]

The CR's gay power rights discourse throws up several difficulties for this politics of race, particularly its antistatist dimensions. By depicting lesbians and gays as undeserving because they are nowhere near as poor or as unrepresented as the "truly disadvantaged," the CR would seem to be implying that these truly disadvantaged people do deserve the "special rights" they have. In other words, the pragmatists are *not* suggesting that all antidiscrimination rights are unacceptable; rather, they argue that there are legitimate and illegitimate recipients. This argument may appeal to some nonwhite conservative Christians; however, many white supporters are in favor of rolling back all antidiscrimination laws and policies entirely, including the civil rights reforms of past decades (see, generally, Edsall and Edsall 1992).

The OCA, an organization that continues regularly to propose antigay initiatives despite several failures, provides a good example of these dynamics. In 1987 Bill Lunch, a political scientist at Oregon State University, attended the first statewide convention of the OCA and conducted a survey of the attitudes of delegates (Lunch

1993). Holocaust revisionist literature was sold openly at this conference, and in response to Lunch's questions an overwhelming majority of delegates expressed disapproval of the Civil Rights Act, the Voting Rights Act, and other reforms of the 1960s, indicating that they would like to see this legislation repealed.

In the autumn of 1994, seven years later, I interviewed Lon Mabon, director of the OCA, and Loretta Neet, the organization's public relations coordinator. As I waited in the OCA's front office, instead of Holocaust revisionist literature I found a statement of support from orthodox Jews in New York that the OCA was distributing enthusiastically.[24] In interviews both Mabon and Neet were careful to express measured approval of civil rights for African Americans, though they, as well as others I interviewed in Colorado, suggested that the reforms had "had their day" and were no longer relevant. Only Kevin Tebedo, a leader of CFV (interview by author, 1994), explicitly called for the repeal of civil rights legislation (providing that truly racist individuals were forced, somehow, to change their ways).

It is highly improbable that OCA members during these seven years reversed their position on civil rights; it is more likely that the organization as a whole chose to deemphasize its race politics so that it could both play to other conservative communities potentially sympathetic to the antigay message and appear less illiberal generally (see Bates 1995). Paradoxically, then, as I have suggested, the portrayal of the undeserving gays served to strengthen the legitimacy of laws for the deserving, laws that many CR activists do not, at root, support at all. Indeed, many CR activists, such as Will Perkins of CFV (interview by author, 1994), believe that women's rights, for example, are as undeserving of legitimacy as lesbian and gay rights.

130

The CR's pragmatic rights discourse throws into relief the tortured reasoning of CR rights politics generally. In its efforts to put a stop to gay rights, the CR constructs other groups as deserving rights. Arguably, however, the CR does not believe that African Americans and other people of color deserve rights based on "race" grounds any longer; much CR literature is crystal clear in setting out that the civil rights reforms were motivated by the existence of legalized discrimination—a state of affairs no longer in place. The views of CR activists and constituents reflect, to a large extent, the conservative rights reaction powerfully analyzed by Thomas and Mary Edsall (1992).

I have attempted to make two related points thus far: (1) many CR activists have never supported and do not support civil rights laws of any kind; (2) CR antigay rights discourse paradoxically reinforces the legitimacy of other rights provision. It remains for me to consider how well the CR responds to the needs of the "truly disadvantaged" groups it exploits, without hesitation, in the antigay genre.

131

Several CR discourses and policies stand in stark contrast to its professed concern for the "disadvantaged." One of these is the campaign for school vouchers (allowing parents to choose the "best" school for their children)—a pillar of the CR educational agenda.[25] School vouchers, according to many professional educators, encourage the impoverishment of inner cities, lead to ever diminishing resources for poor pupils, and can result in de facto educational segregation.[26] Second, the CR's vehement opposition to multicultural educational policy also calls into question any commitment it has to the concerns of non–racially dominant families. Recently centered on campaigns against "politically correct" school history texts, much of the CR opposes, among other things, curricula explaining genocidal policies against American Indians, the cultural and political contributions of Third World peoples, any race-based criticism of the "Founding Fathers," and the contributions of African-American poets and writers.[27]

Third, it is beyond question that the CR encouraged, and in several cases instigated, the groundswell of opposition to affirmative action that arose in the late 1980s.[28] Fourth, and perhaps most obvious, is the CR's electoral support of right-wing Republican politicians, often standing in direct opposition to "minority-friendly" Democratic candidates.[29] Yet another example of this was the CR's relentless antagonism directed at the potential presidential candidacy of Colin Powell, a moderate (although antigay) black Republican, in 1995. In conclusion, then, it is clear that the CR cares little for those whom it exploits in antigay propaganda; the "truly disadvantaged" will remain just that—partly as a result of the CR's political agenda.

I have attempted in this chapter to explore the development, inconsistencies, implications, and power of CR antigay rights discourse. As my discussion has tended to range back and forth, it might be helpful if I gather the various threads together. Here is a summary of the key points of the chapter. (1) The CR's traditional antigay rhetoric of sin, disease, seduction, and mutability more recently has been challenged by a secular, pragmatic, rights-oriented discourse. (2) The newer language of gay wealth and power is internally problematic for the CR in several respects: it ironically portrays gay life as highly desirable; it rejects, yet depends upon, several traditionalist assumptions; its effectiveness relies upon its audience believing that sexuality is immutable—a direct challenge to the dominant CR position. (3) The discursive construction of the gay community deploys economic and political power data in a disingenuous, and often inaccurate and misleading, manner. (4) In so doing, it draws from and plays to underlying anti-Semitic ideologies. (5) The CR exploits racially oppressed peoples in its antigay propaganda while pursuing policies elsewhere that further entrench racial disparities.

Despite these contradictions and deceits, CR antigay rights discourse contains some truths with which the lesbian and gay movement must come to terms. In these concluding remarks, I consider whether there is any substance to the CR's antigay rights discourse. I make five interdependent points.

First, it is possible that, on average, lesbian and gay households, particularly the latter, are better off economically than their heterosexual counterparts. While there are poor communities of lesbians and gay men, their poverty is a consequence not solely of their sexuality, but also, in some cases predominantly, of their class, disability, ethnicity, or gender.

Second, there is little point in denying that the lesbian and gay rights movement has been one of the most successful social movements in this century. Within a few short decades the public perception of homosexuality has changed enormously, while professional discourses have similarly shifted in response to lesbian and gay agitation (see chapter 1).

Third, there is no question that out lesbians and gay men have achieved positions within public and private institutions that they have used to advance their sexual politics.[30] The CR's question—why "special rights"?—is apposite, evocative, and important.

Fourth, are gay rights "special rights"? The gay rights

133

movement has devoted a great deal of energy to answering this question in the negative. I would argue, however, that *some* rights are "special" in the sense that they carve out particular bases upon which discriminatory treatment is not acceptable. The inclusion of "sexual orientation" in civil rights laws, for example, does give sexuality a form of legal protection afforded to legally recognized categories such as religion, race, sex, and so on, and not, for example, to body size, or economic position. If one can be denied housing because one is overweight or on welfare, but not because one is heterosexual or gay, then sexual orientation—including hetero-, homo-, and bisexualities—has "special," as in protected, status. There is, however, no status here for lesbians and gay men that is not accorded equally to hetero- and bisexuals.

134   On the other hand, gay spousal/parental rights are somewhat different. Demands for gay marriage, child custody, adoption rights, spousal benefits, and so on seek to open up an exclusive "couples" club to new members; however, in these cases lesbians and gay men are pursuing entitlements currently granted on a basis that completely excludes them. Their inclusion in the terms of marriage, spousaldom, or parenthood simply accords them the same rights available to all heterosexuals (see Duggan 1994).

Rights such as these, then, do not give "special" rank to sexual orientation that other identities or behaviors do not have; rather, spousal benefit rights are analogous to voting rights—they bring an excluded group into full citizenship.[31] This would be true as well of the struggle to remove the quasi-ban on gays in the military: the elimination of a specific policy of discrimination targeted at a particular group is not a "special" right.

I would argue that sexual-orientation rights are special, but only in the sense of being singled out (along with other enumerated categories), and gay spousal/parental rights are not. Although the CR's rhetoric of "special rights" is a powerful one and has been endorsed by three judges of the U.S. Supreme Court (*Evans* v *Romer;* see chapter 6), defining rights one way or the other actually tells us very little about whether they are deserved or not. Special rights for people with disabilities, for example, are acceptable to many on the CR (up to a point).

Finally, how relevant are the facts about gay wealth and political power to these rights debates? Should groups with higher incomes and more political clout be disentitled to all forms of antidiscrimination rights? The answer would have to be no. First of all, even if the gay community is on average more affluent than some other communities, it is both erroneous and deceptive to insinuate that every lesbian and gay man is therefore wealthy. That would be analogous to saying that there can be no poverty in the United States because the average national income is over $25,000 per year, or that Christians are vastly wealthy as a group because some individual Christians wield enormous economic clout.[32] Furthermore, while wealth and political influence are important indicators of social power, they are not the only ones.

It is obvious, but perhaps necessary, to say that neither wealth nor political power protect against all forms of discrimination. While these assets no doubt cushion blows, history is replete with cases where riches were taken, and influence discarded, in the pursuit of policies ranging from discrimination to genocide. Arguably, the existence of antidiscrimination laws would hardly have been helpful in these situations; however, one argument for their exis-

135

tence is that such legislation helps to create a social climate where extremist politics flourishes less easily.[33]

If wealth and power arguments are either specious or, if credible, unpersuasive, there may be another basis upon which gay rights may be denied more legitimately: if the majority of a community vote to repudiate them. That is the subject of chapter 6.

The Christian Right versus Gay Rights
in Colorado, 1992–1996

Thus far I have concentrated on explaining and analyzing the underlying politics of the CR's antigay agenda. As I outlined at the start, my interest in this topic is with the how and why of CR antigay politics, rather than the when or where. But whys are often best understood in specific contexts, and so in this chapter I take one example of an antigay campaign—the fight for Amendment 2 in Colorado in 1991/92—and consider some of its implications.

In the 1992 elections Colorado voters narrowly approved a citizen-initiated ballot measure to amend the state constitution. Amendment 2, drafted and promoted by Colorado for Family Values (CFV), repealed existing local gay rights laws and prevented any similar enactments (local or statewide) in the future. Once passed, the amendment was immediately challenged in the courts. The resulting litigation has been described by one CR activist as "the *Roe* v *Wade* of the homosexual issue" (Jim Woodall, interview by author, 1995). If this is so, the CR has "lost" again; in May 1996 the U.S. Supreme Court declared the amendment unconstitutional.[1]

What happened in Colorado was not an aberration; rather, Amendment 2 was a logical progression in a national, concerted CR antigay effort of over two decades' duration (see chapter 1). The Colorado initiative since its passage provided an inspirational model to CR activists across the nation.[2] The subsequent judicial responses to the amendment addressed fundamental questions of democracy, minority rights, and the nature of citizen lawmaking under the shadow of constitutional review.

I do not, however, intend this chapter to be predominantly an analysis of the Colorado campaign itself, nor an evaluation of the factors leading to the amendment's passage, nor a doctrinal analysis of judicial pronouncements (although I will certainly touch on all these things).[3] Rather, what I hope to do here is, first, consider how the CR's antigay discourse was operationalized in a particular campaign; and, second, give an account and explore some of the implications of subsequent judicial decisions.

138

I first tell the story of how the amendment came to be, including a brief consideration of some of the characters and organizations involved in shaping its content and struggling for its passage. I hope through doing this that issues I have raised in previous chapters will become more real. For instance, Amendment 2 provides a good example of the continuing tension within the CR between the old moralists and the new pragmatists. The second half of the chapter is concerned with the role of the courts and the implications of their decision making for CR antigay politics. This in turn leads to my final chapter, which is concerned with the relationship between the CR and the state.

THE STORY OF AMENDMENT 2

The Amendment 2 story really begins with some of the initial clashes between gay rights supporters and their opponents in Colorado. For example, in 1974 the city of Boulder enacted a local gay rights ordinance, which CR activists successfully fought to have immediately repealed (the city passed it again thirteen years later). But these stories are legitimate subjects in their own right, and I am not feigning to offer here a history of gay rights in Colorado. Instead, I focus on the situation just preceding, and ultimately precipitating, the filing of Amendment 2 (see Gallagher 1994).

By 1990 several cities in Colorado, like others across the country, had enacted gay rights ordinances, normally consisting of antidiscrimination ordinances including "sexual orientation" as a prohibited ground of discrimination. At the time Amendment 2 was filed in 1991, three city councils (Aspen, Boulder, and Denver) and a school district (Boulder Valley School District Re-2) had enacted such legislation. Denver's ordinance, passed in 1990, became an immediate target of that city's CR leaders, and a local effort was launched to have it repealed.

Around the same time, two other events occurred that had a large impact on subsequent developments. First, a statewide bill was proposed to strengthen all existing human rights protections, one provision of which was to add, among other things, "sexual orientation" to a list of grounds upon which "ethnic intimidation" was prohibited. Second, the Colorado Springs local council began hearings on a proposed human rights ordinance for that city, again part of which was directed toward providing protections for lesbians and gay men.

It is worth noting that only the Denver ordinance was explicitly a "gay rights" initiative. Both the state bill and the Colorado Springs proposal were general human rights–strengthening devices, with "sexual orientation" simply being an add-on to a list of existing grounds. While the gay rights provisions became the focus of opposition, many on the CR opposed the measures in whole and in fact hoped to see most existing human rights laws, and their implementation machinery, removed.

Will Perkins (interview by author, 1994), for example, the car salesman who was to become the key spokesman for CFV during the Amendment 2 campaign, first became involved in the Colorado Springs ordinance battle when he heard that it would strengthen the powers of that city's Human Rights Commission. Indeed, CFV continues today the fight to minimize the role of the Colorado Springs human rights machinery, quite apart from any gay rights angle.[4] Thus, as I have argued throughout this book, CR opposition to gay rights is largely inseparable from the movement's wider, antiliberal agenda. Although Amendment 2 was about "gay rights," its proponents have an anti–civil rights agenda generally (see chapter 5).

Nevertheless, gay rights did provide the focus the CR needed to galvanize support, and they quickly organized to contest the state bill and the Colorado Springs ordinance, while Denver activists continued to fight for repeal there. While these three battles continued, a small group of CR activists began to coalesce in Colorado Springs to consider mounting a more coordinated antigay effort. Colorado Springs was a natural focal point for CR antigay activity as the city had, over several years, become home to more than fifty conservative Protestant organizations, including Focus on the Family, James Dobson's multimedia empire (see chapters 1 and 5).[5]

Colorado Springs was also the home of Tony Marco, an important CR activist of the pragmatist variety (see chapter 5), who was to become a key strategist for CFV. In the spring of 1991 Marco contacted David Noebel, the director of Summit Ministries (see below), and they were soon joined by Kevin Tebedo, a "young Noebel associate" and the son of state senator Maryanne Tebedo (Bransford 1994, 18, 24). This group, soon to expand and call itself CFV, began to believe that a more worthwhile tactic might be to kill all these gay rights birds with one stone—a statewide initiative to amend the constitution in order to repeal existing gay rights laws and prohibit any similar enactments in the future. The citizens' initiative had been an important weapon in the new right's arsenal since the early 1980s (Crawford 1980).

Most U.S. state constitutions provide for some form of direct democracy, or citizen lawmaking, usually through an initiative or referendum process. Technically, initiatives make new law while referenda repeal existing law; however, some initiatives, such as Amendment 2, can do both. In certain states, Colorado for example, the initiative process can be used to amend the state constitution (hence the title "Amendment" 2), in which case only another majority vote of the electorate can alter it.[6] In order to place initiatives on an election ballot, proponents must file the measure with the state legislature, where officials subject it to varying degrees of review (depending on the state in question; see Linde 1993). Once approved, the initiative is fixed on the ballot when enough signatures are gathered (again, the requisite number varies by state). Once that has been accomplished, the electorate votes on it, usually during an election year, and it will pass with a simple majority. It then becomes "legislation" and must be implemented by the state government.

The initiative process is rooted in a model of "direct democracy." Citizens, unhappy with acts (or failures to act) taken by their representative legislatures, can bypass governmental structures by directly enacting legislation through a majority vote. As Joshua Miller (1991) has noted, direct democracy and conservatism have often gone hand in hand since the Puritan era. Partly as a consequence of this dynamic, the model has been subject to a barrage of analysis and criticism (e.g., Adams 1994; Collins and Oesterle 1995; Eule 1990; Linde 1993; Magleby 1995; Niblock 1993). I return to some of these concerns later in the chapter. For now I continue with the Amendment 2 narrative.

Colorado antigay activists believed the initiative mechanism might do more than simply put a hold on the progress of gay rights in Colorado generally; they also intended it as a surprise maneuver to outflank the opposition.

142

> I played the Amendment 2 process the way I did based on well-conceived strategic considerations. CFV did not wait until the Denver and Colo. Spgs. "gay rights" battles were finished to start Amendment 2 *precisely because we wanted the gay militants to think we were fighting the very multibrushfire battle they wanted us to fight.* We purposely gave the impression that these two battles, and others looming, were our sole preoccupations. We deliberately let our apparent weakness serve as a smoke-screen to cover our more extensive purposes. Most of the Denver ref[erendum] people didn't even know about our plans—because we wanted to firmly establish a leadership base in Colo. Sprg. and "cut out of the herd" Denver leadership we considered ineffective. (emphasis in original)[7]

While these plans were under way, the CR in Colorado won two out of three "brushfires"—the state bill failed to progress and was killed, and the Colorado Springs city council voted against the proposed changes to the human rights framework in that city. At the same time, however, the CR repeal effort in Denver failed. Despite the fact that no statewide gay rights law existed, CFV continued in its commitment to put a halt to gay rights at the local level through the initiative process. What this would mean, in effect, is that a majority of the state electorate could override decisions made by elected local governments. In other words, the CR, unable to win a local repeal effort, hoped through the initiative process to avoid any future democratic struggle.

By the summer of 1991 CFV had settled into its role of leading the initiative campaign. By this point, the organization was a full-fledged member of the CR. Its founders, Tony Marco and Kevin Tebedo, are conservative Christians, as were its initial board members. Will Perkins (interview by author, 1994), who became the main spokesperson for CFV during the campaign, is a conservative Christian who believes the gay agenda is the devil's agenda. Kevin Tebedo received his activist training from David Noebel at Summit Ministries, a long-standing CR anticommunist organization with origins in Billy Hargis's Christian Anti-Communism Crusade of the 1950s.[8] Bill McCartney, coach of the University of Colorado football team and hence a popular and populist leader of CFV, had founded Promise Keepers, the conservative Christian men's organization, in 1990.[9] Also initially involved in CFV were Barbara Sheldon of the Traditional Values Coalition, Randy Hicks of Focus on the Family, and Jayne Schindler of Eagle Forum.[10] These CR activists and many others anticipated Colorado's Amendment 2 as the realization of their antigay politics.

CFV, after some initial squabbling, particularly between the different styles of Tebedo (an old-style moralist) and Marco (a rights pragmatist), had settled on its core membership and had selected Will Perkins, an amiable, grandfatherly figure, as the key spokesperson. Tony Marco continued behind the scenes for a few months and then officially resigned, citing personal and financial concerns, although he remained an important adviser. With assistance from Pat Robertson's National Legal Foundation, CFV decided on the language of the amendment.

Although the framers of the amendment were devout conservative Christians, and the leaders of the antigay campaigns throughout the state were important figures on the CR,[11] the initiative was to be formulated deliberately in secular, noncondemnatory terms. "Their unifying argument would be to protect freedoms of speech and association against the tyranny of political correctness now enforcing special homosexual laws over the land. Their initiative language would be neither Republican, Democrat, Libertarian, nor Independent. The issue would be framed as inclusive, pluralistic—appealing to fairness in the law, crossing all political and religious lines" (Bransford 1994, 40). This approach would also serve to distinguish the Colorado amendment from Oregon Measure 9, a similar initiative but designed in more traditional moralistic tones, being advanced at the same time by the Oregon Citizen's Alliance (OCA), the leading CR organization in that state.

It is worth considering the language of both these measures. Colorado's Amendment 2 read:

No Protected Status Based on Homosexual, Lesbian or Bisexual Orientation.

Neither the state of Colorado, through any of its branches or departments, nor any of its agencies, political subdivisions, municipalities, or school districts, shall enact, adopt or enforce any statute, regulation, ordinance, or policy whereby homosexual, lesbian or bisexual orientation, conduct, practices or relationships shall constitute or otherwise be the basis of or entitle any person or class or persons to have or claim any minority status, quota preferences, protected status or claim of discrimination. This Section of the Constitution shall be in all respects self-executing.

Oregon's Measure 9 provided:

(1) This state shall not recognize any categorical provision such as "sexual orientation," "sexual preference," and similar phrases that includes homosexuality. Quotas, minority status, affirmative action, or any similar concepts, shall not apply to these forms of conduct, nor shall government promote these behaviors.

(2) State, regional and local governments and their properties and monies shall not be used to promote, encourage, or facilitate homosexuality, pedophilia, sadism or masochism.

(3) State, regional and local governments and their departments, agencies and other entities, including specifically the State Department of Higher Education and the public schools, shall assist in setting a standard for Oregon's youth that recognizes homosexuality, pedophilia, sadism and masochism as abnormal, wrong, unnatural, and perverse and that these behaviors are to be discouraged and avoided.

While the Oregon measure was clearly couched in the language of traditional conservative moralism, CFV activists chose to go down a different path. State activists were aware that the differences between the two measures effectively made Colorado the first statewide testing ground for the rights pragmatists (see chapter 5). The amendment was filed in Denver on 31 July 1991, and was inconsequentially reviewed and approved by state bureaucrats shortly thereafter.[12]

In order to have the amendment placed on the November 1992 ballot, CFV needed 49,279 petitioners by 12 March 1992. Their campaign got off to a slow start. As Stephen Bransford (1994, 49), a CFV activist, explains in his analysis of the process, initial fund-raising problems, coupled with a certain amount of infighting, led to the organization having gathered only 4,000 signatures by January 1. By early February the petition process seemed doomed; in order to step up publicity, CFV began to run spots on Christian radio stations, hoping to attract activists to take petitions out into the state. This proved a wise decision; not only did cadres deluge CFV offices requesting petitions, but national CR figures, such as James Dobson of Focus on the Family, took notice and began to assist CFV with strategy and marketing. Bransford (1994, 54–55), one of the architects of Amendment 2 publicity, also notes how two further incidents, the vilification of Bill Armstrong and Bill McCartney in the mainstream press, led to a huge increase in support. By the March 12 deadline activists had managed to gather 84,445 signatures, far more than needed to place the amendment on the ballot.

The campaign for a yes vote then began in earnest. To some extent, CFV adhered to its decision to fight a rights-based, rather than a morality-based, battle.[13] They also made the strategic decision to avoid holding large demonstrations, marches, or other spectacles. CFV hoped the image of the organization and the campaign itself would remain unsullied by accusations of "religious mania." However, this was not to be the case. And, as CFV campaigners and other sources note, the yes movement was quickly, and in my view accurately, identified with the "religious right," and the mainstream press was largely unsympathetic.[14]

Nevertheless, CFV continued to persevere in its attempts to convince voters. Shortly before election day, CFV had 750,000 copies of a tabloid printed and individually distributed to Colorado homes ("Equal Rights— Not Special Rights," 1992). As I explained in chapter 5, the document mixed new CR rights discourse with old-fashioned "disease and seduction" rhetorics. It was also clearly targeted at Christian homes as direct appeals to churchgoers were made on the final page (although Bransford's discussion [1994, 145] of the tabloid does not make this clear). CFV's concern that rights-based arguments were too weak and might lose them the amendment is also apparent in activists' decision, during the final weeks of campaigning, to run television ads using clips from *The Gay Agenda* (see chapter 3), a move not supported by Tony Marco (Bransford 1994, 146–53). Despite its protestations to the contrary, the Colorado CR was clearly not unwaveringly devoted to pragmatic rights discourse.

On 3 November 1992 the amendment passed with 53.4% of the vote, although it lost by a considerable margin in the three cities with gay rights ordinances.[15] Clearly, CFV had done something right, although how

147

individual voters were influenced by campaigning remains the subject for a large-scale research project not undertaken here. That CFV marshaled the conservative Christian vote is without question; it is also certainly beyond dispute that less orthodox, and even secular, Coloradans must also have voted for the amendment in large numbers. At the end of the day, however, Colorado did not prove an unblemished testing ground for the new rights rhetoric; CFV campaigners simply could not resist introducing older discourses at the crucial stage, and it is difficult to assess what effect, if any, this had on voting patterns.

On the same day the OCA lost its battle for Measure 9 with a yes vote of 44%. The OCA put another, similar measure on the ballot in 1994 (Measure 13), and lost again, although by a smaller margin. OCA's protégé organization, the Idaho Citizen's Alliance, also very narrowly lost its statewide initiative that year. In 1995 the electorate of Maine voted on a similar measure—it, too, failed.

In Colorado, however, as 1992 drew to a close, the story was far from over. In addition to calling for a national boycott of Colorado, a contested proposal that had mixed success, lesbian and gay activists in the state immediately sought to have the amendment declared unconstitutional by the courts. They succeeded in having an injunction placed on the amendment's enforcement pending the outcome of litigation, and therefore Amendment 2 was never implemented. In fact, in the aftermath of the initiative's passage, additional towns in Colorado passed gay rights ordinances.[16] Having traced a narrative of Amendment 2's origins and progress, I now turn to consider the diverse judicial pronouncements emanating from the resulting litigation.

THE LITIGATION

Nine days after the vote, opponents to Amendment 2 filed a constitutional challenge in district court. The gist of the claim was that Amendment 2 violated the right to equal protection guaranteed in the Fourteenth Amendment (see below).[17] The plaintiffs in the litigation consisted of eight lesbian and gay individuals, a heterosexual, HIV-positive woman, and the cities of Denver, Boulder, and Aspen (where there were gay rights ordinances). Once the amendment had been passed by a majority of the state's population, it effectively became government legislation, and thus the defendant was the state government. This was indeed rather ironic, as the Colorado government had little desire to fight in the amendment's corner. The governor at the time, Roy Romer, had marched with antiamendment campaigners, and lawyers in the attorney general's office reportedly refused initially to prepare the state's defense.[18]

The Colorado Amendment 2 case is legally known as *Evans* v *Romer,* Evans being one of the individual plaintiffs. In addition to the parties, various gay, libertarian, and Christian organizations intervened on either side. Prior to the appearance of the case on the docket of the U.S. Supreme Court in 1995, there were four separate judgments in the courts below.

The first, delivered by Jeffrey Bayless, a judge of the state's district court, on 15 January 1993, resulted in an injunction preventing Amendment 2 from taking effect. Judge Bayless found, after a four-day hearing, that the amendment violated a fundamental constitutional "right not to have the State endorse and give effect to private biases" and, therefore, triggered "strict-scrutiny" analysis (*Evans* v *Romer,* 60 Empl. Prac. Dec. [CCH] 73839).

Strict scrutiny is the highest level of constitutional review under equal protection doctrine. In order to pass its muster, defendants must show a "compelling state interest" being advanced by the legislation under question. Strict-scrutiny review is reserved for legislation implicating "suspect classes," or "fundamental rights." The only classification truly qualifying as "suspect" in American law is the category of "race"; as lesbians and gay men have not been held to be a "suspect class," strict-scrutiny review can only be triggered by antigay measures if a fundamental right is violated. If not, legislation is subject to "rational-basis" review only; meaning, there must be *some* rationality to the measure. In practice, few laws survive strict-scrutiny review, and most emerge unscathed from the rational-basis test. Judge Bayless, as I have noted, did find a fundamental right to be potentially impinged. As a result, he suspended the offending proposed legislation until a full trial could be held and issued an injunction prohibiting its implementation.

The defendant state immediately appealed this decision to the Colorado Supreme Court, where judgment was given on 13 July 1993 (*Evans* v *Romer*, 854 P2d 1270). In a decision upholding the result at district court, a majority of the supreme court found that a different constitutional right was at play. Chief Justice Rovira, writing for the majority, did not endorse Judge Bayless's approach but instead found that the Constitution provided for a fundamental "right to political participation" (1284). "Amendment 2," the court argued, "alters the political process so that a targeted class is prohibited from obtaining legislative, executive or judicial redress from discrimination absent the consent of a majority of the electorate" (1285). In other words, the Colorado Supreme

Court claimed that it was unconstitutional for a majority effectively to deny a minority group's very ability to fight for its rights.

As the supreme court found a fundamental right to be implicated, strict-scrutiny review was therefore appropriate, and the injunction consequently justified. The supreme court remanded the case to Judge Bayless for a decision on whether the state's interest in the legislation was compelling enough to satisfy strict-scrutiny review.[19]

Back in district court the burden was upon the state to defend the amendment on the basis that such legislation was necessary to fulfill compelling state objectives. There were five arguments made in the amendment's defense, and Judge Bayless dismissed them all.[20] Judgment was rendered in favor of the plaintiffs on 14 December 1993, and the case moved back to the supreme court on appeal.

Close to two years following the passage of the amendment, the Colorado Supreme Court issued its final decision in the case—again, in favor of those challenging the amendment's constitutionality (*Evans* v *Romer*, 882 P2d 1335). In the first part of the supreme court's judgment, Chief Justice Rovira, again writing for the majority, affirmed the position that a fundamental right to participate in the political process existed, and that strict-scrutiny analysis was in order. The court then proceeded to consider the justificatory arguments made by the state in its attempt to show compelling interests were being advanced by Amendment 2.

First, the court considered the state's position that the interest of protecting freedom of religion was served through the amendment's enactment (1342). This argument was based on the notion that gay rights laws violate

151

religious freedoms through forcing those with antigay religious views to house and hire lesbians and gay men. While the court agreed that "freedom of religion . . . is among the highest values of our society," the judges did not find the amendment narrowly tailored to meet this interest.

Instead, the court suggested that a simple religious exemption in civil rights laws would be the suitable means of addressing this issue. Religious exemptions, releasing churches, other religious organizations, and sometimes orthodox individuals from obligations under civil rights law, are often a standard accompaniment to gay rights measures. However, exemptions implicitly construct religious believers as a minority, and gay rights as part of majoritarian culture. For reasons that I hope are obvious by now, this is not how the CR wishes to perceive itself and its mission. Nevertheless, the supreme court, given the strict standard of review, argued that the amendment was too widely drafted and insufficiently precise to pass constitutional muster on grounds of religious freedom.

The next state interest assessed by the judges was that of preserving "familial privacy," defined by the state to mean the right of parents to teach their children traditional moral values (1343). Gay rights laws, the state contended, undermine this interest by having government promote a "gay is OK" message which may be in conflict with the values parents wish their children to learn. The court dispensed with this argument using classically liberal discourse.

152

> This argument fails because it rests on the assumption that the right of familial privacy engenders an interest in having government endorse certain values as moral or

immoral. While it is true that parents have a constitutionally protected interest in inculcating their children with
their own values . . . defendants point to no authority,
and we are aware of none, holding that parents have the
corresponding right of insuring that government endorse
those values.

The amendment, according to the court, does not in any
way impinge upon familial privacy; its subject matter,
civil rights laws, has no impact upon what parents can
teach their children.

The court's approach to this argument lies at the heart
of what conservative Christians find most distressing
about the modern state—its failure to act as moral leader.
The initiative process provides a means by which "the
people" can force the state to take a particular moral
stand whether it wants to or not. In the case of Amendment 2, a majority of Coloradans had sent a clear message
to government—"we've had enough of gay rights." The
direct democracy model means little if it cannot bind the
state to furthering a moral interest declared significant at
the ballot box. It may not be the interest of "familial privacy" that is in question, however, but the interest of furthering "the family."

And the court did go on to address this issue directly.

Defendants next argue that Amendment 2 "promotes the
compelling governmental interest of allowing the people
themselves to establish public social and moral norms."
In support of this proposition, defendants define two related norms which are promoted by Amendment 2:
Amendment 2 preserves heterosexual families and heterosexual marriage and, more generally, it sends the soci-

etal message condemning gay men, lesbians, and bisexuals as immoral. (1346)

In a move that must surely have made CR activists' blood run cold, the majority found that there was "no authority to support the proposition that the promotion of public morality constitutes a compelling governmental interest" (1347). The court did suggest, however, that while not compelling, such an interest might be "substantial"—perhaps indicating that this interest could be invoked for rational-basis review.

The court then argued, even though finding no compelling family interest at stake, that the amendment was not a necessary response to this interest in any case. According to Justice Rovira, there was no evidence to show that marriage rates went down, or divorce rates up, subsequent to the passage of gay rights laws. He further argued that the granting of civil rights protections for a specified group did not condone the practices of that group, but only protected individuals from discrimination due to membership. Hinting perhaps at the rational-basis review later adopted by the U.S. Supreme Court, the court's implication here was that the amendment was an irrational response, even if the interest was valid.[21]

Justice Erikson was the lone voice in dissent.[22] He opposed the recognition of a "right to participate in the political process" and scathingly remarked that, "judicial review of Amendment 2 has accomplished exactly what the voters who passed Amendment 2 sought to prevent—the majority has effectively created heightened protection for homosexuals, lesbians, and bisexuals" (1356). The dissent insisted that it was not the role of the court to set "social policy," and that there was an important distinction be-

154

tween citizen-enacted and state-enacted legislation. According to Justice Erikson, the courts must be especially careful not to tamper with the latter. In this sense, Justice Erikson's voice was clearly that of a judicial conservative; it is not for the courts to usurp the policymaking role of government.

Justice Erikson also reiterated that the precedent cited by the majority concerned "suspect classifications" and not "political participation." In other words, these courts were distressed about the restriction of participation only because the group in question was already one that received the strictest of constitutional protection. Lesbians and gay men had no such claim to scrutiny, and thus the courts should not be overly concerned with majoritarian impositions (1357–58). In a sense, this reasoning is tautological; a minority has rights because it has rights.

Finding that strict-scrutiny review was inappropriate, Justice Erikson went on to consider whether Amendment 2 could pass the "rational-basis" test. As he notes, almost any rationality will suffice, and the amendment ought to be judged with a "strong presumption of validity" and given "great deference" (1360).

155

> This is so because: The Constitution presumes that, absent some reason to infer antipathy, even improvident decisions will eventually be rectified by the democratic process and that judicial intervention is generally unwarranted no matter how unwisely we may think a political branch has acted. Thus, we will not overturn such a statute unless the varying treatment of different groups or persons is so unrelated to the achievement of any combination of legitimate purposes that we can only conclude that the legislature's actions were irrational. . . . It is the

prerogative of the people of the State of Colorado, and not this or any other court, to weigh the evidence and determine the wisdom and utility of the purposes behind a measure adopted through the initiative process. . . . [Constitutional review] is satisfied if the people of Colorado could have rationally decided that prohibiting homosexuals, lesbians, and bisexuals from enacting certain legislation might further a legitimate interest. (1361)

Justice Erikson went on to find several such legitimate interests rationally addressed by Amendment 2, including religious freedom; "state-wide uniformity," meaning when issues are divisive the citizens have a right to override local determinations in favor of statewide standardization; and resource conservation (1363–65). Even more provocatively, Justice Erikson found a legitimate interest in the state's "ensuring that the traditionally suspect classes remain respected" (1365). Quite explicitly, the dissent argued that gay rights demean the currency of rights for everyone—an argument astutely advanced by CR rights pragmatists (see chapter 5).

Before moving on to the U.S. Supreme Court's judgment, it is worth noting two serious problems with Justice Erikson's analysis. First, he conflates the interests of majority voters with the interests of the state. One of the ironies of this direct democracy process is that, under constitutional review, legitimate state objectives must be advanced by the impugned legislation, rather than the desires of a voting majority. The interests of the state as a whole do not necessarily coincide with the will of its population (see also Michelman 1989). Second, Justice Erikson's approach suggests that if voters believed Amendment 2 was rational then it was rational. This, too,

156

is a highly problematic assumption. Leave to appeal the Colorado Supreme Court's decision was granted 21 February 1995, and argument was presented to the U.S. Supreme Court that fall. Their decision was rendered on 20 May 1996, over three years after the amendment's passage.

The U.S. Supreme Court, in a relatively short, 6-3 judgment, found the amendment unconstitutional on the basis that it was too broadly drafted to meet a legitimate state interest.[23] The Court avoided directly answering the question of whether there was a fundamental right to participate in the political process (triggering strict-scrutiny analysis) and instead argued that Amendment 2 failed rational-basis review.[24] In an interpretation that relied on the "authoritative construction of Colorado's Supreme Court," Justice Kennedy, writing for the majority, stated that the amendment was "invalid even on a modest reading of its implications" (4). In other words, there was no need to find "fundamental rights" at play, as Amendment 2 violated even the lowest stage of constitutional review under equal protection doctrine.

According to the Court a "solitary class" of homosexuals was singled out and targeted by the initiative (6). This in itself raised constitutional suspicions, but the key issue for the Court was the "reach" of Amendment 2 (15). The broad sweep of the amendment, according to the Court, was evidence of the "animus" behind it. In other words, if the state's motivation for the amendment was to protect children and traditional families or religious liberty, less disabling measures could have been taken; the fact that they were not demonstrated that the principle animating Amendment 2 was to punish and attack a targeted group (20–26). "The resulting disqualification of a class of persons from the right to seek specific protection from the law is unprecedented in our jurisprudence" (22).

Interestingly, Justice Kennedy explicitly countered the CR "special rights" rhetoric by stating that, on the contrary, the initiative imposed a "special disability" upon lesbians and gays: "We find nothing special in the protections Amendment 2 withholds" (18). Civil rights laws, according to the Court, provide "protections against exclusions", not special privileges (18–19). Inclusion within them, in other words, is something any group has a right to fight for: "A state cannot so deem a class of persons a stranger to its laws" (26).

In coming to this conclusion as to the lack of proper state rationale, the U.S. Supreme Court explicitly relied on the reasoning of the Colorado Supreme Court discussed above. Although the latter's reasons for judgment differed, in that strict scrutiny was applied to a fundamental-right violation, the Colorado Supreme Court's answer to the state's case stands as the final word on measures such as Amendment 2. The U.S. Supreme Court simply reaffirmed that response and found it sufficient to invalidate the amendment on rational-basis review alone. For the majority, then, Amendment 2 is insupportable on the simple ground that it covers too wide an area—this in itself is evidence that the amendment was motivated by animosity and not by legitimate preservation of state interest.

Justice Scalia, in a sarcastic dissent (joined by Justices Thomas and Rehnquist), chose to endorse the antigay discourse of the CR quite explicitly. His first statement, that "the Court has mistaken a Kulturkampf for a fit of spite" (27), signaled his recognition that Amendment 2 voiced the concerns of one side in a significant social struggle. At stake was the victory in the "culture war" between conservatives and liberals. According to Justice Scalia Amendment 2 symbolized the citizenry's judgment that homosexuality was to be condemned, not protected; its overturn by the courts represented an impermissible taking of sides in this war.

For two primary reasons it is worth giving the dissenting judgment serious consideration. First, it is more interesting than the majority's. Justice Scalia's argument is wide, confrontational, and relevant to several issues explored in this book. Second, the dissent's reasoning, largely unanswered by the majority in *Evans* v *Romer*, will have to be considered more seriously in future cases. Justice Scalia's legal argument revolved around three key points.

First, the minority judges relied on *Bowers* v *Hardwick* (478 US 186). In that 1986 case the U.S. Supreme Court held that homosexual sex was not protected by a right to privacy, and hence state sodomy statutes, as they applied to "homosexuals," were lawful. The right to privacy, part of the "due process" guarantees, was rooted in the "nation's traditions"—homosexual sodomy, according to the Court, not being one of these. The ruling in *Bowers* led Justice Scalia in *Evans* v *Romer* to argue that, "if it is constitutionally permissible for a State to make homosexual conduct criminal, surely it is constitutionally permissible for a State to enact other laws merely disfavoring homosexual conduct" (35). To the contention that *Bowers* was irrelevant because Amendment 2 targeted homosexual identity/orientation and not conduct, Justice Scalia concluded that the two were indistinguishable—it was reasonable to sweep up the "non-practicing homosexuals" with the others in an effort to disable homosexuality itself (36–37).

The dissent did concede that a "non-practicing homosexual" could bring a challenge to Amendment 2; however, Justice Scalia asserted that "the record indicates none of the respondents is such a person" (38). However, the record indicates the sexual identity of the applicants and does not discuss what sort of sexual practices, if any, they engage in (see Gallagher 1994, 156–57). Nevertheless, *Bowers* v *Hardwick*, as far as the dissenting judges were concerned, was the final word. If homosexual sex can be criminalized, and sex and orientation are one and the same (at least at a prima facie level), then a legislative "targeting" of gay and lesbian orientation is constitutionally valid.

As Justice Scalia noted with disapproval, the majority judgment simply ignored *Bowers*. However, *Bowers is* arguably irrelevant, and while a discussion of the case by the majority might have been useful, it was not strictly necessary. The conduct/orientation distinction in gay rights cases has been explored by several writers (e.g., Currah 1995; Halley 1994a; Eaton 1994). For the most part, scholars have argued that the distinction is false, arbitrary, and theoretically untenable. For many lesbian and gay legal theorists the "being and doing" dichotomy has been analyzed as desexing, depoliticizing, and exclusionary. However, Carl Stychin (1996) has argued that the distinction may have some merit after all. I would agree; the relationship between *Bowers* v *Hardwick* and *Evans* v *Romer* highlights why and how this may be so.

In *Bowers*, at issue was a statute prohibiting oral/anal sex. While the U.S. Supreme Court chose to discuss homosexual sex exclusively, finding no right to privacy for such acts, the decision itself held nothing more than that there was no constitutional right to engage in homosexual sodomy. Sodomy statutes are analogous to, for example, laws prohibiting soliciting for the purposes of prostitution or perhaps the use of guns in certain circumstances. Amendment 2 cannot derive its (un)constitutionality from *Bowers* any more than an initiative to prevent prostitutes or gun lobbyists from seeking civil rights protections can derive its authority from laws that criminalize selling sex or firing guns. It is almost the antithesis of civil rights raison d'être for such rights to be dependent upon the moral approbation of the majority population as expressed through the enactment of criminal sanctions.

To provide further illustration, imagine a society called Empiria. Empiria has a bill of rights that is similar, but not identical, to that of the United States. The country's constitutional adjudication process is also similar. But Empiria is a profoundly atheistic society, where religious expression has no constitutional protection. For example, a law originating in the previous century criminalizes any form of religious worship. Those found engaged in such conduct, even in the privacy of their own homes, are liable to arrest and imprisonment. In practice, however, only Christians are targeted for prosecution. In Empiria, Christians have been historically despised and discriminated against in the society at large, for a range of reasons.

Over time, perhaps many decades, Christian communities began to organize and demand equality. They appeared openly as Christians and began to try to ameliorate the society's antipathy to Christianity. They went to court to have the religious-worship prohibition overturned but were unsuccessful. The country's supreme court endorsed the law and its effects, finding no constitutional right to engage in acts of Christian worship, particularly because such acts were not grounded in the nation's traditions. Nevertheless, Christians continued their strug-

161

gle, an important aspect of which was to achieve inclusion in Empiria's civil rights laws. This they slowly began to do, as their movement became more organized and powerful. The law criminalizing religious worship remained on the books, even as, in some places, Christians began to worship publicly in a climate of increasing tolerance.

Soon, however, a small group of committed, traditional atheists became alarmed at this threat to their belief and value system. As Christianity became more and more acceptable in Empiria, even trendy in some places, so hard-line atheists resolved to try to roll back the gains the Christians had made. One of their tactics was to convince a majority of voters that not only should all rights won by Christians be removed, but that *Christians should forever be prohibited from seeking inclusion in civil rights laws* (unless they could sway back the majority in a referendum). The atheists ran a campaign arguing that Christians did not deserve special privileges, and implying that they loitered in schoolyards preaching to unsuspecting children. In a climate of economic deprivation and hard times, the measure passed, much to the delight of the small group of traditionalists who had drafted and advocated for it. The Christians went back to Empiria's courts, launching a challenge of this new law.

In determining the constitutionality of the measure, the questions ought *not* to be, is the measure too broad? (the majority's approach in *Evans* v *Romer*), nor should it be whether the religious-worship prohibition legitimizes the measure (the *Evans* minority). Rather, the issue ought simply to be, is there a rational basis to removing civil rights for Christians and prohibiting them from ever lobbying for state-sponsored law reform?

In Empiria the rationales offered could be anything

from a general need "to teach our children there is no god" to defending the traditional institution of "the sciences" from being undermined. The courts would then first have to decide whether these were legitimate *state* interests (rather than simply the will of a political majority). In the period when the religious-worship prohibition was passed, many years before, the state's interests were perhaps clearer. Today in Empiria the state has become a site of struggle—identifying "its" interests is far from easy.

Perhaps, however, the interest of preserving the primacy of "the sciences" as the foundation of social life *was* deemed a legitimate state interest. The courts would next have to decide whether the atheists' measure was a rational meeting of this objective. It would not be difficult to argue that it was not; only in a vague, symbolic way were "the sciences" imperiled by the inclusion of Christians in civil rights laws. The religious-worship prohibition is not relevant to this inquiry; neither is the "breadth" of the measure, per se. There is simply not enough, if any, rational connection between the interest (assuming one can be identified) and the impugned measure.

163

To take this story further. Suppose Empiria suddenly came to have its legislatures dominated by traditional atheists. Some of these legislatures passed laws allowing only professed atheists to adopt children, or prohibiting religious believers from joining the prestigious scientific institutions (membership in which provided several benefits, including enhanced social status and pharmaceutical discounts). It is perhaps more likely that these new laws would pass rational-basis review. *If* the interest is legitimate[25] (preserving the atheistic way of life or the "sanctity of the sciences"), the measures clearly have enough rational connection to sustain this sort of review. The question for the courts must be whether, in a pluralistic society, the state's interests can remain fixed. If, through a process of social change, "the sciences" have become less sanctimonious, and people now accept that there may be a spiritual dimension to life, are these still legitimate *state* interests? Is it the business of the *state* to enforce one belief system in a pluralistic society (see Michelman 1989)?

If the court does determine that the interest is indeed legitimate, the new laws outlawing Christian adoption and scientific membership would likely easily pass rational basis review. At this stage, however, other rights might come into play, for example, a right to privacy or free association. While the religious-worship law *may* be relevant at this stage, in that a previous court had found that Christians had no right to privacy to practice their religion, it is not necessarily determinative.

164

For example, Christians may have no right to worship, but they may still have a right to family life or to free association. In other words, Christian conduct might be illegal, but Christian identity could receive constitutional protection. In a changing society, such as the one I suggest, it is almost to be expected that these two seemingly contradictory states could coexist. Whether Christians were to be punished for acts of worship would be a matter of criminal law enforcement; whether they were protected from job discrimination on the basis of their religious identity would be a matter of civil rights law. Arguably, a minority group whose beliefs or behaviors are criminalized need civil rights protections all the more. What "criminalized groups" should qualify for civil rights protections is a matter of political and ethical judgment, not law (similar to defining a legitimate state interest). It is a judgment that is historically and culturally contingent.

In the case of antigay legislation, then, such as that at issue in *Evans* v *Romer*, *Bowers* v *Hardwick* (the gay equivalent to the religious-worship prohibition) is not relevant for two key reasons. First, criminalization and rights holding are not, as I have argued, mutually exclusive. Second, due process and equal protection doctrines have different visions—the former tends to look backward, the latter forward.

To return to *Evans*. The dissent's second point was that the amendment is not overbroad. Justice Scalia found that lesbians and gays were excluded not from the general laws of Colorado but only from obtaining civil rights inclusion through legislative means (31–32). To suggest that any group had a right to avail itself of every means of law-reform machinery available, Justice Scalia remarked, amounted to "terminal silliness" (32). In other words, lesbians and gays were not being made a "stranger" to "the laws" of Colorado, but were only having the possibility of *legislative* action closed off in the area of civil rights.

Arguably, the readings of majority and minority judges are both unbalanced. Amendment 2 would likely not have had all the sweeping effects claimed by Justice Kennedy, but at the same time Justice Scalia's interpretation was unduly narrow. The wholesale exclusion of one group from winning legislative reform in their favor is a far more serious denial of rights than the dissent acknowledges. For the Court's majority, however, the broadness of the initiative was only a symptom of a more fundamental problem: that Amendment 2 was motivated by antigay "animus." The dissent, then, had to grapple with this claim.

Justice Scalia concluded that it was the moral right of the citizenry to disapprove of homosexuality. Not only was this feeling legitimate, but Amendment 2 reflected the "smallest conceivable" amount of antigay hostility, given the provocation (41). According to the dissent, by the time Amendment 2 was passed, the patience and tolerance of Coloradans had been tested beyond endurance. Homosexuals, according to Justice Scalia, were disproportionately powerful, and their social achievements, particularly in large urban centers, had led to a legitimate fear on the part of the majority population that their own values and way of life were threatened (42–44). For the dissent this development was so obvious that no evidence for the "power" of homosexuality needed to be provided (other than the perverse tautology that gay rights exist, therefore gays are powerful). Amendment 2 was the product not of "animus" but of a threatened population fighting back.

166   The dissent's final coup de grâce was to invoke as precedent a nineteenth-century state law denying polygamists the right to vote. This legislation, Justice Scalia argued, represented the "effort by the majority of citizens to preserve its view of sexual morality statewide" (46), and was upheld by the U.S. Supreme Court in 1890 (*Davis* v *Beeson*, 133 US 333). If an attack on such a fundamental right passed constitutional muster, the dissent insisted, so should Amendment 2. As Justice Kennedy rightly pointed out, however, *Davis* v *Beeson* may no longer be good law (23–25). Justice Scalia suggests that, if this is so, it is because the right to vote is "fundamental" and would trigger strict-scrutiny review, something that Amendment 2 does not (50 n. 3). Not only that, Justice Scalia continues, but *Davis* v *Beeson* was cited with apparent approval by the U.S. Supreme Court (indeed, by Justice Kennedy himself) as recently as 1993 (51).

While Justice Scalia is right to accuse the majority of

sidelining the relevance of *Davis*, it is far from clear whether the majority judges in *Evans* v *Romer* rejected or simply did not avail themselves of the fundamental-right argument. In other words, the Court did not explicitly say there was no fundamental right to participate in the political process—the majority simply invalidated Amendment 2 for other, more straightforward reasons. It is also quite possible that the current Supreme Court *would* invalidate a law that denied polygamists the right to fight for inclusion in civil rights laws. No doubt this, too, would displease the dissenting judges, for they, like the CR, despair that the U.S. Supreme Court itself is now little more than a tool of the liberal elite.

Throughout the dissenting judgment, Justice Scalia utters scathing remarks impugning the objectivity of the majority judges. It is not, he argues, the business of the U.S. Supreme Court to impose "upon all Americans the resolution favored by the elite class from which Members of this institution are selected" (28). Justice Scalia insisted that a position against Amendment 2 was more than legally incorrect. Striking down the amendment was indeed more crucially an act of undemocratic superiority engaged in by a judiciary that had fallen prey to the homosexual agenda (55). Indeed, Justice Scalia concludes his judgment by waxing on at length about how the progay policies of American law schools are evidence of a legal elite out of control (53–55). By this point in his judgment, there is little to distinguish it from the texts of antigay materials I have discussed in previous chapters.

At the end of the day, there are at least three clear points to make about the final judgment in *Evans* v *Romer*. First, future antigay measures will have to be more carefully

167

tailored. Second, *Evans* v *Romer* says nothing about the potential constitutionality of less expansive legislation. For example, it is quite possible, indeed even likely, that statutes banning same-sex marriage would comfortably pass rational-basis review. Third, the Court in *Evans* had an opportunity to make a clear statement endorsing "suspect class" status for lesbians and gay men and explicitly to restrict *Bowers* to its facts. They chose to do neither.

What the majority did do was read Amendment 2 for what it was: a measure designed to condemn homosexuality, drafted by leading figures on the CR, and passed after a campaign that featured showings of *The Gay Agenda* and broadsheets accusing lesbians and gays of molesting children. Given everything I have argued in previous chapters, Amendment 2 was obviously the product of the CR's antigay agenda, targeted at a particular social group and motivated by "animus." It was surely with careful thought that Justice Kennedy and his supporters in the Court invoked the infamous *Plessy* decision in the first sentence of their decision (5).[26] This time they wanted the Supreme Court to "do the right thing."

Anti-same-sex marriage laws will appear less hostile on paper; however, their etiology will be the same. Antigay measures in the United States are, at their heart, orthodox Christian measures. Arguably, when they become legislation, the establishment clause is violated.[27] Ironically, as Linde (1993) has pointed out, the original constitutional framers (revered by the CR) in drafting the establishment clause sought to control the passions of religious majorities, not institutionalize them in state practice.

But leaving aside these points of law, Amendment 2's passage and the subsequent litigation suggest that activists on both sides have much with which to contend. The ini-

168

tiative process, as deployed in gay rights struggles, throws into relief key questions about the nature of democracy, minority rights, and the reviewing authority of the courts. Arguably, at a general level civil rights laws are not an appropriate target for the citizens' initiative process, partly because they are inherently, and justifiably, anti-majoritarian. Oddly, in *Evans* v *Romer* only Justice Erikson, in dissent at the Colorado Supreme Court, analyzed the distinction between citizens' initiatives and legislative action.

For the CR, however, citizen-initiated antigay measures represent attempts to control the perceived liberal tendencies of elite institutions out of touch with "real" people's fears and concerns. They capitalize on a populist ethos that could be harnessed by activists of any political persuasion (see, e.g., Hertzke 1993). Gay rights laws symbolize state excess: government out of control. Judicial rejection of populist attempts to rein government in only confirms what the CR already knows to be true: the courts are in the hands of the enemy.

By the mid-1990s the CR's use of the citizen's initiative was slowing down; *Evans* v *Romer* no doubt provides a legal setback. Antigay politics continue to play out in legislative arenas, as the CR focuses its energies on seizing control of state institutions. What does the CR want from the state? My final chapter addresses this question.

169

Regulation, Restoration, Reconstruction
Conservative Christianity and the State

Up to this point my focus has been almost exclusively on the CR's antigay agenda and politics. I have discussed the historical emergence of the gay subject in conservative Christian discourse (chapter 2), the representation of gay and lesbian sexuality by the CR (chapters 3 and 4), issues to do with the CR's "rights politics" (chapter 5), and the operationalization of the CR's antigay agenda in the Colorado Amendment 2 struggle (chapter 6). In this final chapter I move from this focus to consider the CR's relationship with the state at a wider level (see Diamond 1995; Fields 1991; Lienesch 1993; Moen 1995).[1]

One important tactic in CR antigay politics is to decry the edicts of a "Big Brother" state. As I discussed previously, the CR has been quite successful at capitalizing on a general feeling of discontent and demoralization with government. Much of this has involved the CR in supporting calls to downsize the state and to prevent it from impinging upon the intimacies of people's lives. Gay rights laws, in this mind-set, have come to symbolize government out of control, the state having taken one step too many in interfering with individual freedom. The CR, in supporting these arguments, has found a natural ally in the secular economic right.

As I will argue, however, the CR is not antistatist per se. Unlike their secular allies, the CR very much wants the state to play an important role in people's lives—but not the liberal role it is playing now. The CR intends to make the state act as a conservative moral leader, by example and by edict: hence the CR's insistence that the "Founding Fathers" never intended the American state to be nonreligious. This desire for a proactive Christian state in turn fosters constant conflict between the CR and less orthodox conservatives, a clash particularly noticeable and public in Republican Party politics.[2]

171

The CR's relationship to the state also causes friction within the conservative Christian movement itself. In contrast to CR activists, many conservative Christians continue to emphasize religious mission above political engagement; perhaps more importantly, they do not view the state as a proper vehicle in which to convey Christian values and precepts. In this sense the views of these other conservative Christians are more compatible with the politics of the economic right.

Finally, in order to understand the CR's state politics, the increasing importance of postmillennial theory and the reconstruction movement must be considered. While the CR publicly plays down its postmillennial perspectives and its reconstructionist connections, the relationship is more intimate and significant than the CR would like to admit. Less tangible, but equally important, is the CR's relationship to the extremist wing of conservative Protestantism—the Christian Identity and militia movements. The influence of postmillennial reconstructionism, however, provides one such link.

In examining the CR's antigay agenda, these issues go to the heart of that program; hence I am giving them special consideration here. I first return to the pages of *Christianity Today* (*CT;* see chapter 2) to trace a recent history of conservative Christian state perspectives. Next I explore how the CR envisions the state, and continue by assessing some of the implications of this politics.

HISTORICAL BACKGROUND

172

I have explained my use of the journal *CT* in chapter 2. Throughout its forty-year history, *CT* has provided a window into the politics of and debates within conservative Protestantism in the United States. In considering the articulation of the state in *CT,* I focus on two debates in particular: the appropriate behavior of believers in the political realm and the correct relationship between church and state. I explore each in turn.

Mission versus Politics

The question of whether, and to what extent, evangelical Protestants should "get involved in politics" has been an emotive one throughout the movement's history. As I noted in chapter 1, American evangelicalism has undergone significant shifts in outlook on this question over many decades. On the one hand, many believe that individuals come to faith through a process of conversion and personal salvation, through witness, personal experience, and the effects of missionary work. In this view, the realm of politics is intrinsically ungodly; its remit is not what Jesus' armies have been called forth to pursue. Indeed, evangelical involvement in politics, many argue, diverts Christian energies and pollutes the purity of the faith.

On the other side are those who believe strongly that it is an integral part of the Christian mission to struggle in the political realm; to withdraw is to give up power to Satan and to neglect biblical lessons connecting individual salvation with social duties. As many scholars have observed, the history of evangelical Protestantism is partly a history of the waxing and waning of these irreconcilable worldviews (see, generally, Hunter 1987; Marsden 1984).

In the latter half of this century, *CT* was one place where this debate was played out often. Mark Toulouse (1993) in his study of the journal has characterized the opposing views as "pietistic" versus "priestly" faith. At the very start of the journal's operation, pietism was thus expressed by one editorialist:

173

> The issue on which the greatest debate centers is *how* shall the Christian and the Church exercise influence for righteousness in the social order? . . . The primary task of the Church is to win individuals to Christ. It is a spiritual mission, a mission not only alien to but completely obscure and meaningless to the unregenerate world in which it works. . . . To substitute political and other factors for this spiritual force is to exchange the seamless robe of the Lord of Glory for the toga of a modern Caesar. . . . when the Church, in the name of the Church, enters the secular arena and exerts political pressures for righteousness in the social order, then the Church is prostituting her mission and adding to the confusion of the world.[3]

But pietistic withdrawal was not necessarily the dominant ideology of *CT*. Just two years later, in 1958, another editorial insisted that the church *must* get involved in protesting the excesses of the state.

> If America has crossed the Rubicon; if the nation's heritage is now beyond preservation; if the drift to the power-state and to a controlled society cannot be stayed, communist penetration from the outside is not alone to blame. Equal judgement falls upon the churches for indifference and ineffectiveness in the hour of America's greatest trial. Amid the world's subtle conflict between political and spiritual loyalties, the churches sin by their silence. Today not Nero but the churches fiddle while Rome burns.[4]

The debate over the appropriate political role, not just of the church, but of individual Christians, continued throughout the pages of *CT* during the 1950s, 1960s, and 1970s.[5]

174

By the 1980s the tenor of debate within *CT* began to change, as the journal no doubt sought to keep pace with a vibrant, growing, grassroots conservatism. The new mood was inaugurated by *CT*'s general editor in a five-page feature report on the state of the evangelical movement in the United States.[6] Using, interestingly, the "closet" metaphor, Carl Henry noted that evangelicals were a more obvious force in American politics, but the gains they had achieved were minimal.

> Lack of wide-scale penetration of our society by evangelicals suggests that we need to implement two priorities. First, the evangelical movement must place worldly culture on the defensive. . . . Second, no less do we need a well-formulated statement of evangelical goals in contemporary society, and an elaboration of strategy and tactics for moving beyond principles to policies and programs

that enlist the movement's resources for specific objectives. . . . devotional vitality of itself will not compensate for the lack of orderly vision and cooperative engagement. (19)

While some, such as theologian Richard Neuhaus, sounded a cautionary note,[7] others, such as John Whitehead (who in the 1990s runs a CR legal firm, the Rutherford Institute), praised the growing Moral Majority for standing up to the state.[8]

Debates over the question of "cultural intervention" continued into the 1990s. By this point, however, pure pietists were hard to find. Instead, the debate centered not on whether but *how* to be political. While most conservative Protestants, at least as reflected in *CT,* acknowledged that it was appropriate for evangelicals to engage politically, many were less than enthusiastic about the language and tactics of the CR activists who were seen to represent the movement (see chapter 1).

175

In 1995 an exchange between historian John Woodbridge and James Dobson of Focus on the Family exemplified the terms of the argument. Woodbridge argued that, when conservative Christians used war metaphors and other inflammatory rhetoric to advance political objectives, more harm was done than good—that this was not the way in which Christians ought to convey their message in the secular world.[9] In reply Dobson contended that war terminology was both necessary and rooted in the Bible; in language similar to one of the quotations above, he accused Woodbridge of standing on the sidelines while America was on fire.[10] If the letters pages of *CT* are anything to go by, most readers appreciated Woodbridge's, not Dobson's, sentiments.[11]

While *CT*'s relatively mainstream readers often find

CR activists excessively polemical and at times embarrassing, it remains the case that by the 1990s there were few pure pietists among them. And *CT*, reflecting this, had given up any claim to withdrawal and instead advocated a less right-wing, or at least less confrontational, form of intervention. Thus, activists had become polarized into two camps: the CR, on the one hand, and a related but distinct conservative evangelical politics, on the other.

Church and State

The debate over the proper relationship between church and state overlapped, in some respects, the conflict between pietism and activism. For example, pietists were far more likely to hold up the separation of church and state as justification for evangelical political reticence. This had always been the case, however; until relatively recently most conservative Christians shared a commitment to maintaining the "wall"—a commitment that now is far from evident.

In the 1950s and 1960s the strict separation of church and state was part of conservative Protestantism's anti-Catholic agenda.[12] Catholics were struggling to achieve some level of public funding for their school system, a demand vigorously opposed by *CT*'s editors and other Protestant evangelicals (see chapter 2). A key argument in the anti-Catholic arsenal was to accuse Catholics of reinterpreting the First Amendment to enable state support of religion. One ad, placed in *CT* by a group calling itself "Protestants and other Americans united for separation of church and state" (*CT* 4, 25 [1960]: 30), made this accusation in no uncertain terms, insisting that the wall of separation be maintained absolutely. As I explore below, the ironies of this position today are enormous, for the CR now interprets the First Amendment in exactly the same terms attributed to Catholics in this ad.

In 1957 Carl Henry, an eminent theologian and *CT*'s editor at the time, described the wall of separation as a "precious heritage of democracy."[13] In 1961 the National Association of Evangelicals, the conservative Protestant umbrella organization, affirmed its adherence to the separation principle in a conference resolution.[14] Perhaps one of the most interesting discussions about church and state resulted from two decisions by the U.S. Supreme Court in 1962/63. The first, *Engel* v *Vitale* (370 US 421 [1962]), found unconstitutional a state-composed interfaith prayer for use in the schools. While several conservative figures railed against the decision, including evangelist Billy Graham and theologian Reinhold Niebuhr, many others, including the editors of *CT*, believed the judgment to be a correct interpretation of the First Amendment.[15]

The second decision, *Abington School District* v *Schempp* (374 US 203 [1963]), banning required Bible reading and recitation of the Lord's Prayer in Pennsylvania and Maryland schools, was similarly defended, particularly as the justices did not prohibit religion per se from the classroom.[16] As far as *CT* was concerned, "public schools do not exist for the conduct of religious exercises."[17] This commitment to strict separation continued, with some refinements, through this period, although it must be stressed that conservatives were insistent that the wall was not a means by which to ban religion from public discussion.[18]

In 1985 the Christianity Today Institute (CTI), *CT*'s think tank, published a special feature on the relationship between religion and politics/church and state. Again

177

contributing to this debate, by directly addressing the question of whether the state should promote the Christian religion, Carl Henry argued, contrary to constitutional revisionists, that a "law-mandated religious society has no scriptural support."[19] Government had one purpose, religion another, and the First Amendment necessitated that government not act as a religious agent unless a majority of the citizenry established state structures explicitly to further such an objective (11).

At the same time, however, Henry insisted that this did not mean religion had no place in the public sphere or that Christians should stay out of politics—on the contrary. For example, Henry argued that "uncritical acceptance of devious moral behavior in the name of tolerance . . . has costly consequences" (11–12). At root Henry's piece is ambiguous in its attempt to affirm both the U.S. Constitution and the Christian mission. Henry applauds yet criticizes the radicalism of Jerry Falwell's Moral Majority;[20] he maintains both the necessity of separation and the right of evangelicals to promote biblical values in the public realm, including, in certain instances such as abortion, through state legislation.

While the nuances of Henry's argument may be meaningful to a fellow believer, an outsider cannot help but be struck by the inconsistencies and contradictions. The entire CTI feature appears to tread this fine line between the need to respect and obey the state, and putting "God's Law" first—remaining true to and fighting for Christian beliefs. For the conservative Christian movement as a whole, this debate has always been and continues to be a primary source of tension and conflict. Most mainstreamers agree, however, as Kenneth Kantzer put it in his summing up for the CTI, that "they are unutterably opposed to any form of 'theocracy,' " and that, barring exceptional cases, "evangelicals should support their government" (how much today's CR has in common with these views is a question to which I return below).[21] All of this is not to say that these evangelicals did not desire a "Christian America"—they clearly did (see Handy 1984)—however, the state was not the means to achieve this end.

Given the mainstream's support for the separate spheres of church and state during this period, what was legitimate governmental action? Stephen Monsma and others asserted that the state's role is to preserve and promote order and justice, while the church proclaims the faith.[22] But what exactly is meant by order and justice? Clearly, in the first decades of the journal *CT*, a large, dominating state was viewed as a symbol of communism: "socialism is state capitalism."[23] Indeed, writers during the 1950s and 1960s identified the state as the idol worshipped by atheistic Communists.[24] And even as early as 1960, a *CT* editorialist charged that the U.S. state had overextended its legitimate remit through the expansion of welfare policies: "Instead of hailing state welfare programs as an extension of Christian social ethics, it is high time Christian clergy and laymen consider the premise that state welfare programs are inherently anti-Christian."[25] The minimalist state, facilitating and not impeding the free market, was always the state advocated by conservative Christians; indeed, one *CT* editorial in making this argument contended that "a good case can be made for private capitalism from Scripture."[26]

In keeping with this view, conservative Christianity, as reflected in *CT*, was also in favor of a minimalist legal framework: God's law, not man's law, must rule supreme. Consequently, law was not to be used by Christians as a

179

moral weapon.[27] At the same time, however, Christians were not to sit idly by while atheists and others infiltrated the state and used lawmaking powers to further their own agendas.[28] A rich example of the tensions around law and the activist state is provided by *CT*'s response to the black civil rights movement in the 1950s and 1960s (see also Hadden 1969). Interestingly, the state's involvement in promoting civil rights was seen by many to be an unacceptable "legislating of morality."[29] Desegregation was equated with "forced integration"; as one editorialist noted, "Paul did not outlaw slavery legally, but he outlawed it spiritually."[30] The merits of civil rights laws were debated time after time in the pages of *CT* in the lead-up to the passage of the Civil Rights Act, legislation not endorsed by *CT*'s editors until the final hours.[31]

180   Arguably, then, several points can be made about the relationship between conservative Christianity and the state in this era. First, individual evangelicals had a right and a duty to be politically involved in some capacity, but faith and mission must always come first. Second, the spheres of church and state were rightly separate, but neither the First Amendment nor the Scriptures required that religion be banished from public discourse. Third, the state was due respect and allegiance; only in exceptional cases ought laws to be disobeyed.[32] Fourth, the state must not usurp the role of religion by imposing a morality or by taking for itself the role of welfare provision. How, then, does the CR recast these tenets?

Christian Right Representations of the State

The CR's understanding of the state involves, I would argue, three primary, and contradictory, beliefs. First, the

state is "too big"; governmental bureaucracies overinter-
fere in the lives of individuals and in the work of the
church. Second, the Founding Fathers did not intend the
state to be atheistic; indeed, religious faith, and more particularly the Christian faith, lies at the heart of the Constitution and the American polity itself. Third, and following
from the second, the state has a duty to act as a moral
leader, not to usurp the church, but to imbue its activities
with the values and principles of Christianity (or its euphe-
mism "the Judeo-Christian tradition"). For many (but not
all) this includes, indeed necessitates, that the state legis-
late morality.

The first principle is what aligns the CR with both the
economic right and the populist revolt against a perceived
big, corrupt, and biased government (see chapter 5;
Crawford 1980). However, the two final postulates stand
in some contradiction to the first, for they entail an activist, interfering state, furthering a very specific moral
agenda. Arguably, neither the economic right nor the majority of American people support such a program.

Regulation: Big Government

The big-government critique of the CR's state politics is
perhaps the most well known, and as a result I will canvass
its dimensions relatively briefly. In keeping with conservative economic and social thought generally, the CR argues that the state is overextended, its reach penetrating
too far into commercial and civil life.[33] But more than
this, for many on the CR the American state has become
identified with a range of totalitarian characteristics formerly reserved to describe foreign, socialist governments.

Welfarist policies are discussed by the CR as if they
were Soviet desensitization programs, lulling the populace
into laziness and soporific ignorance (e.g., Christian Co-

181

alition 1995, chap. 7; Robertson 1993, 179–83).[34] Public funding of the arts is represented as furthering official state liberalism: hence the CR call to defund the Public Broadcasting System, the National Endowment for the Arts, and similar organizations (e.g., Christian Coalition 1995, chap. 9; Dobson and Bauer 1990, chap. 11).[35]

The Department of Education is also a prime target of the CR; officials there and in the National Education Association, the CR argues, contrive and impose an anti-God agenda, aimed at instilling socialist values and indoctrinating the youth of America (e.g., Dugan 1991; Robertson 1993, chap. 9).[36] Similarly, the Bureau of Alcohol, Tobacco, and Firearms is seen to weave an increasingly tangled web of red tape in its efforts to prevent individuals from exercising their constitutional rights. Arguably, the extreme right crystallized this view with the bombing of Oklahoma federal offices in 1995.

The CR also takes a public stand against state interference in religious freedom. Occasionally, this interest is overtly self-serving and hypocritical, as when the CR vociferously spoke out against the FBI's handling of the Branch Davidian community at Waco in 1993 (e.g., Marrs 1993). The CR is no friend to religious cults, and "its" state would likely have taken exactly the same actions. Nevertheless, the U.S. government is represented by the CR, and many others, as a monolithic, left-wing bloc of power, stamping out all dissension, controlling and manipulating people's very thoughts. Pat Robertson (1993, 197–98, 301) expresses it thus:

> What you have to realize is that the goal of the Radical Left is never to build up society but to tear down existing structures and replace them with a massive social bureau-

182

cracy. . . . The dialectic of socialism is that existing ortho-
doxies are constantly being replaced by new ones. That
is what the liberal wing of the Democratic party in this
country is dedicated to doing. . . . The cultural elites who
orchestrate and bring about change are a privileged cadre
here, just as they were in the Soviet Union—a small, well-
educated core of liberal leaders who are entitled to have
the fantastic dreams, while the rest of us do as we are told.
That elite cadre, or politburo, was one of the principal
instruments of Marxism, expressed in the principle of
"the dictatorship of the proletariat." It is hardly different
from the inner circle of the president's cabinet in Washington today. . . . the Radical Left controls all of the cita-
dels of power—the presidency, the Congress, many
courts, public education, the universities, the press, the
motion picture and television industry, the major founda-   183
tions, and the National Council of Churches.

Thus, as the Cold War cooled down, the CR and others came to identify a new "enemy within"—the American state itself. Forces once seen largely as external threats
are now viewed as wielding complete power over a disen-
franchised and downtrodden people. In previous decades
the U.S government was for many Americans, including
most conservative Christians, a glorified focus of patriotism; while there may have been bad apples within, the
basket itself was beyond reproach. Now this reverence
has evaporated, and the state itself is a symbol of un-
Americanism. And the former patriots are now the
subversives—a shift starkly highlighted in the 1995 Oklahoma bombing and the 1996 standoffs with the "Free-
men" communities.

As I discussed earlier in this chapter, the idea that the

state is too big is not new to conservative Christianity. What is different now, however, about both the CR's representation of the state and popular antistatist feeling in general, is this disidentification *from* the state and its objectives. Furthermore, the state is now identified as being controlled by a liberal elite, intent on pursuing its own agenda through governmental prerogatives (see below and chapter 3): "As secularism triumphs, the god of the state eats away at the religious symbols of yesteryear" (Staver 1995, 178). But for many on the CR, the state does not simply need to be rolled back; rather, ownership must be transferred. Indeed, as I will argue below, many in the CR would welcome an activist, interventionist state—providing that state's agenda was their own.

184

Restoration: Church and State

An integral part of the CR's state agenda involves the production of a revisionist historiography. Christianity, the CR contends, was the foundation upon which America was built. This history begins with a reinterpretation of Columbus. He was not an explorer, but a missionary: "He wasn't primarily looking for a trade route to the Indies at all, he was looking to bring the gospel of Jesus Christ into the western hemisphere."[37] Similarly, the Pilgrims were not fleeing religious persecution; they were evangelists, coming to spread God's word among the natives.[38]

Following from this, CR historians maintain that the Founding Fathers were devout believers, the populace at the time was resolutely God-fearing, and the Constitution itself a statement of religious values and principles (see Staver 1995; Whitehead 1994).[39] The First Amendment, prohibiting the "establishment" of religion, was never intended to secularize the state; rather, its drafters simply sought to ensure that no one Christian denomination could use the state for its own ends and in the process persecute others. Several CR organizations propagate this message[40] (see also Lienesch 1993, chap. 4).

One of the most important CR historians is David Barton (1989), president of Wallbuilders, a leading organization constructing this revisionist historiography. Wallbuilders describes itself as "an organization dedicated to the restoration of the moral and religious values on which America was built,"[41] and Barton appears regularly on the CR circuit. He is a frequent guest, for example, on James Dobson's Focus on the Family radio program. He also appears on the roster of experts relied on by the extreme right-wing movements, such as Christian Identity (see Anti-Defamation League 1994, 54–56). Other important figures in this genre include Peter Marshall,[42] Gary DeMar (1995), and John Whitehead (1994), president of the Rutherford Institute.

In making these arguments about church and state, the CR fixes blame on the Supreme Court for its wrongheaded interpretation of the First Amendment. In this genre the Court is often identified as an agent of the secular state, composed of its appointees, advancing state plans to remove religious faith from the public sphere altogether (e.g., Whitehead 1994). Like the state itself, law, as personified by the Supreme Court, has been reviled and identified with the agenda of the "enemy" (see Herman 1994, chap. 6). The U.S. Supreme Court's decision in *Evans* v *Romer* only confirmed this diagnosis.

The predominant theme of the CR revisionist historiography is to reject the expression "wall of separation," used first in a letter by Thomas Jefferson in 1802 and relied on subsequently by the state and its courts. The CR contends that the separation of church and state is a "myth" that has no foundation in the original construction of American constitutionalism.

> Everyone of us was taught the pilgrims came to America for freedom of worship—that is flatly not true. . . . they were led to America by the Lord Jesus himself to propagate the gospel among the Indians, which they did. And to become themselves stepping stones for the furtherance of the gospel to the outermost parts of the earth. They were missionaries. . . . They had a vision of a new society based on the word of God. . . . The only time in human history that free Christian men and women had the opportunity to build a whole new society based on the biblical principles of self-government was at Plymouth, in 1620. And that's exactly what they did.[43]

186

Thus, this perspective is more than just a critique; it is also visionary. In other words, the CR seeks to *restore* Christianity to the American polity. The word "restoration" is used consistently by the revisionists. Its connotations aptly signal the project in which the CR is engaged: to rebuild America as a Christian nation. Indeed, many CR activists view this project as divinely inspired (e.g., LaHaye and LaHaye 1994; Robertson 1993); it is God's desire that the United States fulfill this role in the world.[44]

To complete this project, the CR needs, not a minimalist state, but an expansive and activist one. I would argue that it is far more accurate to view the CR (but not all conservative Christians by any means) as hoping for, and indeed building (restoring), a *Christian* state—a Christian state that will actively promote Christian tenets through its lawmaking powers. The CR pays lip service to neoconservative economic theory requiring a "lean, mean state," but their aspiration and agenda is to take control of the existing state in order to "restore" its Christian character. While some state action would certainly be rolled back (e.g., welfare policies), other areas of state practice would be extended dramatically. The CR is not so much against the state as it is for the Christianization of worldly states generally. As Keith Fournier, director of the American Center for Law and Justice, has said: "Constantine opened the door in ancient Rome and the Christians of that age transformed the whole empire."[45]

The Christianization project is evident throughout the CR agenda. For example, Focus on the Family and the FRC advocate governmental activism in a wide range of areas, including abortion, divorce, pornography, family tax incentives, penal sanctions, and antigay measures.[46] Similarly, Tim and Beverly LaHaye (1994, 269) support laws banning abortion, homosexuality, pornography, and instituting the establishment of "decency standards" throughout the arts and entertainment industries. CR voter's guides rate candidates according to whether they support such things as tax relief for married couples, antiabortion measures, legislation requiring young women to obtain parental consent prior to having an abortion, a statutory ban on any form of euthanasia, and, of course, antigay rights legislation.[47]

The Christian Coalition's *Contract with the American Family* (1995) provides yet another example of this mendacity. Although the *Contract* is replete with images of "big government out of control," the coalition's actual agenda requires massive governmental intervention. For example, the *Contract* promotes legislation to expand religious and parental rights (including "right to know" legislation),

187

provide "family-friendly tax relief" (including child and married-couple tax credits), ban abortion, control and restrict pornography on the Internet and cable television, and impose mandatory drug and HIV testing on prison populations. The huge and complex bureaucracy needed to implement these and other CR measures would surely make up for that lost from cuts to welfare and arts subsidies.

The tensions this state-activist agenda throws up for the CR alliance with the secular "new right" minimalists are perhaps obvious. So serious are these potential conflicts that intensely pragmatic organizations, such as the Christian Coalition, prefer to keep this activist agenda much in the background, emphasizing instead liberty issues such as freedom of worship, which on their surface involve a reduction in state regulation. This shift has the added benefit of making CR politics more palatable to the evangelical pietists—an important potential CR constituency put off by calls for the "legislation of morality."

But, in my view, it is incontrovertible that the CR does aspire to govern a Christian state.[48] "It would be nice," according to Jim Woodall of Concerned Women for America (interview by author, 1995), if the government "professed Christ." "I would like to see America governed by biblical principles" (Robert Knight, interview by author, 1995). Interestingly, this agenda in itself poses questions for conservative Protestant theology. As I discussed in chapter 1, the CR and conservative Protestants generally are, or have been for most of this century, premillennialists. The eschatological centrality of premillennialism is that the world will descend into greater and greater chaos, degeneration, and war before Christ returns. Activist conservatives have never taken this to mean that they must withdraw and simply await rapture; however, the task of building God's kingdom *now* was always associated with *postmillennialism*—a theology insisting that Christ will return only when Christianity rules the earth.

Arguably, these eschatologies, once starkly separate and antagonistic, have, in the form of the CR, come together in a kind of cloudy synthesis. Pre- and postmillennialists work side by side in CR organizations (Jim Woodall, interview by author, 1995), and it would appear that many CR activists have come to accept that they must strive to establish the United States as a Christian nation now (Fournier 1993; LaHaye and LaHaye 1994; Robertson 1993). An effect, or possibly an instigator, of this shift has been the increasing influence of reconstructionist theology on the mainstream CR.

189

Reconstruction: Postmillennial Theology

The "father" of reconstructionism is Rousas John Rushdoony, who has written over one hundred books articulating the theology (e.g., 1978, 1991). Other important figures in the movement include Gary North, Greg Bahnsen, David Chilton, and Joseph Morecraft.[49] The three basic tenets of reconstruction are generally agreed to be presuppositional apologetics, meaning all truth is presupposed in the Bible; theonomy, or the rule of strict biblical law in the here and now; and postmillennialism—God's kingdom will be established on earth *before* the Second Coming of Christ.

Thus, reconstructionism, also known as dominion theology, posits that the literal meaning of the Bible be observed (as do many conservative Protestants), that social life be governed according to Old and New Testament laws (for example, some forms of slavery are permitted, and the death penalty for recalcitrant homosexuals is advocated), and that "true" Christians battle now to make Jesus' law reign supreme over all the earth. According to Rushdoony (1978, 185), "Christ is King of the nations. This is the Christian expectation and must be the Christian program for action; the sovereignty of Christ over all things and all nations." "This means to ground the totality of our lives, thinking, institutions, and world, including church, state, and school on the Name of Christ the King, *under* His authority, power, law-word, and government . . . the state must serve the Lord" (Rushdoony 1991, 8–9). Rushdoony's basic call (1991, 63–68) is for what he unabashedly terms a "theocracy," a Christian state run by Christian men—because "the Christian man is the only truly free man in the world, and he is called to exercise dominion over all the earth" (1991, 1115).

190

Many in the mainstream CR do not subscribe formally to theonomic imperatives or postmillennial eschatology, and a pietist premillennialism is quite opposed to the sorts of battle cries issued by Rushdoony and his ilk. However, it is possible that as more Christian orthodox become active politically, the desirability (and possibility) of achieving Jesus' rule *now* increases. And it is clear that reconstruction has had an important influence on the thinking of CR activists.

Rushdoony and Gary North have been frequent guests of the CR, including several appearances on Pat Robertson's 700 Club and D. James Kennedy's televangel show.[50] Several prominent CR activists have written of their admiration for some reconstructionist tenets, while disavowing formal allegiance to the movement as a whole. For example, John Whitehead, president of the Rutherford Institute, credits Rushdoony with being an important influence on his thought (Boston 1993, 191). Indeed, it seems likely that the Rutherford Institute originated as a project of Rushdoony's Chalcedon Foundation (Clarkson 1994, 6). Prominent CR figures have contributed large funds to the Chalcedon Foundation—described by one U.S. magazine as the premier think tank of the religious right.[51]

The Coalition on Revival, a CR umbrella group formed in the early 1980s with postmillennial and reconstructionist leanings, contained a number of leading CR figures, including Tim and Beverly LaHaye, Donald Wildmon (American Family Association), Robert Dugan (National Association of Evangelicals), and D. James Kennedy, among others, some of whom are no longer with the organization.[52] Interestingly, several CR activists particularly devoted to antigay politics are associated with reconstructionism, including Tim and Beverly LaHaye, George Grant, William Dannemeyer, and Paul Weyrich.

Because reconstructionism sounds extreme and excessively intolerant to many mainstream Americans, the CR has sought to distance itself publicly from the movement. Several members of the Coalition on Revival jumped ship after an article appeared in *Mother Jones* exposing the organization's reconstructionist agenda. All of those whom I interviewed for this book disavowed reconstructionism, although the rhetoric of some (e.g., Kevin Tebedo of Colorado for Family Values) was imbued with a strong reconstructionist flavor. Similarly, Pat Robertson, for example, has maintained that he is a premillennialist, with no interest in theocracy, despite believing that reconstruction offers important insights (Boston 1993, 190). However, Robertson's premillennialism is tempered by his belief that God is withholding judgment on the United States

(Robertson 1993, 300–301). In other words, Robertson believes that America will be spared the Tribulation, but only if conservative Christianity asserts its dominion—a position with obvious reconstructionist overtones.

As others have noted, reconstructionism is not, in itself, a powerful movement in imminent danger of taking control of the CR, much less the United States in general. It remains in many ways a fringe theology. Its effects may still be important, however, if not so direct, particularly its reasoned, persuasive postmillennialism. For an eschatology requiring Christians to build God's kingdom now is far more in keeping with the agenda of an activist, interventionist branch of conservative Protestantism—the CR—than a premillennialism seemingly in constant conflict with such a politics.

192

Many critics of the CR argue that its "real" agenda is to create a theocracy. This is no doubt the requirement of reconstruction, and probably the logical outcome of any postmillennial perspective. To the extent that the CR continues to be dominated by premillennialism, however, the most one can say, I would argue, is that the question is unsettled. If one believes that the world will descend into a final abyss, and that it will end as Jesus returns, then the possibility of establishing his reign on earth now is simply not there. Furthermore, some members of the CR sincerely believe in the "good" of church/state separation.

However, the more the CR actively seeks to impose its orthodoxy on government, to take control of the state, and to use state power to achieve religious ends, the more theocracy becomes the necessary culmination of these efforts—despite public disavowals. As Pat Robertson has written, quoting God: "I desire mature sons and daughters who will in My name exercise dominion over the earth and will subdue Satan, the unruly, and the rebellious. Take back My world from those who loot it and abuse it. Rule as I would rule" (Robertson and Slosser 1982, 201).

Ironically, however, the more the CR moves in this direction, the less support it may have from the American people. For although Americans are among the most Christian in the world, they are also, it would seem, among the most libertarian—and this is a source of antipathy to both the CR and the gay rights agendas. In one opinion study, for example, while 78% of respondents believed the president should be a moral and spiritual leader and 84% agreed that governmental policies should reflect moral values, 91% expressed the view that "individual freedom was critical to democracy."[53] And, although 93% of those surveyed believed in God or a universal spirit, only 34% thought that the Bible was God's literal word.[54] While the CR does attract support for its antistatist posturing, only a small minority of Americans may stay with the movement as its activist, interventionist, and fundamentally orthodox agenda becomes more apparent.

Afterword

Thoughts on Backlash and Utopia

Intuitively, antigay activism seems like a response to the power and successes of the movement for lesbian and gay rights. Similarly, antifeminism seems a reactionary impulse, a rejoinder to the demand for gender equality made by an increasingly demanding women's movement. These understandings interpret such reactions as a form of "backlash." Backlash, the argument goes, consists of a series of maneuvers, coming to the fore by the mid-1980s, taking aim against advances won by feminists, gay activists, liberal educators, and so on (e.g., Faludi 1991). Backlashes signal a desire to return to a status quo where orthodox truths were not questioned, nor traditional authorities undermined. In some respects it is quite possible, and indeed justifiable, to read my book in such a way as to confirm this narrative.

In other ways, however, I have challenged some of the assumptions contained in this story. My argument has been that many of these developments, particularly antigay activity, are being spearheaded by a social movement with a long history and a clear vision: conservative Protestantism, as led today by the elite I have called the Christian Right. It is, I would argue, unhelpful at best to conceptualize this movement's political activities as "backlash," and I would like to use this short afterword to clarify why this is so.

There are four dimensions to my argument. First, the CR is itself a "victim" of backlash and not simply or unilaterally a perpetrator. Second, the CR is divided and does not constitute a monolithic block of force in any direction. Third, while some CR activists do idealize a mythical past, a cursory glance at their literature historically shows that they were *never* happy with the status quo and have no wish to return to it. For example, their vehemence against immorality in the 1950s was as strong as now (although there is a level at which they currently idealize this earlier period in a way they did not at the time). Unless we say that backlashes last decades (in which case the point of the term is unclear), then it would seem that the concept itself sheds little light on the sources and trajectories of "morality politics" at any rate.

Fourth, and perhaps most important, the CR is a movement with a comprehensive, progressive future *vision*. It is, I would argue, a paradigmatic movement for social change, and no more (nor less) a backlash impulse than feminism, gay rights, and others. As the first two points are somewhat self-evident (and perhaps less controversial), I will expound only briefly on them. The third I hope I have adequately addressed in chapter 2. For the most part I will concentrate on the last issue.

195

"Victims" and "Perpetrators"

The concept of backlash tends to suggest a unidirectional flow of action. First, a force for change appears and has some success—for example, the lesbian and gay rights movement. This, in turn, causes a reaction, the backlash; a counterforce emerges to thwart this change—for example, antigay activism. Within this understanding is a clear perpetrator of backlash, and a clear victim of it. The perpetrators are the attackers, the regressive bloc calling for a halt to perceived changes in sexual relations. The lesbian and gay movement is the victim; fighting for equality, it finds itself confronting reactionary forces set on denying change in the name of tradition.

In my view, deploying backlash in this way serves to cloud historical shifts and contemporary politics. First, the lesbian and gay movement itself is, within this understanding, a form of reaction. In other words, demands for lesbian and gay equality are an attack upon the hegemony of heterosexual culture, a reaction against the imposition of a particular construction of normalcy. In this sense the lesbian and gay movement is the counterforce, the backlash, and the CR merely the establishment "victim" fighting for survival.

Second, with respect to certain social movements, feminism for example, a simple notion of victim/perpetrator obscures an understanding of historical developments within movements. Given the different forms feminist struggle has taken over the last century, it may be more helpful to conceptualize social movements as fluid, dynamic, contradictory, and contingent, rather than simply as forces meeting counterforces in the evolutionary spiral for supremacy that "backlash" would seem to imply.

196

Split at the Root?

Following from the above, it is also worth emphasizing that social movements are not cohesive blocs of power, with a collective and harmonious vision and politics. In the case of the CR in North America, internal strife and division is intense, extending to both short-term strategizing and longer-term goals. The CR is riven with a matrix of fissures, including Protestant versus Catholic; diverse forms of Protestantism; elites versus grassroots; and challenges from within by, among others, pragmatists and opportunists.[1]

If the CR is a backlash, then it has spawned offspring that themselves have turned against the parent. There are thus backlashes within the backlash, and the relationship between these "children of backlash" and the original target—say, the lesbian and gay movement—are more complex and ambivalent. For these reasons as well, I do not find the term very helpful.

Rather than viewing any of this as backlash, I prefer to conceptualize conservative Christianity, and its contemporary political advocate the CR, as a bona fide social movement in its own right. The CR is not new, nor are its internal divisions. Its presence *seems* new (or backlashlike), or did in the 1980s anyway, because it has in fact lost a hegemony it was struggling to regain.

Instead, I would argue that we understand current social struggles as just that—struggles for hegemony between competing belief and value systems. The CR has a long pedigree of social criticism, and as I discuss next, it also possesses a comprehensive, progressive social vision. The CR is, I would suggest, a utopian movement driving toward the establishment of Christ's kingdom on earth.

A FORWARD MARCH

Conservative Protestantism looks forward to a world where peace reigns, hunger and want are unknown, and happiness, even ecstasy, is everywhere. This world, of course, is populated entirely by Protestant orthodox (everyone else being dead by then). This is not a "look back with longing," but forward looking of the highest order. Given the popular (and legitimate) association of this movement with right-wing politics, it may seem disingenuous to portray the CR as utopian, ultimately seeking to establish a kingdom of peace and tranquillity where goodness prevails. But to some extent, with certain caveats, it is indeed such a world to which they aspire.

198   In my view, it is essential to understanding key social struggles today that we come to grips with this dimension of conservative Protestantism. In as much as feminism, or radical lesbian and gay politics, seeks to re-create sexuality in a world where gender matters differently, so conservative Protestantism, as represented by the CR, seeks to build its own version of the good life. Much current social conflict, particularly in light of the failure of mass class mobilizations, is between these competing utopian paradigms and their attendant social-movement representatives. The concept of backlash, then, does not do justice to these dynamics. I do think, however, that backlash has some utility when defined specifically as an attitudinal culture on the part of the "nonaligned" public. In other words, feelings commonly associated with backlash impulses—alienation, resentment, and so on—can be coopted by populist discourses emanating from social-movement actors.

In this way the CR has exploited successfully what are

largely nonreligious sentiments held by white Americans who are not well off—particularly the so-called angry white male. Backlash may be useful here as a way of describing a particular culture, perhaps an ascendant one, where individuals are prepared to fight against the perceived gains of upstart "others"—gains that they believe have come at their direct expense.

But although this resentment exists, there is no logic propelling its holders into the CR camp (see Hertzke 1993). Indeed, while the CR endorses a set of "moral absolutes" (Lon Mabon, interview by author, 1994) or "fundamentals" (Kevin Tebedo, interview by author, 1994), the American public does not. American religiosity is not synonymous with orthodoxy. In fact, Americans are extremely morally relativistic. For example, a majority of the population does *not* believe that there is a single set of correct values that government should promote.[2] Most Americans believe that the individual should determine what is right and wrong.[3]

It is this battle for the hearts and minds of the nonorthodox that lesbian and gay rights activists must win— not with an assertion of gospel truth, but with a thoughtful argument for "living with uncertainty" (Weeks 1995). And as Stephen Carter (1993) has argued, by taking religious faith seriously. In my view, this can happen successfully only when gay rights are tied to a wider, emancipatory social agenda with an alternative, long-term vision.

Liberalism is an unsteady opponent to the CR. It is woolly and indefinable, and those who subscribe to it often run scared. An invigorated, emancipatory left-wing movement would prove a more formidable foe. In the meantime the CR is perhaps best opposed in two primary ways: on its own turf in the churches, by out lesbian and gay evangelicals; and through exposing the inherent exclusivity and grand ambitions of CR orthodoxy, antigay and otherwise. For ultimately the CR activists look forward to "a new heaven and a new earth" (Rev. 21:1), where they are not simply the most prosperous, but the only people who exist. It is one thing to have faith that this utopia is inevitable; it is another to impose its imperatives in the here and now.

Notes

CHAPTER ONE

1. *Bowers* v *Hardwick*, 478 US 186 (1986). This decision of the U.S. Supreme Court denied "a right to privacy" to homosexual sexual acts occurring in private, upholding a Georgia sodomy statute in the process.

2. For summations and extensions of this research see, e.g., Wald, Button, and Rienzo 1996; Kirkpatrick 1993; Seltzer 1992; Joseph Shapiro, "Straight Talk about Gays," *U.S. News and World Report,* 5 July 1993, 42–48.

3. See, e.g., Nugent and Gramick 1989–90; Prager 1993.

4. Of course, there are orthodox lesbians and gay men. My focus here is on antigay politics, however, not gay activism within orthodoxy. On the latter see Thumma 1991 and White's personal account (1994).

5. The ideological origins of the CR go back further than the 1970s; see sources below in note 6 and in "Terms and Limitations."

6. See, e.g., Bromley and Shupe 1984; Bruce 1990, 1994; Crawford 1980; Diamond 1989, 1995; Hertzke 1988, 1993; Himmelstein 1990; Hunter 1991; Jorstad 1987; Liebman and Wuthnow 1983; Lienesch 1982, 1993; Moen 1989, 1992, 1994; Wilcox 1992, 1994— to name just a very few.

7. E.g., contrast Diamond 1989 and Hertzke 1988 with Moen 1989 and Bruce 1990, 1994.

8. Gay rights ordinances were repealed in St. Paul, Wichita, and Eugene, OR; see Crawford 1980, 314.

9. E.g., Lebanon, OR, 1993; Albany, OR, 1994; Alachua County, FL, 1994; Cincinnati 1994; see also resulting litigation, *Equality Foundation of Greater Cincinnati* v *City of Cincinnati*, 54 F3d 261 (12 May 1995).

10. Colorado 1994 (passed, but see chapter 6); Oregon 1992 and 1994 (rejected); Maine 1995 (rejected); see also *Wagner* v *Secretary of State*, 1995 WL 458937. In 1994 such measures were proposed but failed to make the ballot in Arizona, Florida, Maine, Michigan, Mississippi, Nevada, Ohio, and Washington.

11. E.g., an ongoing challenge to New Jersey's law banning sexual-orientation discrimination can be followed in *Presbytery of New Jersey* v *Florio* (as of writing, latest installment 13 September 1995, Civ. No. 92-1641).

12. See "Hostile Climate" 1993.

13. One could also question to what extent the CR is deserving of the term "social movement." For various reasons, which I hope will become clear as the book progresses, I think that it is.

14. On the CR itself, see sources in note 6. On religion and new social movements, see Lechner 1990; Hannigan 1991; Himmelstein 1990; Fields 1991. On the CR and the Republican Party, see the special issue of *Political Science and Politics* 28 (1995): 1–23; Penning 1994; Wilcox 1994.

15. Gallup and Castelli 1989, 45–48. See also Wald 1991; "Spiritual America," *U.S. News and World Report,* 4 April 1994, 48–59.

16. This approach is carried through my work generally; see, e.g., Herman 1993, 1994, 1996.

17. On antigay CR activity in Britain, see, e.g., Cooper 1994; Durham 1991. On Canada see Herman 1994.

18. Indeed, CR constituencies are not uniformly economic conservatives; see Iannaccone 1993.

19. Witness "corporate America's" gradual extension of employment benefits to lesbian and gay workers, and the increasing phenomenon of out gay conservatives; see, e.g., Khan 1996.

20. See O'Sullivan 1993 for a good overview of the Catholic right.

21. See Sara Diamond on this point in M. Slaughter, "An Interview with Sara Diamond," *Z Magazine,* January 1993, 28–33.

22. See Wilcox 1990 and various issues of the magazine *National Minority Politics.* One important black conservative feted by the CR is Alan Keyes, who ran for the Republican presidential nomination in 1996.

23. For an interesting debate on the nature of Jewish support for the CR, see Decter 1994; Levitas 1995. See also Feder 1993.

24. It should be noted that very little of the literature on the extremist right deals with its antigay politics—this work remains to be done.

25. Peters n.d. See also L. Zeskind, "And Now, the Hate Show," *New York Times,* 16 November 1993, A27.

26. Gallup and Castelli 1989, 13. Close to half the population would describe themselves as "born again," but this is a different measure than I am using. See "Spiritual America."

27. Of course, the word "fundamentalist" does not have to be used pejoratively; see Ammerman 1987.

28. See, e.g., the diverse and in some cases contradictory definitions of the term in Marty and Appleby 1993, not to mention the huge diversity of movements surveyed. For example, "fundamentalist" is sometimes used to refer to religious people who are separate from mainstream society, who look, talk, and behave "distinctly"—all they wish is to preserve their separation. On other occasions the term is used to describe biblical literalists who hope to seize state power to impose their own moral vision. The CR that I focus on resembles the latter far more than the former.

29. Note that I only minimally address antigay discourse in Christian radio/television, hence, for example, the obscure presence in my text of Pat Robertson's 700 Club, one of the largest antigay producers. For continuing monitoring of the 700 Club, see cc.watch (Internet).

30. Profiles of Dobson can be found in Rodney Clapp, "Meet James Dobson, His Father's Son," *Christianity Today (CT)* 26, 9 (1982): 14–19; Tim Stafford, "His Father's Son: The Drive behind James Dobson, Jr.," *CT* 32, 7 (1988): 16–22; Steven Roberts, "The Heavy Hitter: James Dobson Speaks for a 'Parallel Culture' Washington Has Ignored," *U.S. News and World Report,* 24 April 1995, 34–39.

31. "Our Faith Values Mission and Guiding Principles," pamphlet, Focus on the Family, n.d.

32. See also K. Lawton, "The Family Man," *CT* 36, 13 (1992): 26–28.

33. For a profile of Rutherford and several other CR legal organizations, see Tim Stafford, "Move Over, ACLU," *CT* 37, 12 (1993): 20–24.

34. For an outsider's account of a previous Christian Coalition conference, see Donna Minkowitz, "Undercover with the Religious Right," *Out,* February–March 1994, 56–61.

35. There is some speculation that the CR's downplaying of its antigay rhetoric is related to its attempts to court a greater Catholic constituency; see cc.watch (Internet), 20 April 1996.

36. E.g., James Dobson of Focus on the Family criticized the coali-

tion's Ralph Reed for the latter's failure to denounce adequately Colin Powell's presidential candidacy.

37. Note that Christian Identity and similar extreme movements embrace a different form of millennialism; see Barkun 1990.

38. Other less significant but important passages are found in Ezek. 37–39, Dan. 7:12, and Mark 13.

39. Klaus Koch (1983, 21–24) has provided a useful definition of the genre. Characteristics he identifies include urgency of expectation, cosmic catastrophe, presence of angels and demons, new salvation possible, and the ultimate enthronement of God and his kingdom. For further discussion of the rhetorical dimensions of the genre, see Brummett 1984.

40. On the Jewish apocalyptic genre and its influence on Christianity, see Collins 1984.

41. Pat Robertson's writing reflects this sort of pro-Israeli anti-Semitism; e.g., 1990, chaps. 11, 12. See also Skipp Porteous, "Anti-semitism: Its Prevalence within the Christian Right," *Freedom Writer*, May 1994, 1–8. For a fascinating account of how premillennialists interpret the Holocaust in terms of their eschatology, see Ariel 1991.

204

CHAPTER TWO

1. For an excellent review of the overall history, theology, and politics of *CT*, see Toulouse 1993. In this chapter my concern is solely with a discursive analysis of selected journal texts, rather than with the role and philosophy of *CT* itself.

2. See, e.g., Focus on the Family's video *Children at Risk* (1993).

3. Ralph A. Cannon and Glenn D. Everett, "Sex and Smut on the Newsstands," *CT* 2, 10 (1958): 5.

4. For further discussion of the CR and the idealized family, see sources noted in Herman 1994, chap. 5. Also Lienesch 1993, chap. 2.

5. Pitirim A. Sorokin, "Demoralization of Youth: Open Germs and Hidden Viruses," *CT* 3, 20 (1959): 3. Homosexuality is mentioned specifically, but I address that separately below.

6. Ibid., 3–4. See also Pitirim A. Sorokin's peculiar follow-up piece, "The Depth of the Crisis: American Sex Morality Today," *CT* 4, 20 (1960): 3–5.

7. "Sex in Christian Perspective," *CT* 4, 20 (1960): 6–8.

8. Later conservative Christians took up this challenge, and, indeed, a large literature on sex, and sexual pleasure within marriage, has been produced.

9. "The Press and Sex Morality," *CT* 5, 9 (1961): 20–22.

10. Stanley C. Baldwin, "Sodom in America," *CT* 8, 2 (1963): 14;

"Diagnosis Is Not Enough" (editorial), *CT* 8, 2 (1963): 24–26; Howard Carson Blake, "The New Morality," *CT* 8, 12 (1964): 7–9.

11. David L. McKenna, "The Morals Revolution and the Christian College," *CT* 8, 19 (1964): 10–13.

12. Sorokin, "Demoralization of Youth," 4.

13. Sorokin, "Depth of the Crisis," 3.

14. "Press and Sex Morality," 6.

15. Baldwin, "Sodom in America," 14; Blake, "New Morality," 8.

16. A Supreme Court decision allowing gay magazines through the public mail is also noted (without comment); see *CT* 6, 21 (1962): 29.

17. J. Marcellus Kik, "Combating Juvenile Delinquency," *CT* 3, 20 (1959): 13–16.

18. Emma Fall Schofield, "Will Alcohol Destroy Our Youth?" *CT* 3, 20 (1959): 6–8.

19. Dirk W. Jellema, "Faith and Madness: The Post-Modern Mind," *CT* 5, 16 (1961): 3.

20. Charles Lowry, "A Plea for Realism: Perspective on the Power Struggle," *CT* 6, 16 (1962): 3–6.

21. Carl F. Henry, "Christian Responsibility in Education," *CT* 1, 17 (1957): 11.

22. See "NCC, God, and the Schools" (editorial), *CT* 3, 18 (1959): 20–22.

23. *Abington School District* v *Schempp*, 374 US 203 (1963).

24. But see reaction to an earlier decision (*Engle* v *Vitale*, 370 US 421 [1962]) in *CT* 6, 21 (1962): 29–31, and 6, 22 (1962): 25. For comment on the 1963 judgment in *CT*, see "Is the Supreme Court on Trial?" (editorial), 7, 11 (1963): 28; "The Meaning of the Supreme Court Decision" (news report), 7, 20 (1963): 29–31; John M. Stuart, "Give Me Back My Child!" 7, 23 (1963): 9–10; "The Schoolyard Becomes a Battleground" (editorial), 7, 24 (1963): 29.

25. "America's Future: Can We Salvage the Republic?" (editorial), *CT* 2, 11 (1958): 4. See also "Foundations: Tilt to the Left" (editorial), *CT* 2, 15 (1958): 20–24.

26. "Christ and the Campus" (editorial), *CT* 3, 16 (1959): 20; Robert M. Smith, "Famine on University Campuses," *CT* 6, 10 (1962): 13.

27. Smith, "Famine on University Campuses," 15; Ernest Gordon, "The Word and the Campus," *CT* 8, 16 (1964): 5. See also "The Storm over Academic Freedom" (editorial), *CT* 7, 14 (1963): 28–30.

28. "The Christian-Pagan West" (editorial), *CT* 1, 6 (1956): 34.

29. See, e.g., Forster and Epstein 1964; Roy 1960. On Catholicism and anticommunism see Frank 1992.

30. "Red China and World Morality" (editorial), *CT* 1, 5 (1956):

21. See, e.g., "Lessons from the Slavery Crisis" (editorial), *CT* 3, 7 (1959): 22.

31. J. Edgar Hoover, "Communism: The Bitter Enemy of Religion," *CT* 3, 19 (1959): 3. See also "The Communist Menace: Red Goals and Christian Ideals," *CT* 5, 1 (1960): 3; "Communist Propaganda and the Christian Pulpit," *CT* 5, 2 (1960): 5; "Soviet Rule or Christian Renewal," *CT* 5, 3 (1960): 9; "Spiritual Priorities: Guidelines for a Civilization in Peril," *CT* 6, 19 (1962): 3; "Storming the Skies: Christianity Encounters Communism," *CT* 7, 6 (1962): 3; all by J. Edgar Hoover.

32. Frederick G. Schwarz, "Can We Meet the Red Challenge?" *CT* 3, 14 (1959): 13. For specific discussions of Fred Schwarz's Christian Anti-Communism Crusade, see Forster and Epstein 1964, chap. 3; Koeppen 1967; Wilcox 1992, chap. 4. Note that Fred Schwarz continued his anticommunist activity through the 1980s; see Diamond 1989, 47. See also Fred Pierce Corson, "Facing the Communist Menace," *CT* 6, 15 (1962): 4.

33. Charles Lowry, "Judgement on the Christian West," *CT* 1, 7 (1957): 24; Hoover, "Communism"; "Red China and World Morality," 22.

34. "Red China and World Morality," 22; William K. Harrison, "Reminiscences and a Prophecy," *CT* 1, 11 (1957): 13; Lowry, "Judgement on the Christian West," 25.

35. Harrison, "Reminiscences and a Prophecy," 13; "What of Tomorrow?" (editorial), *CT* 2, 11 (1958): 20.

36. Lowry, "Judgement on the Christian West," 25.

37. Schwarz, "Can We Meet the Red Challenge?" 14.

38. Harrison, "Reminiscences and a Prophecy," 15.

39. Lowry, "Judgement on the Christian West," 24.

40. Billy Graham, "Facing the Anti-God Colossus," *CT* 7, 6 (1962): 6.

41. See John Sutherland Bonnell, "A Challenge to Christianity," *CT* 7, 6 (1962): 11; "What about the Atheists?" (editorial), *CT* 7, 9 (1963): 28.

42. E.g., "We Christians commonly speak of Marx as a Jew, and in favor of this is the fact that he was very Jewish in his mind and soul" (Lowry, "Judgement on the Christian West," 24).

43. Oswald T. Allis, "Israel's Transgression in Palestine, *CT* 1, 6 (1956): 6.

44. I am not suggesting that anti-Zionism is per se anti-Semitic, only that this form is.

45. Wilbur M. Smith, "Israel in Her Promised Land," *CT* 1, 6 (1956): 10.

46. Jacob Gartenhaus, "Evangelizing the Jews," *CT* 2, 14 (1958): 8. The author is described as "Founder and President of the International Board of Jewish Missions, Inc." and a "convert." On Jewish obstinacy, see also "What about the Atheists?" 28.

47. That Jews are a chosen people is an important point of difference between the millennialism of mainstream and extreme conservative Christianity.

48. For an account of Protestant anti-Catholicism in earlier periods, see Lipset and Raab 1971.

49. Andre Lamorte, "The Moral Sag in France," *CT* 1, 19 (1957): 11.

50. C. Stanley Lowell, "Rising Tempo of Rome's Demands," *CT* 1, 7 (1957): 11.

51. "A New Protestant Awakening," *CT* 2, 1 (1957): 3. The reaction of conservative Protestants to the Kennedy campaign and presidency provides additional insight into anti-Catholicism.

52. I am not suggesting that anti-Catholicism lost its appeal to *CT* constituencies, only that it no longer featured prominently in the journal.

53. James Huffman, "Sex Education in Public Schools," *CT* 13, 25 (1969): 5–8; Harold Lindsell, "Sex, SIECUS, and the Schools," *CT* 14, 9 (1970): 10–13; Lewis Penhall Bird and Christopher T. Reilly, "Sex Education and the Church," *CT* 14, 18 (1970): 10–13.

54. E.g., Hoover articles; Daniel J. Evearitt, "The Rolling Stones: The Darker Side of Rock," *CT* 22, 10 (1978): 18–19.

55. A key proposal in Wolfenden was to decriminalize same-sex sexual acts occurring in a narrowly defined private sphere.

56. "Church Channel to Homosexuals" (news report), *CT* 10, 11 (1966): 53–54.

57. "The Homosexual Church" (news report), *CT* 14, 24 (1970): 48–50.

58. See, e.g., coverage of both a seminar sponsored by the Council on Religion and the Homosexual and the activities of the Gay Liberation Front at an Episcopalian convention, in " 'Gays' Go Radical" (news report), *CT* 15, 5 (1970): 40–41; "Sexuality and Ministry," *CT* 19, 9 (1975): 28–30; "The NCC: Equal Rights for All (Homosexuals, Too)," *CT* 19, 13 (1975): 38–39; "United Presbyterian Church: Deciding the Homosexual Issue," *CT* 22, 18 (1978): 38–41.

59. See "The Bible and the Homosexual" (editorial), *CT* 12, 8 (1968): 24–25; B. L. Smith, "Homosexuality in the Bible and Law," *CT* 13, 21 (1969): 7–10; "Not Because They Are Gay" (editorial), *CT* 16, 21 (1972): 23; Klaus Bockmuhl, "Homosexuality in Biblical Perspective," *CT* 17, 10 (1973): 12–18; "Can Homosexuals Inherit the

Kingdom?" (editorial), *CT* 21, 16 (1977): 27; Bennett J. Sims, "Sex and Homosexuality," *CT* 22, 10 (1978): 23–30; "Homosexuality: Biblical Guidance through a Moral Morass" (editorial), *CT* 24, 8 (1980): 12–13.

60. It is not my intention in this book to engage in any debate on the validity of scriptural interpretation.

61. "Bible and the Homosexual," 25.

62. Smith, "Homosexuality in the Bible," 8–10.

63. Sims, "Sex and Homosexuality," 30.

64. "The Laws against Homosexuals" (editorial), *CT* 14, 3 (1969): 32.

65. Lindsell, "Sex, SIECUS," 11.

66. "Gay Demands" (editorial), *CT* 15, 5 (1970): 26; "Gay Ground-Gaining" (editorial), *CT* 16, 19 (1972): 27–28.

67. Harold Lindsell, "Homosexuals and the Church," *CT* 17, 25 (1973): 8.

68. Letha Scanzoni, "On Friendship and Homosexuality," *CT* 18, 25 (1974): 11.

69. Guy Charles, "Gay Liberation Confronts the Church," *CT* 19, 24 (1975): 16.

70. Carl F. Henry, "Evangelicals Jump on the Political Bandwagon," *CT* 24, 18 (1980): 21–25.

71. But see John R. Stott, "Homosexual 'Marriage': Why Same-Sex Partnerships Are Not a Christian Option," *CT* 29, 17 (1985): 21–28.

72. Tom Minnery, "Homosexuals Can Change," *CT* 25, 3 (1981): 36–41.

73. See, e.g., Randy Frame, "The Homosexual Lifestyle: Is There a Way Out?" *CT* 29, 11 (1985): 32–36. However, note that this piece includes a front-page photo of a gay rights march, with a "leatherman" in the foreground. See also Tim Stafford, "Coming Out," *CT* 33, 11 (1989): 16–24; Randy Frame, "The Evangelical Closet," *CT* 34, 16 (1990): 56–57.

74. See, e.g., Susan Thomas, "Everybody, It Seemed, Supported the Homosexuals in Palo Alto (except the Voters, That Is)," *CT* 26, 1 (1982): 32; Beth Spring, "Gay Rights Resolution Divides Membership of Evangelical Women's Caucus," *CT* 30, 14 (1986): 40–42; Robert Digitale, "San Francisco Set to Define 'Family,' " *CT* 33, 15 (1989): 44–46.

75. "Homosexuals in the Church" (editorial), *CT* 27, 8 (1983): 8–9.

76. "The Devil Who Is There" (editorial), *CT* 34, 11 (1990): 32.

77. Clinton E. Arnold, "Giving the Devil His Due," *CT* 34, 11 (1990): 16–19.

78. See also J. I. Packer, "The Devil's Dossier," *CT* 37, 7 (1993): 24.

79. E.g., Tim Stafford, "Campus Christians and the New Thought Police," *CT* 36, 2 (1992): 15–17.

80. Joe Laconte, "The Battle to Define," *CT* 37, 12 (1993): 74–77.

81. But see Joe Dallas, "Born Gay? How Politics Have Skewed the Debate over the Biological Causes of Homosexuality," *CT* 36, 7 (1992): 20–23.

82. "The New Ex-Gay Agenda" (editorial), *CT* 36, 3 (1992): 21.

83. Alexander F. C. Webster, "Homosexuals in Uniform?" *CT* 37, 2 (1993): 23.

84. Dale Buss, "Homosexual Rights Go to School," *CT* 37, 6 (1993): 70–72.

85. David Neff, "Two Men Don't Make a Right," *CT* 37, 8 (1993): 14–15.

86. Note *CT*'s apparent acknowledgment of a biological foundation to homosexuality. See chapter 3 for further discussion on how conservative Christians conceptualize the "causes" of homosexuality.

87. Stanton L. Jones, "The Loving Opposition: Speaking the Truth in a Climate of Hate," *CT* 37, 8 (1993): 18–25.

88. See, e.g., Tim Stafford, "The Post-closet Era," *CT* 39, 13 (1995): 51, 60; and the journal's neutral reporting of the failed antigay initiative in Maine, "Maine Curbs on Rights Fail," *CT* 39, 14 (1995): 71.

CHAPTER THREE

1. See chapter 1 for a discussion of how I use these various terms, such as conservative Protestant, Christian Right, conservative Christian.

2. Short biographies, such as this of Tim LaHaye, are synthesized from organizational material, autobiographical accounts, and reports of CR monitoring groups and journalists. Where I allege anything controversial about an individual, I provide specific sources.

3. See the Anti-Defamation League 1994 and Political Research Associates 1993 for a useful discussion of Weyrich and the Free Congress Research and Education Foundation. On Weyrich's role in the CR generally, see sources in chapter 1, note 6.

209

4. In 1994 Dannemeyer surfaced again, reportedly accusing Bill Clinton of being linked to a series of suspicious deaths. See Keith Clark, "Dannemeyer's Latest Political Conspiracy Theory," *Lesbian and Gay News-Telegraph,* 22 July–11 August 1994, 15.

5. See chapter 1 for an overview of Focus on the Family.

6. Tony Marco, "Oppressed Minority, or Counterfeits?" *Citizen* 6, 4 (1992): 1; "Special Report," *Citizen* 7, 8 (1993). I discuss the Colorado example in detail in chapter 6.

7. Jeff Hooten, "What's Wrong with This Picture?" *Citizen* 10, 4 (1996): 1–4.

8. Susan D. Martinuk, "What's Wrong with Gay Rights?" *Citizen* (Canada) 3, 4 (1994): 1–3; Susan D. Martinuk, "A Critical Time for the Family," *Citizen* (Canada) 3, 5 (1994): 1–2; Susan D. Martinuk, "Understanding the Gay Agenda," *Citizen* (Canada) 4, 2 (1995): 1–3; "The Egan Case: A Landmark Ruling for Marriage," *Citizen* (Canada) 4, 6 (1995): 1–3; Susan D. Martinuk, "Why You Should Get Involved," *Citizen* (Canada) 4, 4 (1995): 1–3.

9. For further discussion of lesbian and gay rights in Canada and the role there of Focus on the Family, see Herman 1994.

10. See various issues of *Washington Watch, Insight,* and *Family Policy.* In chapter 1 I give a brief biography of the FRC and its principle actors.

11. The packet includes Gary Bauer, "Beware the Hidden Gay Agenda," *USA Today,* 26 April 1993, 12; "Platform of the 1993 March on Washington for Lesbian, Gay, and Bi Equal Rights and Liberation," flyer; Robert Knight, "The Homosexual Agenda in Schools," *Insight,* 1993; Robert Knight, "A Queer Car Ride," *Chronicles,* March 1993, 48; Gary Bauer, "Compelling Evidence" (n.d.).

12. See, e.g., American Family Association 1994. The American Family Association produces several packages of material on homosexuality, some of which I discuss below. On Concerned Women for America, see LaHaye 1991 and other material discussed below. The Free Congress Research and Education Foundation distributes the Rueda (1982) summary, among other things.

13. See chapter 1 for a discussion of Colorado Springs as a center of CR activity. See conference documents (on file with author). Note that the details of CR antigay *strategy* (as opposed to *politics*) are not my concern in this book. However, it is worth noting that the documents from this conference are very illuminating on the former topic. An account of this conference is provided by the Institute for First Amendment Studies in *Freedom Writer,* August 1994.

14. Such organizations include Exodus International (CA), Homosexuals Anonymous (PA), LIFE (NY), and Love in Action (CA). The

conservative Christian ex-gay genre is a world unto itself, and for the most part I have chosen not to consider its politics and literature directly. For a critique, see Ide 1987; Pennington 1989.

15. See, e.g., Burtoft 1994, chap. 1; Dannemeyer 1989, chap. 1; Farrar 1994, 142–43; Magnuson 1994, chap. 4.

16. E.g., Robert Knight, "New Genetic Study Not What It's Cracked Up to Be," *Infocus*, Family Research Council, 1993; American Family Association 1994; "Homosexual Behaviour: Choice or Chance," Family First, MA, 1992.

17. This research suggests that gay and heterosexual genes (and/or brains) are different. See, e.g., Allen and Gorski 1992; Bailey and Pillard 1991; Hamer et al. 1993; LeVay 1991.

18. See interview with Nicolosi in "A Doctor Offers Life-Changing Therapy," *Citizen* (Canada) 3, 7 (1994): 1–3.

19. See discussion in Burtoft 1994. I discuss the lesbian theories more comprehensively in chapter 4.

20. Thanks to Carl Stychin for passing on this anecdote.

21. See discussion of the apocalyptic genre in chapter 1.

22. For an excellent review of this debate (and its legal implications) within lesbian and gay communities, see Halley 1994b.

23. In constitutional equality law, "sex" receives less protection than "race." This is because, in the former case, judges have held biological differences to be relevant in certain circumstances. See also Currah 1995.

24. It remains to be seen how *Evans* v *Romer* (1996 US Lexis 3245) alters this landscape, if at all.

25. Some poll data suggest that this is so. See, e.g., Joseph Shapiro, "Straight Talk about Gays," *U.S. News and World Report*, 5 July 1993, 46. See also Halley 1994b, n. 62.

26. I discuss in chapter 5 how some CR activists theorize gay identity in the context of rights struggles.

27. For further discussion of this point, see Herman 1994, chap. 5 and afterword.

28. This secularization process does pose problems for a religious movement; see discussion in Herman 1994, chap. 6.

29. Note that most radical feminist and sexuality theorists similarly dispute the assumptions upon which this figure is based.

30. E.g., J. Gordon Muir, "Homosexuality and the 10% Fallacy," *Wall Street Journal*, 31 March 1993, A14; Robert Knight, "Sexual Disorientation," *Family Policy* 6 (1992): 1–8; American Family Association 1994. See also general discussion in David Tuller, "Studies Question Kinsey's '10 Percent,'" *San Francisco Chronicle*, 29 March 1993, A1.

31. The Kinsey rating represented a point along a continuum of

sexuality; the scale is used to suggest that many people have had homosexual desires and experiences.

32. In my view, "counting" the number of lesbians and gays in the population is impossible, as *any* estimation is merely speculative. The vast majority of people involved in same-sex sexual relations either do not identify as gay, or certainly would not do so to survey researchers. If sexuality is socially constructed, any talk of a fixed percentage is meaningless. If it is not, we will only know how much of the population is gay and lesbian when (if) it becomes entirely safe to come out.

33. See, e.g., Herman 1994, chap. 5; Patton 1985; Seidman 1992, chap. 4; Stychin 1995; Weeks 1985.

34. The CR's response to HIV/AIDS has been explored well by others. See, e.g., Patton 1985; Palmer 1990.

35. For profiles of Cameron, see Ann Guidici Fettner, "The Evil That Men Do," *New York Native*, 23 September 1985, 23; Dave Walter, "Paul Cameron," *Advocate*, 29 October 1985, 28–32.

36. "Notice to Members," American Psychological Association, 2 December 1983; *ASA Footnotes*, February 1987, 14. See, e.g., Gonsiorek and Weinrich 1991, 4–5; Robert Brown and James Cole, letter to the editor, *Nebraska Medical Journal* 20, 9 (1985): 410–14, in reply to Cameron et al. 1985. Regarding the journal in which Cameron publishes some of his material, *Psychological Reports*, see George Pramenko, "Letter to Colorado for Family Values," 30 November 1993 (copy on file with author).

37. "Medical Consequences of What Homosexuals Do," Family Research Institute, 1993; Cameron et al. 1985; *Family Research Report*, various issues.

38. "Murder and Homosexuality," *Family Research Report*, May–June 1994, 2.

39. The CR's citation of such studies is often inaccurate and self-serving; see, e.g., Eric Lichtblau, "Gay 'Facts' in Mailer Disputed," *Los Angeles Times*, 3 November 1989, B1.

40. E.g., book publishers participating in a "queer theory" conference in Iowa in 1994 received "I know you were there" letters from LaBarbera.

41. Paglia is cited approvingly by Grant and Horne (1993), among others.

42. Reisman and Eichel 1990, 212–13); Judith Reisman, "Transcript of Speech to National Antigay Conference," Colorado Springs, 1994 (on file with author); "Child Molestation and Homosexuality," Family Research Institute, 1993.

43. For a profile of the ministry, see David Colker, "Anti-Gay

Video Highlights Church's Agenda," *Los Angeles Times,* 22 February 1993, A1.

44. For a history of *Gay Agenda* showings, see Clarkson 1993.

45. See, e.g., American Family Association 1994; Nancy Sutton, "The Homosexual Agenda from Stonewall to the White House," pamphlet, Family First, 1994.

46. The American Family Association, for example, constantly monitors the perceived "pro-gay bias" of the media; see various issues of *AFA Journal* and "Top Sponsors of Pro-homosexual Programs," American Family Association, leaflet, 1994.

47. See Tom Minnery, "Feeding Frenzy!" *Citizen* 7, 8 (1993): 1–3.

48. See American Family Association material in note 46; various issues of *Education Reporter,* Eagle Forum.

49. See also *Infocus* publications, Family Research Council. I discuss the relationship between the CR and the state in chapter 7.

50. See also special issues of Concerned Women for America's *Family Voice,* July 1992, May 1994.

51. I discuss the counteridentity of the conservative Christian activist further in Herman 1994, chap. 5.

52. Indeed, I could arguably be accused of doing just that in this book (by distinguishing between "conservative Christians" and the "Christian Right").

53. Quoted in Grant and Horne 1993, 39, citing "Congressional Record 1987." Full text quoted in McIlhenny, McIlhenny, and York 1993, 212, citing *AFA Journal,* which cited *Gay Community News.* Also quoted in Farrar 1994, 136–37, citing McIlhenny, McIlhenny, and York.

54. *After the Ball* is discussed in Burtoft 1994; Grant and Horne 1993; and McIlhenny, McIlhenny, and York 1993, among many others.

55. I discuss this further, in relation to the state, in chapter 7.

56. See also Davis 1971 and Johnson 1983 for a discussion of themes of conspiracy.

57. The issue of gays and lesbians in the church is one I am not able to consider in this book. As I noted in chapter 1, the struggles, and partial successes, of lesbian and gay Christians within mainline Christianity was an important factor precipitating the CR's focus on gay rights.

CHAPTER FOUR

1. In a note (1994, 111 n. 179) Burtoft acknowledges that this "threefold typology is taken from a personal conversation with Joseph Nicolosi, Ph.D." See chapter 3 for a discussion of Nicolosi.

2. Burtoft references Theo L. Dorpat, *The Homosexualities: Reality, Fantasy, and the Arts* (Madison, CT: International Universities Press, 1990).

3. Young 1992, 12. See also the personal stories in "Once Gay, Always Gay?" *Focus on the Family Magazine*, March 1994, 2–5.

4. Given that this study ostensibly concerned the behavior of HIV-positive women in prisons, the argument is hardly surprising. For a more useful analysis of lesbianism and criminality, see Robson 1995.

5. "Lesbian 'Marriage' and Violence," *Family Research Report*, January–February 1995, 6. Cameron's quotations from the book do not in any way substantiate this allegation.

6. "Leading Gay Group Picks S/M Advocate for Director," *Lambda Report* 1, 5 (1993): 1, 4; see also follow-up, "Gay Leader Describes Herself as S&M 'Leatherwoman,'" *Lambda Report* 1, 6 (1993): 1, 10.

7. See, e.g., "Heather's Two Mommies Publisher Endorses Female 'Fisting,'" *Lambda Report* 1, 3 (1993): 10.

8. "Lesbian Avengers Pass Out Phone Sex Fliers to Grade Schoolers," *Lambda Report* 2, 1 (1994): 6–7.

9. "Lesbians Recruiting Girls," *Lambda Report* 1, 7 (1993–94): 7.

10. See, e.g., de Hart 1991; Diamond 1989; Himmelstein 1986, 1990; Klatch 1987; Mathews and de Hart 1990.

11. Phyllis Schlafly, "Women in Combat? What It Means for American Culture and Defense," Heritage Lectures 317, Heritage Foundation, 1991. See also Phyllis Schlafly, "The Feminization of the U.S. Military," *Phyllis Schlafly Report* 23, 2 (1989).

12. Elsewhere I have considered this debate in more depth; see Herman 1996.

13. See, e.g., some of the contributions to Bad Object-Choices 1991.

14. Another exception was Pat Robertson's attack on a black gay video *(Tongues Untied)* during his 1992 bid for the Republican nomination.

CHAPTER FIVE

1. Tony Marco, interview by author, 1994. See also Morken 1994 for a somewhat hagiographic account of Marco and his sexual politics.

2. I have over a dozen of Marco's position papers on file, as well as a ninety-page gay rights analysis.

3. See, e.g., Focus on the Family (e.g., *Citizen* 6, 4 [1992]: 1–4); Grant and Horne 1993, 35, 40, 42, 125; re Marco's influence in Colo-

rado, see Bransford 1994; re his influence in Maine, see Carolyn Cosby, Open Letter, Concerned Maine Families, December 1993 (on file with author).

4. See, e.g., Tony Marco, *Gay Rights: A Public Health Disaster and Civil Wrong* (Ft. Lauderdale: Coral Ridge Ministries, 1992), cited in Grant and Horne 1993, 264.

5. Tony Marco, "Ultimate Nix to Old 'Disgust' 'Gay Rights' Opposition," memo, 7 August 1994 (on file with author).

6. Tony Marco, "Oppressed Minority, or Counterfeits?" *Citizen* 6, 4 (1992): 2.

7. Robert Knight, "Homosexuality Is Not a Civil Right," *Infocus*, Family Research Council, 1993. See American Family Association 1994. McIlhenny, McIlhenny, and York (1993, 76–77) cite a similar piece in the *San Francisco Chronicle,* and Farrar (1994, 135) cites the McIlhennys.

8. The Cincinnati material is reprinted in the FRC's *Infocus* (1993). See also "Equal Rights—Not Special Rights," broadsheet, Colorado for Family Values, 1992; "Ballot Measure 13," campaign literature, Oregon Citizen's Alliance, 1994.

9. See, e.g., *San Francisco Chronicle,* 27 August 1991, cited in McIlhenny, McIlhenny, and York 1993, 77. See also Schacter 1994, 299 n. 84.

10. L. Stoesen, "Census Yields Snapshot of Black Same-Sex Households," *Washington Blade,* 8 September 1995. See also Badgett 1995.

11. Tony Marco, "Shaky Foundation: Twelve 'Big Lies' the 'Gay Rights' Movement Is Built On," memo, 1993, 1994 (on file with author).

12. See chapters 3 and 4 for discussion of other, related themes.

13. See, e.g., Joseph Shapiro, "Straight Talk about Gays," *U.S. News and World Report,* 3 July 1993, 48.

14. See, e.g., Knight, "Homosexuality Is Not a Civil Right"; Robert Knight, "The Homosexual Agenda in Schools," *Insight,* 1993 (and many other *Infocus* and *Insight* publications); Robert Knight, interview by author, 1994.

15. "Ballot Measure 13"; "Equal Rights—Not Special Rights"; "Community Watch Action Kit: Monitoring and Defeating Homosexual Extremism in Your Community," Colorado for Family Values, 1993.

16. In 1995 one state campaign largely based on the pragmatic discourse failed (Maine). I discuss the contradiction in the Colorado campaign more fully in chapter 6.

17. See, e.g., Marco documents (on file with author); Robert Knight, interview by author, 1995.

18. In chapter 1 I explain why I view the CR (as opposed to conservative Christianity generally) as a "white" movement.

19. In chapter 7 I explore how these divisions played out during the black civil rights struggles of the 1950s and 1960s.

20. See, e.g., various issues of the magazine *National Minority Politics*.

21. For example, in 1996 the Christian Coalition offered a $25,000 reward for information leading to the arrest of perpetrators of fire bombings of black churches; see cc.watch (Internet), 23 April 1996. See also D. J. Gribbin, "Bridge-Building across Racial Lines," *Christian American* 5, 7 (1995): 20–21; Reed 1994, chap. 16; F. Chideya, "How the Right Stirs Black Homophobia," *Newsweek*, 18 October 1993, 73. Bridges are also being built between the CR and orthodox Jews, Muslims, Hindus, and other non-Christian faith communities (see chapters 1 and 7).

22. See, e.g., Jeff Hooten, "Making Their Voices Heard," *Citizen* 10, 5 (1996): 1–4. Some of these tensions are well illustrated in Frum 1994. See also Randy Frame, "The Cost of Being Black," *CT* 30, 13 (1986): 19–20.

23. See Edward Gilbreath, "Manhood's Great Awakening," *CT* 39, 2 (1995): 20–28.

24. "New York City Orthodox Jews Support Your Continuing Efforts to Ban Special Protection for Homosexuals," petition to Lon Mabon, Oregon Citizen's Alliance, 1994 (on file with author).

25. See, e.g., Christian Coalition 1995, chap. 3; Frum 1994, 91–94; Dobson and Bauer 1990, 299–300.

26. It should be noted that some black nationalists endorse educational segregation and support vouchers on this basis.

27. See Bennett 1992; Dobson and Bauer 1990, 197–203; various issues of *Citizen, Washington Watch*, and *Family Policy;* materials from the Oregon Citizen's Alliance.

28. For a good review of some of the legal maneuvers used to oppose affirmative action, see Richard Perez-Peña, "A Rights Movement That Emerges from the Right," *New York Times*, 30 December 1994.

29. Indeed, two such figures, Trent Lott and Edwin Meese, appeared in an antigay video targeted at black communities; see Chideya, "How the Right Stirs Black Homophobia," 73.

30. The acknowledgment of these truths does not mean that homophobia and antigay discrimination are not a part of everyday life.

In my view, however, such an acknowledgment does begin to come to grips with the power of CR rhetoric. By calling this rhetoric a "lie," we simply continue an accusatory and unproductive spiral. By responding to the substance of the critique, we can perhaps move the public discussion onto different terrain.

31. The conservatism of spousal-benefit rights is well-defended by Andrew Sullivan (1995). Note I am not suggesting gay marriage rights are inherently conservative; see Herman 1994, afterword.

32. See, e.g., Dan McGraw, "The Christian Capitalists," *U.S. News and World Report*, 13 March 1995, 52–63.

33. See discussion in Herman 1994. See also Henry Louis Gates's perceptive piece "Blacklash?" *New Yorker*, 17 May 1993, 42–44.

CHAPTER SIX

1. *Evans* v *Romer* (1996 US Lexis 3245).

2. E.g., in Florida (see Salokar 1994) and Maine.

3. On the campaign, see Bransford 1994. On sociolegal factors leading to the success of law reform campaigns, and a problematization of the notion of "success," see Herman 1994. For doctrinal analyses of the judgments in the Colorado and similar litigation, see, e.g., Batterman 1995; Burke 1993; Coukos 1994; Gallagher 1994; Niblock 1993; *Ohio State Law Journal* 1994; Rankin 1994; Wagner 1993.

4. See "CFV's Analysis of the Human Relations Commission's 'Proposal for Change,' " memo, Colorado for Family Values, 28 October 1994 (on file with author).

5. In 1995 Paul Cameron's Family Research Institute (see chapter 3) moved to Colorado Springs as well. Profiles of the city can be found in Steve Rabey, "Focus under Fire," *CT* 37, 3 (1993): 48, 60; Sam Stanton, "Cold Shoulder in Colorado," *Sacramento Bee*, 26 July 1993, A9; "New Hub for Family Values Movement," *Los Angeles Times*, 19 December 1992, B5; Jim Impoco, "Fatigue on the Right," *U.S. News and World Report*, 23 October 1995, 48–49. An interesting feel for the city can be found in PBS's *Bill Moyers Journal: The New Holy War*, aired 19 November 1993.

6. For a thorough review and critique of these processes, see Magleby 1995; Collins and Oesterle 1995.

7. Tony Marco, memo re errors of fact in Bransford's *Gay Politics*, 1994 (on file with author).

8. For a profile of Summit Ministries, see Tom Morton, "The Summit," *Colorado Springs Gazette-Telegraph*, 1 July 1990, F1. On the Christian Anti-Communism Crusade, see chapter 2.

9. For a profile of Promise Keepers, see Edward Gilbreath, "Manhood's Great Awakening," *CT* 39, 2 (1995): 20–28.

10. See Bransford 1994; Political Research Associates 1993, part 3.

11. Aside from CFV, Denver activists included Barbara Sheldon, Jayne Schindler, and Beatrice Nelson of the Christian Coalition (Bransford 1994, 47).

12. On the role of state reviewing procedures in the initiative process, see Linde 1993.

13. See, e.g., "Statement by John N. Franklin" (past chairman, Colorado Civil Rights Commission), 4 March 1992; Tony Marco, "Scope of the 'Gay Rights' Issue," memo, 1992 (on file with author).

14. See Bransford 1994 and Focus on the Family's analysis of press coverage in Tom Minnery, "Feeding Frenzy!" *Citizen* 7, 8 (1993): 1–3.

15. See Dirk Johnson, "Colorado Homosexuals Feel Betrayed," *New York Times*, 8 November 1992, sec. 1, 38.

16. See, e.g., Kathy Deitsch "Ruling Tossing Out Colorado Anti-Gay Law Dampens Fires of Hate," *Arizona Republic*, 28 December 1993, B5.

17. There were other grounds pleaded, but these were not significant subsequently.

18. Deitsch, "Ruling Tossing Out Colorado Anti-Gay Law," B5; Thaddeus Herrick, "Not Everyone in Holly Backs Romer," *Rocky Mountain News*, 28 March 1994, 24.

19. Leave to appeal this decision to the U.S. Supreme Court was denied 1 November 1993.

20. For an interesting account of the trial, see Jeffrey Rosen, "Sodom and Demurrer," *New Republic*, 29 November 1993, 16–19.

21. The Colorado Supreme Court considered several other state interests that I do not explore here.

22. A separate but concurring judgment was written by Justice Scott.

23. *Evans* v *Romer*, 1996 US Lexis 3245. Pages in the text refer to this Lexis version.

24. The dissent suggests in a note that the majority implicitly rejected the Colorado Supreme Court's judgment that Amendment 2 violated a fundamental right to participate in the political process. I disagree and would suggest the opposite; the majority implies that such a right may exist; see, e.g., ibid., 24.

25. This is the necessary political and ethical inquiry avoided by the courts in *Evans*.

26. In *Plessy* v *Ferguson*, 163 US 537 (1896) the Supreme Court validated racial segregation in public transport.

27. Interestingly, this argument appears to have been made in the early stages of the *Evans* litigation; see Gallagher 1994.

CHAPTER SEVEN

1. On "fundamentalisms and the state" generally, see Marty and Appleby 1993.

2. As I explained in chapter 1, my concern in this book is not with party politics. On the CR and the GOP, see many of the sources in chapter 1, note 6.

3. "What Is the Way to a New Society?" (editorial), *CT* 1, 4 (1956): 23–24.

4. "America's Future: Can We Salvage the Republic?" (editorial), *CT* 2, 11 (1958): 2–7.

5. See, e.g., "Sex in Christian Perspective" (roundtable), *CT* 4, 20 (1960): 6–8.

6. Carl F. Henry, "Evangelicals: Out of the Closet but Going Nowhere?" *CT* 4, 1 (1980): 17–22.

7. Richard John Neuhaus, "Who, Now, Will Shape the Meaning of America?" *CT* 26, 6 (1982): 16–17. See also J. I. Packer, "How to Recognize a Christian Citizen," *CT* 29, 7 (1985): 4–8; David L. McKenna, "Political Strategy for the Local Church," *CT* 29, 7 (1985): 19–23.

8. John Whitehead, "The Christian Connection," *CT* 26, 18 (1982): 31–35.

9. John D. Woodbridge, "Culture War Casualties," *CT* 39, 3 (1995): 20–26.

10. James Dobson, "Why I Use Fighting Words," *CT* 39, 7 (1995): 27–30. In the same issue Woodbridge offers a mild response to Dobson, "Why Words Matter," 31–32.

11. See, e.g., letters to the editor, *CT* 39, 6 (1995): 6.

12. For an interesting discussion of church and state in an earlier period, see Smith 1994.

13. Carl F. Henry, "Christian Responsibility in Education," *CT* 1, 17 (1957): 11–14.

14. "News," *CT* 5, 15 (1961): 29.

15. See "Church-State Separation: A Serpentine Wall?" *CT* 6, 21 (1962): 29–31; "Repercussions of Supreme Court Prayer Ruling," *CT* 6, 22 (1962): 25.

16. See "The Meaning of the Supreme Court Decision," *CT* 7, 20 (1963): 29–31.

17. "Is the Supreme Court on Trial?" (editorial), *CT* 7, 11 (1963): 28.

18. See, e.g., "America's Future," 4; Harold Lindsell, "Sex, SIECUS, and the Schools," *CT* 14, 9 (1970): 12.

19. Carl F. Henry, "Church and State: Why the Marriage Must Be Saved," *CT* 29, 7 (1985): 10.

20. See also the more strongly critical piece by Carl F. Henry, "Evangelicals Jump on the Political Bandwagon," *CT* 24, 18 (1980): 21–25.

21. Kenneth S. Kantzer, "Summing Up: An Evangelical View of Church and State," *CT* 29, 7 (1985): 28–32.

22. Stephen V. Monsma, "Windows and Doors in the Wall of Separation," *CT* 29, 7 (1985): 14–18.

23. "Capitalism vs. Communism" (editorial), *CT* 15, 16 (1971): 34.

24. E.g., William K. Harrison, "Reminiscences and a Prophecy," *CT* 1, 11 (1957): 14.

25. "The State in Welfare Work" (editorial), *CT* 4, 8 (1960): 23.

26. "Capitalism vs. Communism," 35. See also Lienesch 1993, chap. 3.

27. See, e.g., Ralph A. Cannon and Glenn D. Everett, "Sex and Smut on the Newsstands," *CT* 2, 10 (1958): 7.

28. "What about the Atheists?" (editorial), *CT* 7, 9 (1963): 28–30.

29. "Race Tensions and Social Change" (editorial), *CT* 3, 8 (1959): 21. See also Smith 1994.

30. "The Church and the Race Problem" (editorial), *CT* 1, 12 (1957): 21.

31. "Civil Rights and Christian Concern" (editorial), *CT* 8, 16 (1964): 28. See Findlay 1990.

32. See "Christians Must Obey the Laws—but Which Ones?" (editorial), *CT* 26, 13 (1982): 10–12.

33. Note that this desire for minimalism does not extend to "law and order" measures. This is an irony I do not pursue further.

34. See also various issues of *Citizen*, *Family Policy*, and *Washington Watch*.

35. See also Robert Knight, "The National Endowment: It's Time to Free the Arts," *Insight*, 1995.

36. See also "Freeing America's Schools: The Case against the U.S. Education Department," *Family Policy*, April 1995, 1–8.

37. Peter Marshall, "Recovering America's Christian Heritage," in *America's Christian Heritage* 1993.

38. Ibid.; David Barton, "A Grateful Nation," in *America's Christian Heritage* 1993.

39. This story stands in some contrast to Bellah's famous account of "civil religion" (1967).

40. E.g., Wallbuilders (TX); the American Center for Law and Justice (VA); the Foundation for American Christian Education (San Francisco).

41. "A Word about Wallbuilders," in *Wallbuilder Report,* summer 1995.

42. Marshall, "Recovering America's Christian Heritage."

43. Ibid. See also Barton 1989; David Barton, "Our Spiritual Heritage," in *America's Christian Heritage* 1993; LaHaye 1994, chap. 3.

44. See, e.g., Marshall, "Recovering America's Christian Heritage." See Smith 1994 and Crowther 1992 for a discussion of how proslavery Protestants similarly had "God on their side." See also discussion in Lienesch 1993, 141–69.

45. Keith Fournier, "Christ and Caesar," *Law and Justice* 4, 1 (1995): 3–4.

46. See various issues of *Citizen, Family Policy,* and *Washington Watch.*

47. See, e.g., "Oregon Christian Voter's Guide," broadsheet, Traditional Values Coalition (Oregon), 1994 (on file with author).

48. Matthew Moen (1994) seems to suggest that the pragmatic discourse indicates a shift in CR aspirations; I disagree and consider the shift tactical, rather than ideological (see also chapter 5).

49. See Boston 1993, chap. 9; Skillen 1990, chap. 8; DeMar 1995; Clarkson 1994; Diamond 1995, 246–49.

50. Rodney Clapp, "Democracy as Heresy," *CT* 3, 3 (1987): 17–23.

51. The Institute for First Amendment Studies provides a useful portrait of the Chalcedon Foundation in *Freedom Writer,* January 1995, 1, 8.

52. See, e.g., Boston 1993, 187–88; Diamond 1995, 247; other sources in chapter 1, note 6.

53. "Spiritual America," *U.S. News and World Report,* 4 April 1994, 48–59.

54. See also NY Times/CBS Poll, cited in cc.watch (Internet), 30 October 1995.

AFTERWORD

1. See sources in chapter 1, note 6.

2. NY Times/CBS Poll, cited in cc.watch (Internet), 30 October 1995. See also chapter 7.

3. "Spiritual America," *U.S. News and World Report,* 4 April 1994, 51.

References

INTERVIEWS BY AUTHOR

Knight, Robert. 1995. Director of Cultural Studies, Family Research Council. Washington, DC, 11 September.

Mabon, Lon. 1994. Director, Oregon Citizen's Alliance. Brooks, OR, 31 October.

Marco, Tony. 1994. Cofounder, Colorado for Family Values. Colorado Springs, CO, 3 November.

Minnery, Tom. 1994. Vice President, Public Policy, Focus on the Family. Colorado Springs, CO, 2 November.

Neet, Loretta. 1994. State Communications Director, Oregon Citizen's Alliance. Springfield, OR, 31 October.

Perkins, Will. 1994. Chairman of the Board, Colorado for Family Values. Colorado Springs, CO, 3 November.

Tebedo, Kevin. 1994. Cofounder, Colorado for Family Values. Colorado Springs, CO, 3 November.

Woodall, Jim. 1995. Vice President, Concerned Women for America. Washington, DC, 12 September.

NEWSLETTERS, MAGAZINES, JOURNALS, VIDEOS, AUDIOCASSETTES

AFA Journal. American Family Association.

America's Christian heritage. 1993. Colorado Springs, CO: Focus on the Family. Audiocassette.

CFV Report. Colorado for Family Values.

Children at risk. 1993. Focus on the Family. Video.

Christianity Today.

Citizen. Focus on the Family.

Education Reporter. Eagle Forum.

Family Policy. Family Research Council.

Family Research Report. Family Research Institute.

Family Voice. Concerned Women for America.

Focus on the Family Magazine. Focus on the Family.

The gay agenda. 1992. The Report. Video.

The gay agenda in public education. 1993. The Report. Video.

The gay agenda: March on Washington. 1993. The Report. Video.

Infocus. Family Research Council.

Insight. Family Research Council.

Lambda Report.

Law and Justice. American Center for Law and Justice.

National Minority Politics.

Phyllis Schlafly Report. Eagle Forum.

Rutherford. Rutherford Institute.

Stonewall: 25 years of deception. 1994. The Report. Video.

Washington Watch. Family Research Council.

OTHER SOURCES

Adam, Barry D. 1987. *The rise of a gay and lesbian movement.* Boston: Twayne.

Adams, William E., Jr. 1994. Pre-election anti-gay ballot initiative challenges: Issues of electoral fairness, majoritarian tyranny, and direct democracy. *Ohio State Law Journal* 55:583–648.

Aho, James A. 1990. *The politics of righteousness: Idaho Christian patriotism.* Seattle: University of Washington Press.

Allen, L. S., and R. A. Gorski. 1992. Sexual orientation and the size of the anterior commissure in the human brain. *Proceedings of the National Academy of Science* 89:7199–7202.

Altman, Dennis. 1982. *The homosexualization of America.* Boston: Beacon.

American Family Association. 1994. *Homosexuality in America: Exposing the myths.* Tupelo, MS: American Family Association.

Ammerman, Nancy Tatom. 1987. *Bible believers: Fundamentalism in a modern world.* New Brunswick, NJ: Rutgers University Press.

———. 1991. North American Protestant fundamentalism. In *Fundamentalisms observed,* ed. M. E. Marty and R. S. Appleby. Chicago: University of Chicago Press.

REFERENCES

Anti-Defamation League. 1994. *The religious right: The assault on tolerance and pluralism in America.* New York: Anti-Defamation League.

Ariel, Yaakov. 1991. Jewish suffering and Christian salvation: The evangelical-fundamentalist Holocaust memoirs. *Holocaust and Genocide Studies* 6:63–78.

Bad Object-Choices, ed. 1991. *How do I look?* Seattle: Bay Press.

Badgett, Lee. 1995. The wage effects of sexual orientation discrimination. *Industrial and Labor Relations Review* 7:WL8477331.

Bailey, J. Michael, and Richard C. Pillard. 1991. A genetic study of male homosexual orientation. *Archives of General Psychiatry* 48:1089–96.

Barkun, Michael. 1987. The language of apocalypse: Premillennialists and nuclear war. In *The god pumpers: Religion in the electronic age,* ed. M. Fishwick and R. B. Browne. Bowling Green, OH: Bowling Green University Popular Press.

———. 1990. Racist apocalypse: Millennialism on the far right. *American Studies* 31:121–40.

———. 1994. *Religion and the racist right: The origins of the Christian Identity movement.* Chapel Hill: University of North Carolina Press.

Barton, David. 1989. *The myth of separation: What is the correct relationship between church and state?* Aledo, TX: Wallbuilders.

Bates, Vernon L. 1995. Rhetorical pluralism and secularization in the new Christian Right: The Oregon Citizen's Alliance. *Review of Religious Research* 37:46–64.

Batterman, Daniel A. 1995. *Evans* v. *Romer:* The political process, levels of generality, and perceived identifiability in anti-gay rights initiatives. *New England Law Review* 29:915–80.

Beckford, James A. 1985. *Cult controversies: The societal response to the new religious movements.* London: Tavistock.

Bell, Daniel. 1964. *The radical right.* Garden City, NY: Anchor.

Bellah, Robert N. 1967. Civil religion in America. *Daedalus* 96:1–21.

Bennett, William J. 1992. *The de-valuing of America: The fight for our culture and our children.* Colorado Springs, CO: Focus on the Family.

Blanchard, Dallas A., and Terry J. Prewitt. 1993. *Religious violence and abortion: The Gideon project.* Gainesville: University Press of Florida.

Bogle, Darlene. 1990. *Strangers in a Christian land: Reaching out with hope and healing to the homosexual.* Old Tappen, NJ: Chosen Books.

Boston, Robert. 1993. *Why the religious right is wrong: About separation of church and state.* Buffalo, NY: Prometheus.

Boyer, Paul. 1992. *When time shall be no more: Prophecy belief in modern American culture.* Cambridge, MA: Harvard University Press.

Bransford, Stephen. 1994. *Gay politics vs. Colorado: The inside story of Amendment 2.* Cascade, CO: Sardis.

224

Bromley, David G., and Anson Shupe, eds. 1984. *New Christian politics.* Macon, GA: Mercer University Press.

Bruce, Steve. 1984. *Firm in the faith.* Aldershot, UK: Gower.

———. 1990. *The rise and fall of the new Christian Right: Conservative Protestant politics in America, 1978–1988.* Oxford: Clarendon.

———. 1994. The inevitable failure of the new Christian Right. *Sociology of Religion* 55:229–42.

Brummett, Barry. 1984. Premillennial apocalyptic as a rhetorical genre. *Central States Speech Journal* 35:84–93.

Bull, Malcolm, ed. 1995. *Apocalypse theory and the ends of the world.* Oxford: Blackwell.

Burke, Craig Cassin. 1993. Fencing out politically unpopular groups from the normal political processes: The equal protection concerns of Colorado Amendment Two. *Indiana Law Journal* 69:275–98.

Burtoft, Larry. 1994. *The social significance of homosexuality: Questions and answers.* Colorado Springs, CO: Focus on the Family.

Byne, William, and Bruce Parsons. 1993. Human sexual orientation: The biologic theories reappraised. *Archives of General Psychiatry* 50:228–39.

Cameron, Paul, Kay Proctor, William Coburn, and Nels Forde. 1985. Sexual orientation and sexually transmitted disease. *Nebraska Medical Journal* 70:292–99.

Carter, Stephen L. 1993. *The culture of disbelief: How American law and politics trivialize religious devotion.* New York: Basic Books.

Cassara, Ernest. 1982. The development of America's sense of mission. In *The apocalyptic vision in America: Interdisciplinary essays on myth and culture,* ed. L. P. Zamora. Bowling Green, OH: Bowling Green University Popular Press.

Chandler, Ralph Clark. 1984. The wicked shall not bear rule: The fundamentalist heritage of the new Christian Right. In *New Christian politics,* ed. D. G. Bromley and A. Shupe. Macon, GA: Mercer University Press.

Chilton, David. 1987. *Power in the blood: A Christian response to AIDS.* Brentwood, TN: Wolgemuth & Hyatt.

Christian Coalition. 1995. *Contract with the American family.* Nashville: Moorings.

Clarkson, Frederick. 1993. The anti-gay nineties. *Freedom Writer* 10, 2: 1–4.

———. 1994. Christian reconstructionism, parts 1 and 2. *Public Eye* 8, nos. 1, 2.

Coates, James. 1987. *Armed and dangerous: The rise of the survivalist right.* New York: Hill & Wang.

Collins, John J. 1984. *The apocalyptic imagination: An introduction to the Jewish matrix of Christianity.* New York: Crossroads.

Collins, Richard B., and Dale Oesterle. 1995. Structuring the ballot initiative: Procedures that do and don't work. *University of Colorado Law Review* 66:47–127.

Cooper, Davina. 1994. *Sexing the city: Lesbian and gay politics within the activist state.* London: Rivers Oram.

————. 1995. *Power in struggle: Feminism, sexuality, and the state.* New York: New York University Press.

Coukos, Pamela. 1994. Civil rights and special wrongs: The Amendment 2 litigation. *Harvard Civil Rights–Civil Liberties Law Review* 29: 581–98.

Crawford, Alan. 1980. *Thunder on the right: The "new right" and the politics of resentment.* New York: Pantheon.

Crowther, Edward R. 1992. Holy honour: Sacred and secular in the Old South. *Journal of Southern History* 58:619–36.

Cruickshank, Margaret. 1992. *The gay and lesbian liberation movement.* New York: Routledge.

Currah, Paisley. 1995. Searching for immutability: Homosexuality, race, and rights discourse. In *A simple matter of justice? Theorizing lesbian and gay politics,* ed. A. Wilson. London: Cassells.

Dannemeyer, William. 1989. *Shadow in the land: Homosexuality in America.* San Francisco: Ignatius.

Davies, Bob, and Lori Rentzel. 1993. *Coming out of homosexuality.* Downers Grove, IL: Intervarsity.

Davis, Angela. 1981. *Women, race, and class.* New York: Vintage.

Davis, David Brion. 1971. *The fear of conspiracy: Images of un-American subversion from the revolution to the present.* Ithaca, NY: Cornell University Press.

Decter, Midge. 1994. The A.D.L. vs. the "religious right." *Commentary* 98:45–47.

de Hart, Jane Sheron. 1991. Gender on the right: Meanings behind the existential scream. *Gender and History* 3:246 ff.

DeMar, Gary. 1995. *America's Christian history: The untold story.* Atlanta: American Vision.

D'Emilio, John. 1983. *Sexual politics, sexual communities: The making of a homosexual minority in the United States, 1940–1970.* Chicago: University of Chicago Press.

Diamond, Sara. 1989. *Spiritual warfare: The politics of the Christian Right.* Boston: South End.

————. 1995. *Roads to dominion: Right-wing movements and political power in the United States.* New York: Guilford.

226

Dobson, Ed, and Ed Hindson. 1986. Apocalypse now? What fundamentalists believe about the end of the world. *Policy Review* 38:16–22.

Dobson, James, and Gary Bauer. 1990. *Children at risk.* Dallas: Word.

Dugan, Robert P. 1991. *Winning the new civil war.* Portland, OR: Multnomah.

Duggan, Lisa. 1994. Queering the state. *Social Text* 39:1–14.

Durham, Martin. 1991. *Sex and politics: The family and morality in the Thatcher years.* Houndsmills, UK: Macmillan.

Eaton, Mary. 1994. Lesbians, gays, and the struggle for equality rights: Reversing the progressive hypothesis. *Dalhousie Law Journal* 17:130–86.

Ebaugh, Helen Rose Fuchs. 1988. *Becoming an ex: The process of role exit.* Chicago: University of Chicago Press.

Edsall, Thomas Byrne, with Mary D. Edsall. 1992. *Chain reaction: The impact of race, rights, and taxes on American politics.* New York: W. W. Norton.

Eule, Julian N. 1990. Judicial review of direct democracy. *Yale Law Journal* 99:1503 ff.

Faderman, Lillian. 1980. *Surpassing the love of men.* London: Junction.

Faludi, Susan. 1991. *Backlash: The undeclared war against American women.* New York: Crown.

Farrar, Steve. 1994. *Standing tall: How a man can protect his family.* Sisters, OR: Multnomah.

Feder, Don. 1993. *A Jewish conservative looks at pagan America.* Lafayette, LA: Huntington House.

Felsenthal, Carol. 1981. *Phyllis Schlafly: The sweetheart of the silent majority.* Chicago: Regnery Gateway.

Fields, Echo E. 1991. Understanding activist fundamentalism: Capitalist crisis and the "colonization of the lifeworld." *Sociological Analysis* 52:175–90.

Findlay, James F. 1990. Religion and politics in the sixties: The churches and the Civil Rights Act of 1964. *Journal of American History* 77:66–92.

Forster, Arnold, and Benjamin R. Epstein. 1964. *Danger on the right.* New York: Random House.

Fournier, Keith A. 1993. *Religious cleansing in the American republic.* American Center for Law and Justice. Pamphlet.

Frank, Robert L. 1992. Prelude to cold war: American Catholics and communism. *Journal of Church and State* 34:39–56.

Frum, David. 1994. *Dead right.* New York: Basic Books.

Gager, John G. 1983. The attainment of millennial bliss through myth:

The Book of Revelation. In *Visionaries and their apocalypses*, ed. P. D. Hanson. Philadelphia: Fortress.

Gairdner, William D. 1992. *The war against the family*. Toronto: Stoddart.

Gallagher, Michael J. 1994. Amendment 2. *Law and Sexuality* 4:123–94.

Gallup, George, Jr., and Jim Castelli. 1989. *The people's religion: American faith in the 90s*. New York: Macmillan.

Gilman, Sander. 1991. *The Jew's body*. New York: Routledge.

Glanz, Dawn. 1982. The American west as millennial kingdom. In *The apocalyptic vision in America: Interdisciplinary essays on myth and culture*, ed. L. P. Zamora. Bowling Green, OH: Bowling Green University Popular Press.

Gonsiorek, John G., and James D. Weinrich. 1991. The definition and scope of sexual orientation. In *Homosexuality: Research implications for public policy*, ed. J. Gonsiorek and J. D. Weinrich. Newbury Park, CA: Sage.

Graham, Billy. 1983. *Approaching hoofbeats: The four horsemen of the apocalypse*. London: Hodder & Stoughton.

———. 1992. *Storm warning*. Dallas: Word.

Grant, George, and Mark A. Horne. 1993. *Legislating immorality: The homosexual movement comes out of the closet*. Chicago: Moody.

Green, David G. 1987. *The new right: The counter revolution in political, economic, and social thought*. Brighton, UK: Wheatsheaf.

Hadden, Jeffrey K. 1969. *The gathering storm in the churches*. Garden City, NY: Doubleday.

Halley, Janet. 1994a. The politics of the closet: Towards equal protection for lesbian, gay, bisexual identity. In *Reclaiming Sodom*, ed. J. Goldberg. New York: Routledge.

———. 1994b. Sexual orientation and the politics of biology: A critique of the argument from immutability. *Stanford Law Review* 46:503–68.

Hamer, Dean H., Stella Hu, Victoria L. Magnuson, Nan Hu, and Angela M. L. Pattatucci. 1993. A linkage between DNA markers on the X chromosome and male sexual orientation. *Science* 261:321–27.

Handy, Robert T. 1984. *A Christian America: Protestant hopes and historical realities*. New York: Oxford University Press.

Hannigan, John A. 1991. Social movement theory and the sociology of religion: Toward a new synthesis. *Sociological Analysis* 52:311–31.

Harding, Susan. 1991. Representing fundamentalism: The problem of the repugnant cultural other. *Social Research* 58:373–93.

Hayton, Brad. N.d. *The homosexual agenda: Changing your community and nation.* Colorado Springs, CO: Focus on the Family.

Henry, Carl F., ed. 1971. *Prophecy in the making.* Carol Stream, IL: Creation House.

Herman, Didi. 1990. Are we family? Lesbian rights and women's liberation. *Osgoode Hall Law Journal* 28:789–816.

———. 1993. Beyond the rights debate. *Social and Legal Studies* 2:25–44.

———. 1994. *Rights of passage: Struggles for lesbian and gay legal equality.* Toronto: University of Toronto Press.

———. 1996. Law and morality re-visited: The politics of regulating sado-masochistic pornography and practice. *Studies in Law, Politics, and Society* 15:147–66.

Herman, Didi, and Carl F. Stychin, eds. 1995. *Legal inversions: Lesbians, gay men, and the politics of law.* Philadelphia: Temple University Press.

Hertzke, Allen D. 1988. *Representing God in Washington: The role of religious lobbies in the American polity.* Knoxville: University of Tennessee Press.

———. 1993. *Echoes of discontent: Jesse Jackson, Pat Robertson, and the resurgence of populism.* Washington, DC: Congressional Quarterly.

Himmelstein, Jerome L. 1986. The social basis of antifeminism: Religious networks and culture. *Journal for the Scientific Study of Religion* 25:1–15.

———. 1990. *To the right: The transformation of American politics.* Berkeley: University of California Press.

Hofstadter, Richard. 1966. *The paranoid style in American politics, and other essays.* London: Jonathan Cape.

Hostile climate: A state by state report on anti-gay activity. 1993. Washington, DC: People for the American Way, November.

Hunter, James Davison. 1987. *Evangelicalism: The coming generation.* Chicago: University of Chicago Press.

———. 1991. *Culture wars: The struggle to define America.* New York: Basic Books.

Iannaccone, Laurence R. 1993. Heirs to the Protestant ethic? The economics of American fundamentalism. In *Fundamentalisms and the state,* ed. M. Marty and R. S. Appleby. Chicago: University of Chicago Press.

Ide, Arthur Frederick. 1987. *Homosexuals Anonymous.* Garland, TX: Tangelwüld.

Ingersoll, Julie J. 1995. Which tradition, which values? "Traditional family values" in American Protestant fundamentalism. *Contentions* 4:91–104.

Johnson, George. 1983. *Architects of fear: Conspiracy theories and paranoia in American politics.* Los Angeles: Jeremy P. Tarcher.

229

Jones, Lawrence. 1992. Apocalyptic responses to the war with Iraq. In *Christianity and hegemony,* ed. J. P. N. Pieterse. New York: St. Martin's.

Jorstad, Erling. 1970. *The politics of doomsday: Fundamentalists of the far right.* Nashville: Abingdon.

———. 1987. *The new Christian Right, 1981–1988.* Lewiston, NY: Edwin Mellen.

Khan, Surina. 1996. Gay conservatives: Pulling the movement to the right. *Public Eye* 10:1–10.

King, M., and E. McDonald. 1992. Homosexuals who are twins: A study of 260 probands. *British Journal of Psychiatry* 160:407–9.

Kintz, Linda. 1994. Motherly advice from the Christian Right: The construction of sacred gender. *Discourse* 17:49–76.

Kirk, Marshall, and Hunter Madsen. 1989. *After the ball: How America will conquer its fear and hatred of gays in the 90s.* New York: Penguin.

Kirkpatrick, Lee A. 1993. Fundamentalism, Christian orthodoxy, and intrinsic religious orientation as predictors of discriminatory attitudes. *Journal for the Scientific Study of Religion* 32:256–68.

Klatch, Rebecca E. 1987. *Women of the new right.* Philadelphia: Temple University Press.

Koch, Klaus. 1983. What is apocalyptic? An attempt at a preliminary definition. In *Visionaries and their apocalypses,* ed. P. D. Hanson. Philadelphia: Fortress.

Koeppen, Sheilah Rosenhack. 1967. Dissensus and discontent: The clientele of the Christian Anti-Communism Crusade. Ph.D. diss., Department of Political Science, Stanford University.

LaHaye, Beverly. 1991. *The hidden homosexual agenda.* Concerned Women for America. Pamphlet.

LaHaye, Tim. 1978. *What everyone should know about homosexuality.* Wheaton, IL: Tyndale House.

LaHaye, Tim, and Beverly LaHaye. 1994. *A nation without a conscience.* Wheaton, IL: Tyndale House.

Lawrence, Bruce B. 1989. *Defenders of God: The fundamentalist revolt against the modern age.* San Francisco: Harper & Row.

Lechner, Frank L. 1990. Fundamentalism revisited. In *In gods we trust: New patterns of religious pluralism in America,* ed. T. Robbins and D. Anthony. New Brunswick, NJ: Transaction.

LeVay, Simon. 1991. A difference in hypothalamic structure between heterosexual and homosexual men. *Science* 253:1034–37.

Levitas, Daniel. 1995. A.D.L. and the Christian Right. *Nation* 260: 882–88.

Liebman, Robert C., and Robert Wuthnow. 1983. *The new Christian Right: Mobilization and legitimation.* Hawthorne, NY: Aldine.

Lienesch, Michael. 1982. Right-wing religion: Christian conservatism as a political movement. *Political Science Quarterly* 97:403–25.

———. 1993. *Redeeming America: Piety and politics in the new Christian Right.* Chapel Hill: University of North Carolina Press.

Linde, Hans A. 1993. When initiative lawmaking is not "republican government": The campaign against homosexuality. *Oregon Law Review* 72:19–45.

Linder, Robert D. 1982. Militarism in Nazi thought and in the American new religious right. *Journal of Church and State* 24:263–79.

Lindsell, Harold. 1984. *The Armageddon spectre.* Westchester, IL: Crossway.

Lindsey, Hal. 1994. *Planet Earth: 2000 A.D.* Palos Verdes, CA: Western Front.

Lindsey, Hal, and C. C. Carlson. 1970. *The late, great Planet Earth.* Grand Rapids, MI: Zondervan.

Lippy, Charles H. 1982. Waiting for the end: The social context of American apocalyptic religion. In *The apocalyptic vision in America: Interdisciplinary essays on myth and culture,* ed. L. P. Zamora. Bowling Green, OH: Bowling Green University Popular Press.

Lipset, Seymour Martin, and Earl Raab. 1971. *The politics of unreason: Right-wing extremism in America, 1790–1970.* London: Heinemann.

Lunch, William M. 1993. The Oregon Citizen's Alliance, social control, and the Republican Party: The political future of the new cultural politics? Paper presented at the Pacific Northwest Political Science Association, 22 October 1993, Coeur d'Alene, ID.

McIlhenny, Chuck, and Donna McIlhenny, with Frank York. 1993. *When the wicked seize a city: A grim look at the future and a warning to the church.* Lafayette, LA: Huntington House.

Magleby, David B. 1995. Let the voters decide? An assessment of the initiative and referendum process. *University of Colorado Law Review* 66:13–45.

Magnuson, Roger. 1994. *Informed answers to gay rights questions.* Sisters, OR: Multnomah.

Marrs, Texe. 1987. *Dark secrets of the new age.* Westchester, IL: Crossway.

———. 1993. *Big sister is watching you: Hilary Clinton and the White House feminists who now control America—and tell the president what to do.* Austin, TX: Living Truth.

Marsden, George. 1984. *Evangelicalism and modern America.* Grand Rapids, MI: William B. Eerdmans.

Marty, Martin E., and R. Scott Appleby. 1993. *Fundamentalisms and the state.* Chicago: University of Chicago Press.

Mathews, Donald, and Jane Sheron de Hart. 1990. *Sex, gender, and the politics of the ERA.* New York: Oxford University Press.

Mayer, William G. 1992. *The changing American mind: How and why American public opinion changed between 1960 and 1988*. Ann Arbor: University of Michigan Press.

Meigs, Anna. 1995. Ritual language in everyday life: The Christian Right. *Journal of the American Academy of Religion* 63:85–103.

Meier, Paul. 1993. *The third millennium*. Nashville: Thomas Nelson.

Melucci, Alberto. 1989. *Nomads of the present: Social movements and individual needs in contemporary society*. London: Century Hutchinson.

Michelman, Frank I. 1989. Conceptions of democracy in American constitutional argument: Voting rights. *Florida Law Review* 41:443–90.

Miller, Joshua. 1991. *The rise and fall of democracy in early America, 1630–1789*. University Park: Pennsylvania State University Press.

Moberly, Elizabeth R. 1983. *Homosexuality: A new Christian ethic*. Greenwood, SC: Attic.

Moen, Matthew C. 1989. *The Christian Right and congress*. Tuscaloosa: University of Alabama Press.

———. 1992. *The transformation of the Christian Right*. Tuscaloosa: University of Alabama Press.

———. 1994. From revolution to evolution: The changing nature of the Christian Right. *Sociology of Religion* 55:345–57.

———. 1995. Political and theological adjustment in the U.S. Christian Right. *Contentions* 4:75–90.

Morken, Hubert. 1994. "No special rights": The thinking behind Colorado's Amendent #2 strategy. Paper presented at the Annual Meeting of the American Political Science Association, New York, 1–4 September.

Mosse, George. 1985. *Nationalism and sexuality: Middle-class morality and sexual norms in modern Europe*. Madison: University of Wisconsin Press.

Mouly, Ruth W. 1985. *The religious right and Israel: The politics of Armageddon*. Chicago: Midwest Research.

Niblock, John F. 1993. Anti-gay initiatives: A call for heightened judicial scrutiny. *UCLA Law Review* 41:153–98.

Nicolosi, Joseph. 1991. *Reparative therapy of male homosexuality*. Northvale, NJ: Jason Aronson.

———. 1993. *Healing homosexuality*. Northvale, NJ: Jason Aronson.

Nugent, Robert, and Jeannine Gramick. 1989–90. Homosexuality: Protestant, Catholic, and Jewish issues. *Journal of Homosexuality* 18:7–46.

Offe, Claus. 1985. New social movements: Challenging the boundaries of institutional politics. *Social Research* 52:817ff.

Ohio State Law Journal. 1994. Symposium: The Bill of Rights vs. the

232

ballot box: Constitutional implications of anti-gay ballot initiatives. 55:1–674.

O'Leary, Stephen, and Michael McFarland. 1989. The political use of mythic discourse: Prophetic interpretation in Pat Robertson's presidential campaign. *Quarterly Journal of Speech* 75:433–52.

O'Sullivan, Gerry. 1993. Catholicism's new cold war: The church militant lurches rightward. *Humanist* 53:27–32.

Palmer, Susan J. 1990. Virus as metaphor: Religious responses to AIDS. In *In gods we trust: New patterns of religious pluralism in America*, ed. T. Robbins and D. Anthony. New Brunswick, NJ: Transaction.

Patton, Cindy. 1985. *Sex and germs: The politics of AIDS.* Boston: South End.

Penning, James M. 1994. Pat Robertson and the GOP: 1988 and beyond. *Sociology of Religion* 55:327–44.

Pennington, Sylvia. 1989. *Ex-gays? There are none!* Hawthorne, CA: Lambda Christian Fellowship.

Peters, Peter. N.d. *Death penalty for homosexuality is prescribed in the Bible.* Laporte, CO: Scriptures for America.

Pieterse, Jan P. Nederveen. 1992. The history of a metaphor: Christian Zionism and the politics of apocalypse. In *Christianity and hegemony*, ed. J. P. N. Pieterse. New York: St. Martin's.

Political Research Associates. 1993. Constructing homophobia: How the right wing defines lesbians, gay men, and bisexuals as a threat to civilization. Parts 1–7. Cambridge, MA. Duplicated.

Prager, Dennis. 1993. Homosexuality, the Bible, and us: A Jewish perspective. *Public Interest* 112:60–83.

Rankin, Lori J. 1994. Ballot initiatives and gay rights: Equal protection challenges to the right's campaign against lesbians and gay men. *University of Cincinnati Law Review* 62:1055–1103.

Redman, Barbara J. 1993. Strange bedfellows: Lubavitcher Hasidism and conservative Christians. *Journal of Church and State* 34:521–48.

Reed, Ralph. 1994. *Politically incorrect: The emerging faith factor in American politics.* Dallas: Word.

Reisman, Judith A., and Edward W. Eichel. 1990. *Kinsey, sex, and fraud: The indoctrination of a people.* Lafayette, LA: Lochinvar–Huntington House.

Robertson, Pat. 1990. *The new millennium.* Dallas: Word.

———. 1991. *The new world order.* Dallas: Word.

———. 1993. *The turning tide: The fall of liberalism and the rise of common sense.* Dallas: Word.

Robertson, Pat, with Bob Slosser. 1982. *The secret kingdom.* Nashville: Thomas Nelson.

Robson, Ruthann. 1995. Convictions: Theorizing lesbians and criminal justice. In *Legal inversions: Lesbians, gay men, and the politics of law,* ed. D. Herman and C. F. Stychin. Philadelphia: Temple University Press.

Ross, Becki. 1988. Heterosexuals only need apply: The secretary of state's regulation of lesbian existence. *Resources for Feminist Research* 17:35–38.

Roy, Ralph Lord. 1960. *Communism and the churches.* New York: Harcourt Brace.

Rueda, Enrique. 1982. *The homosexual network: Private lives and public policy.* Old Greenwich, CT: Devin-Adair.

———. 1987. *Gays, AIDS, and you.* Old Greenwich, CT: Devin-Adair.

Rushdoony, Rousas John. 1978. *Thy kingdom come: Studies in Daniel and Revelation.* Fairfax, VA: Thoburn.

———. 1991. *The roots of reconstruction.* Vallecito, CA: Ross House.

Salokar, Rebecca Mae. 1994. Revisiting the state constitutional initiative process: Gay rights and procedural safeguards. Paper presented at the Annual Meeting of the American Political Science Association, New York, 1–4 September.

Schacter, Jane S. 1994. The gay civil rights debate in the states: Decoding the discourse of equivalents. *Harvard Civil Rights–Civil Liberties Law Review* 29:283–317.

Seidman, Steven. 1992. *Embattled eros: Sexual politics and ethics in contemporary America.* New York: Routledge.

Seltzer, Richard. 1992. The social location of those holding antihomosexual attitudes. *Sex Roles* 26:391–98.

Skillen, James W. 1990. *The scattered voice: Christians at odds in the public square.* Grand Rapids, MI: Zondervan.

Smith, R. Drew. 1994. Slavery, secession, and southern Protestant shifts on the authority of the state. *Journal of Church and State* 36: 261–76.

Staver, Mathew D. 1995. *Faith and freedom.* Wheaton, IL: Crossway.

Stychin, Carl F. 1995. *Law's desire: Sexuality and the limits of justice.* London: Routledge.

———. 1996. To take him "at his word": Theorizing law, sexuality, and the U.S. military exclusion policy. *Social and Legal Studies* 5:179–200.

Sullivan, Andrew. 1995. *Virtually normal.* New York: Alfred A. Knopf.

Thumma, Scott. 1991. Negotiating a religious identity: The case of the gay evangelical. *Sociological Analysis* 52:333–47.

Toulouse, Mark G. 1989. Pat Robertson: Apocalyptic theology and American foreign policy. *Journal of Church and State* 31:73–99.

———. 1993. *Christianity Today* and American public life: A case study. *Journal of Church and State* 35:241–84.

Touraine, Alain. 1985. An introduction to the study of social movements. *Social Research* 52:749–87.

Tucker, Kenneth H. 1991. How new are the new social movements? *Theory, Culture, and Society* 8:75–98.

Vaid, Urvashi. 1995. *Virtual equality: The mainstreaming of gay and lesbian liberation.* New York: Anchor.

Wagner, Robert J. 1993. *Evans* v. *Romer:* Colorado Amendment 2 and the search for a fundamental right for groups to participate equally in the political process. *St. Louis University Law Journal* 38:523–51.

Wald, Kenneth D. 1991. Social change and political response: The silent religious cleavage in North America. In *Politics and religion in the modern world,* ed. G. Moyser. London: Routledge.

———. 1994. The religious dimension of American anti-communism. *Journal of Church and State* 36:483–506.

Wald, Kenneth D., James W. Button, and Barbara A. Rienzo. 1996. The politics of gay rights in American communities: Explaining antidiscrimination ordinances and policies. *American Journal of Political Science* 40:1152–78.

Weeks, Jeffrey. 1985. *Sexuality and its discontents: Meanings, myths, and modern sexualities.* London: Routledge & Kegan Paul.

———. 1995. *Invented moralities: Sexual values in an age of uncertainty.* Cambridge: Polity.

White, Mel. 1994. *Stranger at the gate: To be gay and Christian in America.* New York: Simon & Schuster.

Whitehead, John W. 1994. *Religious apartheid: The separation of religion from American public life.* Chicago: Moody.

Wilcox, Clyde. 1990. Blacks and the new Christian Right: Support for the moral majority and Pat Robertson among Washington, D.C., Blacks. *Review of Religious Research* 32:43–55.

———. 1992. *God's warriors: The Christian Right in twentieth-century America.* Baltimore: Johns Hopkins University Press.

———. 1994. Premillennialists at the millennium: Some reflections on the Christian Right in the twenty-first century. *Sociology of Religion* 55:243–61.

Wilcox, Clyde, and Leopoldo Gomez. 1989–90. The Christian Right and the pro-life movement: An analysis of the sources of political support. *Review of Religious Research* 31:380 ff.

Wilcox, Clyde, Ted G. Jelen, and Sharon Linzey. 1995. Rethinking the reasonableness of the religious right. *Review of Religious Research* 36:263–76.

Wilson, Angelia. 1995. *A simple matter of justice? Theorizing lesbian and gay politics.* London: Cassells.

Wilson, Dwight. 1977. *Armageddon now! The premillennarian response to Russia and Israel since 1917.* Grand Rapids, MI: Baker House.

Young, Michelle. 1992. Leaving the lesbian lifestyle. *Journal of Christian Nursing* (fall): 10–13.

Zald, Meyer, and J. D. McCarthy, eds. 1987. *Social movements in an organizational society.* New Brunswick, NJ: Transaction.

236

Index